PITY FOR THE GUY

By the same author and published by Peter Owen

Robin Hood: The Unknown Templar

PITY FOR THE GUY

A BIOGRAPHY OF GUY FAWKES

John Paul Davis

Peter Owen
London and Chicago

PETER OWEN PUBLISHERS
73 Kenway Road, London SW5 0RE

Peter Owen books are distributed in the USA and Canada by
Independent Publishers Group
814 North Franklin Street, Chicago, IL, 60610, USA

This collection first published in Great Britain 2009 by
Peter Owen Publishers

ISBN 978-07206-1349-0

A catalogue record for this book is available
from the British Library

Printed and bound in Great Britain by
Windsor Print Production Ltd, Tonbridge, UK

'The devil, and not God, was the discoverer.'

– Guy Fawkes, 5 November 1605

CONTENTS

Illustrations Between Pages 144 and 145

PREFACE

He was a man of considerable experience as well as knowledge. Thanks to his prowess he had acquired considerable fame and name among the soldiers. He was also – something decidedly rare among soldiery, although it was immediately evident to all – a very devout man, of exemplary life and commendable reticence. He went often to the sacraments. He was pleasant of approach and cheerful of manner, opposed to quarrels and strife: a friend, at the same time, of all in the service with him who were men of honour and good life. In a word, he was a man liked by everyone and loyal to his friends.[1]

These were the words used by the Jesuit priest Father Oswald Tesimond to describe his friend and former schoolfellow, Guy Fawkes.

Never in the four hundred years since the days of Tesimond has such a glowing account been used to describe the man infamous for his attempt to destroy the Houses of Parliament. Back in 1604, however, such generous praise was not uncommon.

When Guy Fawkes travelled across the English Channel on a ship from Flanders to London in the company of his new friend Thomas Wintour, he did so as a man with a reputation that was celebrated among soldiers. When he arrived in England he was warmly welcomed, and his abilities received considerable praise and respect. Yet within two years he was dead, dying in extreme agony, his reputation not that of an esteemed soldier but as a figure synonymous with treachery and murder.

It was just after midnight on the morning of 5 November 1605 that Guy Fawkes, dressed in a dark hat, cloak and boots, was arrested by government officials following a tip-off from an anonymous whistle-blower of a plot to blow up Parliament. Wearing spurs as though ready for flight and described as a 'very tall and desperate fellow', he was discovered keeping vigil over a vault located beneath the House of Lords. On closer inspection, hidden under a large quantity of wood and other elements of debris were thirty-six barrels of gunpowder. Over the coming days it was learned that the man's name was Guy Fawkes of Yorkshire, one of several men of the Catholic faith that had conspired the regicide of James I by blowing up Parliament and all those within it on its reopening later that very day. When asked of his purpose he denied nothing. When tried for treason against the king he admitted his crime was worthy of death, and he was subsequently executed because of it. In the wake of the plot his image was demonized by a succession of poems, stories and pamphlets characterizing him as being in league with the devil, highlighting his pivotal role in the plot and successfully imprinting a lasting impression on the public consciousness, thereby cementing his place in history as one of England's most ruthless villains.

Over the years, the facts behind the life of Guy Fawkes have continued to be distorted by fiction, ignorance and, in certain cases, propaganda. While the portrayal of Guy Fawkes in the twenty-first century remains as a shady little man skulking around a darkened cellar, dressed in black, lantern in hand and a sinister expression crossing his bearded face partially hidden beneath his hat, the reality was something different. Even in the hours after his capture there is evidence to suggest his image in the eyes of the authorities was not altogether negative. Guy's performance under interrogation was highly praised by many government officials, even earning him a reputation as a Gaius Mucius Scaevola character, famed in ancient Rome for his fearless nature when threatened with torture. Guy's colourful and well-respected career as a soldier fighting in the Spanish Netherlands on the side of hundreds of English Catholics is often overlooked, despite the fact that he was honoured on more than one occasion for his gallantry. As a result of his fine performance as a soldier, in addition to his intellect and language skills, Guy was selected for another highly controversial mission as a diplomat to the Court of Philip III on behalf of England's beleaguered Catholics, a significant moment not only in Guy's own life but in early Stuart history as a whole. Yet this, too, has not been examined in close detail.

In celebration of the foiling of this 'desperate fellow' on that famous night in 1605, every year 5 November remains devoted to his memory. Although for the majority Guy Fawkes Night represents an occasion of carnival – spectacular fireworks, sparklers, glow sticks and countless accidents – Guy Fawkes's role in the proceedings remains immortalized. According to a poll conducted by the BBC in 2002, this man, described by a contemporary account of his execution as 'the great devil of all', is regarded by many in Britain as among the top one hundred greatest Britons of all time. Children throughout Britain continue to frequent the streets with odd-shaped effigies accompanied by the slogan 'penny for the guy'; children and adults alike celebrate his failings through the famous rhyme 'Remember, remember the fifth of November' while similar effigies to those that grace the streets of England in the run-up to 5 November burn on top of bonfires.

Yet despite his considerable influence on English history it is often said that Guy's life is something of an enigma. For previous commentators who have studied the Gunpowder Plot in detail the story of Guy Fawkes is less likely to be viewed so simply – even among academics, portrayal of Guy Fawkes ranges from that of a tyrant, a misguided zealot, a minor accomplice, to a cat's-paw used by the other conspirators to take the fall or even an agent working on behalf of Robert Cecil.

The aim of this biography is to provide an accurate depiction of Guy Fawkes, encompassing his formative years in Yorkshire, his early adulthood, the decade he spent serving in the English Regiment of the army of Albert, Archduke of Austria, in the Low Countries, his mission to Spain in 1603 and his contribution to the Gunpowder Plot. Earlier investigations have tended to centre solely on the plot itself, so in this book the plot is considered primarily from Guy's own perspective rather than as an investigation in its own right. Nevertheless, it has at times been necessary to stray outside Guy's life and touch on the events and the lives of those of direct significance to him – the life of fellow conspirator Thomas Wintour, in particular, features prominently. In addition, since the work of Henry Garnett and Eric N. Simons, authors of the most recent serious biographies of Guy Fawkes – namely *Portrait of Guy Fawkes* and *The Devil of the Vault*, respectively, both penned within a year of one another in 1962 and 1963 – much new information has come to light. As a result there is still much that can be learned about Guy Fawkes, and my aim here is to complete the jigsaw, at least as far as

possible with the still incomplete information at our disposal.
By concentrating on the life of Guy Fawkes as a whole it is my
intention to pull together many different sources of information,
each key to understanding his life and the events that dominated
it. In doing so I hope to present the life of Guy Fawkes, for the
first time ever, in its proper context, incorporating all the key
events of his 35-year life, not just his role in the plot, and thus
establishing an accurate picture of the historical man: an Elizabethan schoolboy growing up in York; a veteran of the wars of
religion that plagued Europe throughout the sixteenth century;
a diplomat at the court of a king; a commander of men; and,
finally, the man who nearly wiped out a government. I have also
attempted to consider the context of Guy's life as a recusant
Catholic growing up against the cultural and social backdrop
of Protestant England, a Puritan-governed Yorkshire and a war-
ridden Europe and, in doing so, attempt to explore the motives
behind the treason for which he has never been forgotten.

I

PORTENTS OF DREAD

A freak storm hit the coasts of the Low Countries on All Saints' Day 1570. Buildings collapsed, houses and churches were destroyed, and over 20,000 lives were lost in the province of Friesland alone as the sea overflowed its banks. Such ill fate was viewed as a portent of dread by the superstitious Catholic Spanish who saw the storm, the likes of which had not been seen for four hundred years, as representing a menacing judgement sent to earth by the saints as a warning against Protestant heretics for their destruction of sacred images. When the senior curate of the town of Hoorn marched out into the streets with the Holy Sacrament in a desperate attempt to calm the waves and save the town, his cries went unheeded, causing the unbelieving burghers to laugh. To the reformed this was no evil portent; quite the contrary. They claimed that the saints were figures of peace not liable to such unrelenting anger. Instead, this event foreshadowed new disturbances, the likes of which were still to become known.[1]

As history recalls, the year 1570 was certainly a year of disturbances. The marriage of the King of Spain, Philip II, to Anne of Austria proved to be deeply unpopular with the Dutch reformists, a situation that would contribute significantly to the ongoing wars of religion that plagued Europe throughout the sixteenth century. In February of that year Pope Pius V signed the Papal Bull that excommunicated Queen Elizabeth I of England, further widening the ever-increasing Catholic–Protestant divide. Following the edict from Rome denouncing Elizabeth and her followers as heretics, Elizabeth's Catholic subjects were excused of their oaths of allegiance and commanded to flaunt her authority or face excommunication. Since the accession of Elizabeth in 1558, bringing with her England's reversion to the Protestantism of her brother Edward VI, the power of the state lay solely with Protestants, and the obedience to Rome required of England's Catholics brought it into opposition with the state. When the Duke of Alba sent copies of the Papal Bull to England, a committed Catholic named Felton fixed it up to the gate of the residence of the Bishop of London – reminiscent of the antics of Martin Luther in Wittenberg – in defiance of the 'pretender' queen. While Felton was executed for his action, the real danger remained hidden from view. Although rumbles of discontent from England's Catholics continued to increase, the threat was not to be found in the form of one organized army but in refugee priests, travelling throughout Europe on a mission to bring the reformed back to the Roman tradition, leading in many cases to hostile rebellion.

Throughout England, Catholics and Puritans, zealous in nature and direct in purpose, were becoming increasingly dangerous. Less than a year earlier, a Catholic conspiracy had been thwarted in Norfolk, leading to further rebellion in the north, demonstrating the great battle of principle that still raged in England against the Protestant state. While at least one Vatican historian of the time commented that the days when 'the thunders of the Vatican could shake the thrones of Princes' were over, new storm clouds were starting to assemble. Oblivious to the thundering winds and torrential rain that battered the Low Countries, a woman of little significance was preparing to give birth in a small house in York. Only in time would history recall this was one child who, had fate been different, would have succeeded in shaking the 'thrones of princes' by thunder.[2]

Guy Fawkes was born into a family of gentlemanly status. According to records of the Church of St Michael-le-Belfrey in York he was baptized into the Protestant faith on 16 April 1570. His date of birth is lost from history, but historians typically place it as 13 April in keeping with the usual three-day gap between birth and baptism. His family had no great claim to fame, he was heir to no titles, no family fortunes, nor could he ever expect to be. His father was a lawyer, as was his father before him, and such an occupation was not without esteem and entitled the family to be considered of gentleman status.

There are records of two families of the surname Fawkes living in York at the time. Most likely they were branches of the same one. The head of one branch had been John Fawkes of Farnley, whose family history can be traced back to around 1320. John Fawkes was steward of Knaresborough Forest during the reign of Henry VII until his death in 1496 and had been survived by three sons, Nicholas, William and Henry.[3] While William appears to have died without issue in 1501, Nicholas married an Anne Pulleyn in 1520. The third son of John Fawkes was Henry, according to some writers, the great-grandfather of Guy Fawkes. Henry Fawkes was a merchant who achieved distinction as a freeman of York. In later years he was also mentioned in the town records as having acted as swordbearer to the Lord Mayor on ceremonial occasions, a proud moment for any family of such status. In 1522 Henry Fawkes achieved further distinction after serving as captain of an army raised by the city to assist the Earl of Shrewsbury in their border skirmish with the Scots.

Following his service as a soldier, Henry Fawkes continued to serve as swordbearer until 1549 when his son, Reginald, also a freeman of the city, was appointed joint swordbearer alongside his father. The family line continued with Reginald's son, another Henry, who also became a freeman and merchant and inherited a substantial property from his father.[4]

This branch of the Fawkes family lived a relatively peaceful existence. Based on the evidence available, the family survived the troublesome events of the Reformation without any indication of discontent and adapted peacefully to the ways of the new Protestant rites. Whether Henry Fawkes, the swordbearer to the Lord Mayor, had another son who would later provide a direct link with the famous gunpowder conspirator is unconfirmed. Some previous commentators have viewed it as extremely unlikely that two families of the same name living in the same locality at the same time would not have been related, yet this does not rule out the possibility that this one had only recently moved to the city from another location. From around 1530 onwards records cite a William Fawkes living in the parish of St Michael-le-Belfrey. Of William's parents nothing is known. Perhaps he was indeed a son of the distinguished swordbearer Henry. Some information about William Fawkes has survived, however. An advocate of the Ecclesiastical Court, he married the most respectable of wives, an Ellen Harrington, daughter of William Harrington, the Sheriff of York in 1531 and also Lord Mayor in 1536. Fawkes was undoubtedly a hard-working, serious character and is recorded as being appointed Registrar of the Exchequer Court by grant under the archiepiscopal seal in 1541, a worthwhile appointment for a man of his status. With his wife Ellen, William fathered four children, and some details survive of each. Thomas, his eldest son, became a wool-stapler; his second son, Edward, a lawyer; his daughter Edith married a

John Foster; while a fourth child, another daughter whose name has vanished from history, married a man named Umfray Ellis and had three daughters.[5]

In the eyes of history it is Edward whose life would be of most significance. Not surprisingly for a child of gentleman status at the time, Edward Fawkes followed his father into the legal profession, becoming a proctor of the Ecclesiastical Court and later an advocate of the Consistory Court of the Archbishop of York, an organization charged with the responsibility of administering ecclesiastical law, located in Peter Prison in Minster Yard.[6] Unlike his brother Thomas, Edward is known to have married. The date of his wedding has been lost, but records show that he married a woman named Edith, surname unknown, probably in 1568. According to a previous commentator, Henry Garnett, who cited evidence such as Edith's inability to write her own name on a lease dated 8 July 1579 and a poorly initialled signature to another document in 1592, it seems probable that the respectable proctor married beneath himself.[7]

This branch of the family has a somewhat diverse ancestry. Ellen, wife of William Fawkes, was from respectable stock as the daughter of a lord mayor. Whether a connection can be made between William Fawkes before his marriage with Ellen and Henry Fawkes, swordbearer to the Lord Mayor, is uncertain. Henry's distinction as freeman and swordbearer appears to be the work of his own efforts rather than nepotism. Yet perhaps a connection can be made between Henry Fawkes, who would have acted as swordbearer to William Fawkes's future father-in-law before William's marriage to Ellen. Nevertheless, what claim the family had to the lower gentry was all but gone by 1570. For the next thirty-five years the activities of this family are little more than footnotes recorded sparsely in the activities of the parish of St Michael-le-Belfrey. A daughter, Anne, is recorded as being baptized into the Protestant faith on 3 October 1568. She was buried seven weeks later. Despite the tragic loss, within a year Edith gave birth again, this time to a boy, born in April 1570, named Guy.

Of the early years of Guy Fawkes's life, very few written accounts have survived. The young boy would have had no recollection of the birth of his younger sister, another Anne, born 12 October 1572, but he may have had some brief memory of the birth of his other sibling, Elizabeth, on 27 May 1575. Guy's grandfather, William Fawkes, had already been dead for five years by the time of Guy's birth, but Guy would probably have been old enough to know his grandmother Ellen Fawkes, née Harrington, and was remembered in her will. Judging from the contents of the will, William and Ellen Fawkes lived a comfortable life at their townhouse in High Petergate with several items of luxury ranging from silver spoons to brass pots, feather mattresses, sheets and pillows, cushions with red roses and many other items that were later passed on to over eighteen beneficiaries. It is also apparent that Ellen remained a widow for the remainder of her life, as she requested in her will that she be 'buried as near my late husband, William Fawkes, as may be'. It is a clear mark of her character that she remembered all of her children and those of her grandchildren who were born at the time in her will, including Guy, who was less than six months old at the time the will was written and who received one angel of gold and her best whistle.[8]

The limited evidence available from contemporary sources suggests that Guy and his cousins were equally loved by their grandmother. A similar conclusion can be drawn from the will of his Uncle Thomas, dated 18 February 1581. It is evident from the will that Thomas and Edward Fawkes had also been close as brothers. By 1578 Edward Fawkes, Guy's father, was also dead, and Thomas is recorded as requesting to be buried 'near as may be to my brother Edward Fawkes'.[9] Thomas leaves no evidence of a family of his own. Judging by Thomas's will his death was expected, as suggested by the words 'being sick in body, but of good and perfect mind and memory'. While his claims that he was still sound of mind at the time of writing implies that he had thought long and hard about the bequests in his will, some of them are strange. He gave generously to Guy's sisters: Anne received a girdle of silver, Elizabeth his carpet of tapestry work, while his entire napery was divided between them; Guy was remembered reasonably well, inheriting his gold ring, his bed and one pair of sheets with appurtenances – the gift of a bed and sheets was a mark of affection at the time – yet his seven silver spoons went to his friend, a Mr Robert Wright, and his cloak and hat to Robert Wright's maid, whereas Guy's mother, Edith, does not seem to be mentioned.[10]

Although far from being blessed by great wealth, Guy grew up in a secure household. Determining the exact place of his birth has become difficult following centuries of unsubstantiated claims and hearsay, but its exact location can be clarified to a degree. By the turn of the twentieth century no less than four traditions existed claiming to be the place in question. Two traditions depicted the house of Guy Fawkes's birth as being on the south side of High Petergate in York; a third suggested it was on the north side; while a fourth claimed Guy was born in the nearby village of Bishopthorpe. Early in the twentieth century, the renowned historian and antiquarian Henry Hawkes Spink investigated the matter in detail. Spink himself had been informed by at least one antiquarian from Bishopthorpe that a house that once stood opposite the old village church was the site in question. By the early 1900s, the time of Spink's investigation, the house had long been demolished and replaced with a pleasure garden marked with a stone to commemorate the site. Spink, however, viewed the tradition as unlikely because of Guy's baptismal record in the parish of St Michael-le-Belfrey in York and favoured the tradition that Guy was born in a house adjoining an alley called Minster Gate on the north side of High Petergate. Writing in 1973, however, historian Katharine Longley presented strong evidence that the house was on the south side of High Petergate in Stonegate.[11] When being questioned in the Tower of London in the aftermath of the Gunpowder Plot, Guy gave his place of birth as Nidderdale in Yorkshire before later admitting he was born in York itself.[12] While it cannot be ruled out that the recently captured conspirator was lying on both occasions, records exist of a lease for a small building in Petergate between Matthew Hutton, Doctor of Divinity and the Dean of York Minster Cathedral, and Edith Fawkes, dated 8 July 1579 – some eighteen months after Edward Fawkes's death – for thirty-one years at an annual fee of ten shillings. Possibly the agreement was for a different house than the one in which Guy was born, but the wording of the lease suggests it was a new lease for the house previously in the name of Guy's father only now made in the name of his mother.

With the exception of the births of his young sisters and the death of his grandmother, the young boy appears to have enjoyed a relatively quiet first eight years. Being the son of a lawyer and classed as a gentleman, Guy was eligible to attend the free school of St Peter's and was sent there when he was old enough. Located close to the city, the school was founded in 1557 under the Royal Charter of Philip and Mary and subsequently placed under the patronage of the Dean and Chapter of the Cathedral.[13] There Guy took his first major step into the world, mixing with children of both gentry and gentleman status alike, including characters of notable Catholic influence.

It is intriguing that during the latter half of the sixteenth century many of the school's pupils were known to have Catholic sympathies. In York itself, many among the population were fined regularly for being recusants, and as late as the end of the seventeenth century as much as a quarter of all nobility and gentry from the West Riding of Yorkshire was still Catholic.[14] It is equally noteworthy that when Guy was four years old the school was the subject of a most unwanted scandal. Following a brief suspension, the headmaster of the time, a Mr Fletcher, was removed from his position with immediate effect for his reversion to the Catholic faith. Following the new Act of Supremacy issued by Elizabeth in 1559 and her own excommunication from Rome, it had become illegal for any person outwardly to conform to the Catholic tradition. To do so incurred a crime punishable by monthly fines and, in some cases, prison. While dismissal and prison greeted Fletcher, many other Englishmen of Catholic sympathy evaded the suffering of recusancy by adhering to the Protestant rites in public while returning to worship the old faith in private. Although the Pope officially forbade such acts, in reality the fines for recusancy and the penalties applied made visible recusancy a difficult option. Bearing this in mind, it is difficult now to estimate with confidence the exact number of Catholics in England during this period. What is clear, however, is that Fletcher's successor could not be a Catholic. In his edict of 1571 the recently appointed Archbishop Grindal of York made clear what was required of a headmaster of the day:

> No schoolmaster shall teach, either openly or privately, in any gentleman's house, or in any other place, unless he be of good and sincere religion and conversation, and be first examined, allowed, and licensed by the ordinary in writing under his seal. He shall not teach

any thing contrary to the order of religion now set forth by public authority. He shall teach his scholars the Catechism in Latin lately set forth, and such sentences of scripture, besides profane chaste authors, as shall be most meet to move them to the love and due reverence of God's true religion, now truly set forth by the Queen's Majesty, and to induce them to all godliness and honest conversation.[15]

Fletcher's replacement was John Pulleyn, BA, from Caius College, Cambridge, and a Protestant reverend. Pulleyn took up his new position on 5 March 1575 and remained there throughout Guy's schooling. During that time, the young Guy would have come to know him quite well. While the duties of 21st-century head teachers usually involve administrative work rather than teaching, during the Elizabethan era the role of the headmaster was far more hands on. It is reasonable to conclude that the new headmaster would have had a notable influence on his students. It is also likely that Pulleyn would have spoken to his students about religion on a regular basis, as was typical at the time. Although officially a Protestant, Pulleyn's own stance on religion has been the attention of much intrigue. Rumour in some quarters suspected him of being a Jesuit, although those allegations were never proven. There were three Pulleyn families in Yorkshire at the time. Among them, records cite the Pulleyn family from Scotton as known recusants. In her family history, Catherine Pullein was somewhat unconvinced about the possibility of a direct link between the Pulleyns of Scotton and Guy's headmaster. Instead, John Pulleyn was identified as the eldest son of Henry Pulleyn of Blubberhouse, also in Yorkshire. Nevertheless, connections between John Pulleyn and the family from Scotton do exist. John Pulleyn is mentioned briefly in the will of Peter Pulleyn of St Michael's, Ousebridge, in 1578, receiving five shillings for his role as supervisor and witness.[16] Without question the family from Scotton had a long history of Catholic sympathy and lived in an area widely known to be home to several powerful recusant families, including a branch of the Percy family, one of whose number, Thomas Percy, would play an integral part in the Gunpowder Plot. A long-standing tradition from the area tells that the young Guy often visited the Roos family in Wetherby, which had strong family ties to the Pulleyns.[17]

It is a startling coincidence that Pulleyn's tenure would see the rise of several important Catholics. Among his pupils were the Wright brothers, John and Christopher. Born in 1568 and 1570 respectively, the brothers, nicknamed Jack and Kit, were the offspring of Robert and Ursula Wright, staunch Catholics who suffered prison for their faith. Hailing from Plowland Hall in Holderness, both brothers attended school at the same time as Guy. Christopher was the same age as Guy, undoubtedly his classmate, while both were famously co-conspirator with Guy in the Gunpowder Plot.[18]

Another of Guy's contemporaries was a boy named Robert Middleton, who, despite having been raised a Protestant, had been born into a strongly Catholic family and converted to Catholicism in adulthood. Following his conversion, Middleton studied for the priesthood in Rome and evaded capture from the Protestant English government until 1600 when he was tried for his Catholicism, which resulted in his execution and martyrdom the following year. Another former alumnus of St Peter's was the Protestant Thomas Morton, later Bishop of Chester, Coventry and Durham and author of several religious works including *The Exact Discovery of Romish Doctrine in the Case of Conspiracy and Rebellion*, which was published in the aftermath of the Gunpowder Plot.[19] Also at St Peter's, albeit nine years Guy's senior, was a boy named Edward Oldcorne. After studying for the priesthood at Rheims and later at the English College in Rome, Oldcorne became a Jesuit and spent several years working on the mission in England, during which time he developed a reputation that continues to be celebrated. He survived throat cancer in 1591 and supported the mission until his eventual capture and execution in 1606, yet another of Pulleyn's students caught up in the aftermath of the Gunpowder Plot.[20] Finally, there was another Jesuit. Seven years Guy's senior, Oswald Tesimond was even more directly implicated in the Gunpowder Plot, and more shall be said about him later.

Coming from a relatively stable background of obedient reformists it is unlikely that Guy Fawkes harboured any Catholic sympathies or that he resented authority in any way during the first nine years of his life. At the time Edward Fawkes was still serving his profession with distinction and, considering his occupation at the Ecclesiastical Court, was almost certainly in favour of the monarch and committed to the Protestant rites. There is certainly no indication given from either branch of the Fawkes family of any rebellion towards the Protestant faith.[21]

How Guy fared at school is unrecorded. According to Spink, he was highly intelligent and well read.[22] A similar account, found in John Hawarde's published reports of cases in the Star Chamber, affirms Guy as being 'of excellent good natural parts, very resolute and universally learned'. As the son and grandson of lawyers and the great-grandson of a former lord mayor, it can at least be deduced that Guy had a solid grounding. Most of the work that he would have undertaken can be confidently deduced from our knowledge of education at that time. During the Tudor period, the curriculum was imposed directly by the monarch. A typical child of his class growing up during the reign of the Protestant Elizabeth would have begun to learn Latin at around the age of seven with the aid of William Lily's Latin grammar textbook, probably under the guidance of an usher – either a junior master or a senior pupil. By the end of their first year they would have grasped the basics of nouns and verbs and be ready to tackle sentence structure and grammar by the age of eight. By the age of nine Guy would have become familiar with Latin-to-English translations and vice versa, something that would develop further over the coming year, while over the next four years his education would have focused on arithmetic, religion, literature and possibly Greek and Hebrew. In his book *The Devil of the Vault* author Eric Simons considers the possibility that Guy was involved in extra-curricular activities. According to Simons, John Pulleyn is known to have put on a presentation of plays for public entertainment at the common hall of the school in 1585, and it is possible that Guy may have been involved in that.[23]

During the five-and-a-half-day weeks of his academic year, of perhaps up to forty-four weeks a year, Guy would have sat through Protestant services every day and conversed with his friends only in Latin. Living at a time when education consisted largely of repetition and frequent examinations it seems Guy would have been forced to adapt to the formality of Protestant life and the military-style discipline that would serve him in good stead as a soldier. At home, his life was probably quite similar. As an advocate at the Consistory Court of the Archbishop of York, Edward Fawkes was intelligent, respectable and serious, in keeping with his profession. Edward Fawkes would undoubtedly have presided over a stable and disciplined household. Then, when he was seven years old, Guy Fawkes's life changed drastically. At the relatively young age of forty-six Edward Fawkes died. Whether he had been ill in the run-up to his death is not known, but what is certain is that he died intestate, surprising for a lawyer. Undoubtedly the loss of Edward had a profound effect on Edith, Guy and his sisters, particularly as the sole bread-winner was deceased. Records of the time, located in the City House Book, reflect the loss of income to the household and the decrease in payment by Mrs Fawkes to the poor:

> Whereas Master Edward Fawkes, late of the parish of St Michael of the Belfrey is lately deceased, who was assessed to pay weekly towards the relief of the poor 4d., it is now agreed by these presents [*sic*] that Edith Fawkes, his late wife, shall pay but only 2d. weekly to the poor.[24]

For Guy life had taken a significant turn. In addition to the tragedy of losing a father, the burden of replacing him as man of the house at such an early age in a household whose income had dropped must have had a profound effect on him. For a time Guy's uncle became a prominent guardian, at least until his own death three years later. For Edith Fawkes, who remained a respectable widow before remarrying nine years later, the task of bringing up her children alone was undoubtedly a difficult one. Guy must have felt the burden, too, perhaps becoming even more serious after this time. As the only son in the family, abruptly deprived of his role model, the child was already growing into a man.

2

THE CATHOLIC RECUSANTS OF
THE WEST RIDING OF YORKSHIRE

Edward Fawkes was laid to rest on 17 January 1578, after which time his property and possessions passed to Edith. According to the lease for the house at High Petergate in 1579, the family continued to live in York, most likely the same house in which Guy had been brought up. It is likely that he continued to be educated alongside Kit and Jack Wright at St Peter's school in York, remaining there until around the age of fourteen, during which time Edith Fawkes raised Guy and his sisters Anne and Elizabeth as a sole parent. Suggestion has been put forward by independent researchers that Edith took in a lodger shortly after Edward's death, but this is unconfirmed. The family continued to reside in the Petergate property until at least 1583, after which the name of a new tenant appears. According to lease records from 1586, the tenant was a Robert Bridge, or Briggs, who had already been in the house for around three years.[1] While Bridge could have been taken in by Edith as a lodger, evidence of a new tenant probably indicates that the family moved from the property when Guy was thirteen. Guy's whereabouts cannot be traced at this period. The possibility that he was living elsewhere offers support for the other three traditions that he lived either in another part of Petergate or in the village of Bishopthorpe, but this cannot be verified. Nevertheless, if these traditions are based on a degree of fact, it is far more likely that if Guy did take up residence in one of these areas, he did so in his later childhood rather than from birth, thus accounting for evidence of his baptism being recorded among parish records of St Michael-le-Belfrey and the lack of information about his teenage years.[2]

During the latter half of the sixteenth century England continued to undergo a period of change. The brief Catholic resurgence during the five-year reign of Mary Tudor and her husband Philip II of Spain had effectively ended following Elizabeth I's passing of an Act of Supremacy and an Act of Uniformity in 1559, decreeing Protestantism as the nation's religion and in doing so banning participation in the Catholic mass. Yet any hopes Elizabeth might have had of a peaceful transition were severely hindered by a series of challenges to her right to rule that threatened to develop into widescale conflict throughout the 1560s. Although Elizabeth managed to see out the decade without any major threat of conflict from abroad, it was the actions of those closer to home that posed the greater test of her authority.

Rarely in England's long and chequered history has there been a more controversial figure than Elizabeth's cousin, Mary Stuart. Often remembered in England as Mary, Queen of Scots, her decision to flee to England in 1568 following her dethronement and imprisonment at the hands of a group of Scottish nobles, who rebelled against her following her marriage to James Hepburn, 4th Earl of Bothwell, proved a significant moment in the future of both nations. The religious divide Elizabeth inherited from her father Henry VIII following his split from Rome before she was born continued to prove problematical throughout her reign. As a product of the late king's second marriage, so a bastard child in the eyes of Rome, Elizabeth's claim to succeed her father by right of right of blood succession was tainted.

Because of Elizabeth's revival of Protestantism in England, Mary Stuart was hailed by certain influential English Catholics as the rightful heir to the English throne despite having an inferior claim to Elizabeth, whose position as Henry's daughter had been further strengthened by her father's decision to bar any member of the Stuart line, the descendants of his sister Margaret Tudor, from inheriting the throne. Nevertheless, this did not prevent Mary's father-in-law, King Henri II of France, from attempting to seize the throne for Mary following the death of Queen Mary Tudor.[3] Mary Stuart had previously spent over ten years in the Court of Henri II before her marriage to the king's fourteen-year-old son, the future King Francis II in 1558, a political arrangement by Henri to stake a claim to the English throne and also ensure Valois rule in Scotland even without Mary's successful delivery of an heir. For Mary, the possibility of securing the English throne was clearly of appeal. Following the death of Mary I (Tudor), Mary Stuart made known her intentions by bearing the royal arms of England, something she continued to do throughout her life, which in turn contributed in no small part to the strained relationship she had with Elizabeth. Although Elizabeth was reluctant to act too harshly against Mary following her escape to England, Elizabeth's decision to imprison her cousin at Carlisle clearly demonstrated that Mary presented a threat. As long as Mary remained alive, Elizabeth's lack of an heir would continue to ensure that Mary was the most obvious heir to the throne, something that generated considerable support for Mary among England's Catholics and in whose name influential Catholic statesmen would betray their sovereign and significantly threaten the security of the realm.

The Secretary of State to Elizabeth was Sir William Cecil, 1st Baron Burghley, a confirmed Protestant and loyal subject of the queen. Although he was not a religious purist like many others at Court, his contribution to the Elizabethan religious settlement of 1559 was extensive, and he was well known for taking a more lenient stance against Puritans than Catholics. For certain members of the Privy Council, often referred to historically as the anti-Cecil faction, the fate of the English Crown and England's Catholics was in far too delicate a state to be left in such uncertainty. It was these same men who were behind the Norfolk Conspiracy against Elizabeth in 1569, a plan involving a marriage between the Duke of Norfolk and the exiled Mary, resulting in Mary replacing Elizabeth as Queen to be followed by the deposition of Cecil as England's Chief Minister. The plan failed when Robert Dudley, the Earl of Leicester, confessed knowledge of it to the queen. For Elizabeth, this conspiracy and the subsequent Northern Rebellion, led by the Earl of Westmoreland, Lord Neville, and the Earl of Northumberland, Lord Percy, in defiance of the monarch for her treatment of English Catholics and her seizing several of their mines, would prove to be merely the first of a number of plots on her life over the next thirty years.

Although Elizabeth had successfully avoided war in Europe, her decision to sign the Treaty of Blois in April of 1572 with Catherine de'Medici on behalf of the King of France would eventually lead England into direct conflict with Spain because of the ongoing Spanish conflict with France. By 1574 Elizabeth faced other problems. Throughout that year the number of 'Seminary priests' – Catholic priests who trained in English seminaries or study houses on the Continent – landing in England with the intention of claiming Catholic converts had increased dramatically. By 1579 the English College had been founded in Rome to train priests, and less than a year later three Jesuit priests – Edmund Campion, Robert Persons and Ralph Emerson – had also reached England's shores, marking the start of the controversial Jesuit mission. Although Campion was captured the following year, his pioneering role in the mission would lead to countless conversions to the Catholic faith over the next two decades as well as a series of trials against influential recusant families, in particular the Tresham, Vaux and Catesby families, all of whom were later connected with the Gunpowder Plot.[4]

Although Elizabeth's accession brought with it reversion to Protestantism as the official religion of the state, the transition was not as smooth as many have assumed. Official enaction of the Acts of Settlement was achieved by May 1559, six months into her reign, yet its changes failed to take effect immediately. In Guy Fawkes's York, the Marian Archbishop, Nicholas Heath, remained in the see until 5 July 1560, and it was not until January 1561 that a Protestant successor, Thomas Young, was finally appointed. Before Heath's departure the possibility cannot be ruled out that Catholic priests continued to be ordained. Furthermore, other attempts to repress Catholicism throughout the West Riding of Yorkshire struggled to gather momentum. Young did not take up office until May 1561, while his first ordinary visitation was not until September. The first attempt at Catholic repression by a York Court of High Commission did not occur before May, and even then many of its members were known for their tendency to affiliate with prominent Catholics.[5]

Following the removal of the Earl of Rutland as Lord President of the Council of the North, the position remained in a vacuum until Archbishop Young's appointment to this role in May 1564. From this time onwards Young acted as both lord president and archbishop until his death in 1568. Despite this, repression of Catholicism in Yorkshire still failed to gather pace, and throughout his tenure Young seemed to favour quiet tolerance as opposed to conflict. Young's successor as lord president, the Earl of Sussex, was equally lenient. Furthermore, appoint-

ment of a new archbishop did not happen until 1570. Had the
Acts of Settlement been implemented more effectively, the
Northern Rebellion of Neville and Percy would probably have
incurred further opposition from the authorities. Appointment
of another new archbishop took place in 1571 with the Puritan
Edmund Grindal, who had previously been Bishop of London,
while another Puritan, Henry of Hastings, the Earl of Huntingdon, replaced Sussex as Lord President in 1572. From this
time onwards the repression of recusants was more acute. Under
Hastings, injunctions and punishments against recusants also
increased, usually in the form of imprisonment and fines.[6] Such
methods were evidently effective. Between 1559 and 1574 records
reveal that 210 lay recusants had been identified in the West
Riding, yet that number had risen to 271 between 1575 and 1580
as Hastings's assaults on Catholicism became more intense. In
1582 the figure is even more surprising. A further government-
led drive judged there to have been somewhere between 1,500
and 2,000 recusants in the West Riding alone. By this time
Hastings's methods had effectively rid the area of the 'mislikers'
brand of Catholicism – those with Catholic leanings but motivated more by a distaste for Anglicanism – while the period from
1572 to 1582 also saw firm attention placed on rounding up
priests.[7] An accurate estimate of the number of priests located in
the West Riding is difficult. There were 178 parishes and roughly
as many chapels. Taking this into consideration, the number of
clergy was probably between three and four hundred, all of
whom were still practising in 1559. From 1559 onwards all
prebendaries – a member of the chapter of a cathedral or
collegiate church, usually a canon, responsible for carrying out
administration – were required to accept special articles trans-
ferring their spiritual authority from Rome to the Crown and
agreeing that the 1559 *Book of Common Prayer* was in keeping

with scripture. Presumably the same was required of Catholic priests. While no records of punishment for failure to comply exist from 1559, in certain cases, clergy in the West Riding were recorded as being deprived of their positions for their refusal to subscribe. Others simply left their cures – pastoral control of a parish – for no obvious reason. Among the remaining Catholic clergy were the chaplains of the gentry and the nobility, parish priests of Catholic sympathy, who for whatever reason avoided deprivation, and a number of other priests from the recent Marian era who roamed the countryside without affiliation to any particular parish. By 1577 most of the benefices – roles of an ecclesiastical office nature, including parish priests – of the West Riding had changed hands, while many other Catholic priests left over from Mary's reign were starting to die off.[8]

Nevertheless, from around 1574 a new form of Catholicism was emerging, stemming from that first wave of Seminary priests coming over from the Continent. By 1582 thirty-five Yorkshire-born priests had returned to the county, eleven of whom were natives of the West Riding, and a further nine had arrived by the end of the year.[9] Notwithstanding that Hastings's efforts to repress Catholicism in Yorkshire were at their greatest at this time, he failed to make any real impact on the area's hardcore recusants. As the number of seminaries increased, so did their following. Hastings's primary intention was to tackle the recusant nobility and gentry, which still accounted for a quarter of the entire nobility and gentry in the West Riding. Despite a system of repression developing through Hastings's control of both ecclesiastical and secular government, his large network of spies and the backing of the Privy Council, attempts to enforce recusancy charges against the nobility and gentry largely failed. In many cases charges against them were not pursued, persecution drives lacked intensity, officials were inefficient and the recusants were highly skilled in avoiding persecution. Despite Hastings's notorious tenure, between 1584 and 1603 the number of lay recusants increased following the arrival of the seminaries, reaching 1,013 between 1590 and 1595 and 1,136 by the year of the Gunpowder Plot.[10]

It is a notable coincidence that Guy's own conversion to Catholicism occurred at a time when the Seminary mission was at its height. If we are to be guided by his answers to interrogation on the morning of 6 November, shortly after his arrest in connection with the Gunpowder Plot, Guy became a recusant around the age of fifteen or sixteen. According to the official report, as witnessed by the Earls of Salisbury, Nottingham, Suffolk and Northampton, 'he confesseth he hath bene a Recusant about this twenty yeares', thus dating his conversion to around 1585 or 1586.[11]

Based on Guy Fawkes's confessions after his arrest for his role in the plot, Guy did not reveal the exact date or the reasons behind his decision. When the subject was brought up on the orders of King James I, Guy sidestepped the question, almost certainly to avoid incriminating any known recusant or priest.[12] The potential consequences had he done so would have been severe. Guy would have been well aware of the execution of several priests in Yorkshire for their Catholicism and is known to have had connections with the 'venerable' William Knight, a yeoman from East Yorkshire, who was executed in 1596 for 'explaining to a man the Catholic faith'.[13]

Considering Guy's traditional Protestant upbringing it seems evident that around the age of fifteen his life underwent something of a transformation. It is almost certain that a degree of Catholic influence came from within his own family. He stated, although he may have been lying, that his mother was a Jackson, perhaps connecting her with the Jackson family listed among the recusants of West Yorkshire. A Jackson is also recorded as witnessing a financial transaction between Guy and a Christopher Lumley in 1591.[14] Other research suggests she was a member of the Blake family, respected merchants and aldermen from Scotton.[15] Should Edith have been born a Catholic, her influence on Guy's later decision to convert is understandable, particularly following his father's death. Among Guy's other relations were the Goodrickes, or Goodriches, of Ribston Park, located between Cowthorpe and Knaresborough, who were owners of a large estate at Ribston Hall that included a chapel.[16] A close friendship is also known to have existed between Guy and his cousin, Richard Collinge, who became a Jesuit and who is recorded as accompanying Guy on his journey to Flanders in 1593. Collinge was not only related to Guy but also to the Harrington family of Mount St John, and it is the view of writer and historian Catherine Pullein that Guy's education in religious matters might well have stemmed from this side of the family. Among their number was William Harrington the elder – Collinge's uncle and cousin once removed to Guy – who was indicted for his role in harbouring the notorious Jesuit Edmund Campion for ten days in October 1581.[17]

Another possibility is that Guy found role models in stories of the city's past. When Henry VIII dissolved the monasteries in 1535, several monks from the nearby town of Beverley, who had been expelled from their religious houses, are recorded as having rebelled against the monarch under the leadership of Yorkshire landowner Robert Aske and his army of some 5,000 horsemen, in what later became known as the Pilgrimage of Grace. The bravery of Aske became fondly remembered in the city, and his continued efforts eventually resulted in negotiations and a royal pardon.[18] According to Spink, the young Guy was a frequent visitor to the village of Cowthorpe, where a Knights

Templar preceptory once stood.[19] Equally, the young student may have been influenced in his own time by the suspension of Archbishop Grindal in 1577 for refusing to bow to the decree of the church to suppress prophesying or news that the Catholic Sir Francis Throckmorton had been caught liaising with an agent of Mary, Queen of Scots in an attempt to promote an invasion of England in 1583.[20] By then his life would have been shaped by eight years under the influence of headmaster Pulleyn in addition to being a contemporary of many children from known Catholic families.

Assuming Guy Fawkes's claim to have converted to Catholicism around the age of fifteen is true, the time period coincides with the martyrdom of Margaret Clitherow. Known as the 'pearl of York' and the wife of a Protestant butcher, Clitherow remains honoured for her devotion to the Catholic cause following her conversion in 1574. Acting on the certainty that her actions represented 'necessary duty to God', Clitherow converted her home into a refuge for priests, leading to the site becoming identified as a centre of fellowship for York's recusant community. Following her indictment for harbouring the priests in 1585, Clitherow refused trial and received the heavy sentence of being stoned to death – despite, as some sources claim, being pregnant at the time – so becoming one of only three women to die for her faith during Elizabeth's reign.[21] While Clitherow's martyrdom alone would have succeeded in capturing the interest of many of York's citizens, it is a notable coincidence that Robert Middleton, the son of Margaret's brother Thomas, was the same Robert Middleton who was Guy's friend at school. Robert, himself later martyred for his faith in 1601, was the same age as Guy, although the future Jesuit adhered to the Protestant faith until the age of eighteen.[22] Curiously it was also around this time that two of Guy's other schoolfriends, Jack and Kit Wright, were introduced at first hand to the harsh realities of religious persecution after being forced to endure the execution of their uncle, a Jesuit priest named Father Francis Ingleby, for his priesthood in June 1586.[23] According to the laws of Elizabeth:

> All Jesuits, seminary and other priests ordained since the beginning of the Queen's reign, should depart out of the realm within 40 days after the end of that session of Parliament; and that all such priests or other religious persons ordained since the same time should not come into England, or remain there, under the pain of suffering death as in case of treason.[24]

Guy may already have converted to Catholicism by the time his mother remarried some time between April 1587 and February 1589.[25] Nevertheless it is probably of some significance that his stepfather – the first significant male-authority figure in his life since the deaths of his father and uncle – should be Catholic. According to the records of York, Edith Fawkes married one Dionis Bainbrigge, or Denis Bainbridge, a country gentleman who hailed from Scotton. Evidence available confirms that Edith spent between nine and eleven years mourning Edward Fawkes as a sober and respectable widow before moving in with her new husband, originally to Timble, a house owned by the Pulleyn family, and then to Bainbridge's home village of Scotton in 1588 or 1589.[26] It is possible that the marriage produced a child as, although no reference to this is found in Catherine Pullein's family history, Spink suggests Guy may have had a brother who was a student at the Inns of Court at the time of the Gunpowder Plot.[27]

Bainbridge's personality differed considerably from that of Edward Fawkes. Whereas Edward was undoubtedly a hard-working and serious character, at least one contemporary report of Bainbridge implied he was more 'ornamental' than 'useful'. In later years he was described as being something of a spend-thrift, a characteristic that evidently had a damaging effect on Guy's inheritance.[28] Nevertheless, through his new stepfather Guy would have become more closely involved in the Catholic community. It might well have been around this time that his admiration for priests, Jesuit, Seminary or other, began to streng-then. By 1591 the Jesuit mission had begun in Yorkshire with the landings of Richard Holtby and John Curry on the northern coast. In his biography of Guy Fawkes, Eric Simons states with certainty that Jesuits were being harboured at Scotton Hall, something of which Guy was probably aware.[29] Undoubtedly Bainbridge as a practising Catholic liaised with priests on a regular basis and may even have harboured them on occasion.

Bearing this in mind, it seems reasonable to believe that Guy's transition from a quiet Protestant worshipper to a fervent Catholic by the time of his death in 1606 developed significantly following his mother's marriage. If Guy was still at school at this time, the young man might suddenly have found himself labelled as something of an outcast, despite being in the company of those he had known all his life. In addition, the Protestant services that were so familiar to him would have lost much, if not all, of their meaning and relevance.

Exactly when Guy left school is not recorded. Some com-mentators have suggested he was eighteen, using it as a means of covering gaps in knowledge about Guy's life, but it is far more likely an Elizabethan schoolboy would have left grammar school at fourteen. Because of the lack of information available, many previous commentators have concluded that Guy worked on his stepfather's estates in Scotton between the ages of eighteen and twenty-one. The possibility is credible enough. As a Catholic,

Guy would have been prevented from obtaining a university degree without accepting the Oath of Supremacy to the queen, something that most recusants refused to do. Nevertheless, the possibility that Guy attended university should not be ruled out altogether. In addition to descriptions of Guy by some commentators as 'universally learned', and 'highly intelligent' and 'well read', his answers to questioning in the aftermath of the Gunpowder Plot are interesting. When responding to the question by James I 'Where he hath lived?' the answer Guy is recorded as having given, as appears on the document, is 'He hath lived in Yorkshyre first at skoole there, and then to Cambridge and after in foure other places.'[30] Guy does not elaborate on his time at Cambridge, however, although he may have lived there some time between leaving Yorkshire and moving to the Low Countries. Equally possible is that Guy attended university at Cambridge around the age of fourteen and left without obtaining a degree for refusing to swear the Oath of Supremacy. Robert Catesby, Guy's future co-conspirator and the leader of the Gunpowder Plot, is known to have attended Oxford but left without a degree for precisely this reason.[31]

In addition to being unable to receive a degree, Guy's conversion to Catholicism would have restricted his career options significantly. Had his father still been alive it seems probable that Guy would have followed him into the legal profession and embarked on a career as a proctor, and it seems reasonable to believe his father had this in mind when he sent Guy to St Peter's. Guy's conversion would inevitably have prohibited him from following in his father's footsteps in the Ecclesiastical Court. However, taking up work on his stepfather's estates would have been a typical employment move for a Catholic at the time but would have offered little opportunity to progress.[32] His earnings would have been very low, undoubtedly adding to any young man's frustration. Alternatively, Guy may have found some brief employment in the household of a local recusant, acting in a servant's capacity, a common move by many young Catholics of gentleman status, thus furthering his learning and developing his military skills, something that would have been of benefit considering his later enrolment in the English Regiment of the Spanish Army in the Spanish Netherlands during the 1590s. The effect of the Wright brothers on Guy's development may have been important here. Both Jack and Kit were described as outstanding swordsmen, and it has been suggested by Henry Garnett that the brothers sparred with Guy during their leisure hours, teaching him much about swordsmanship. There is also suggestion that Thomas Percy was well known to Guy from his time at Scotton. Coincidentally, Bainbridge had acquired the property owned by the Percy family shortly before marrying Edith Fawkes.[33] Previous commentator Harry Speight wrote with certainty of a friendship between Thomas Percy and Guy, referring to Percy as Guy's lifelong 'friend and companion'.[34] Should that be the case, the behaviour of Percy would have had a negative influence on the young man. According to the Jesuit priest John Gerard, who was later implicated in the Gunpowder Plot, Percy

> for the most part of his youth he had been very wild more than ordinary, and much given to fighting, so much that it was noted in him and in Mr John Wright (whose sister he afterwards married) that if they had heard of any man in the country to be esteemed more valiant or resolute than others, one or the other of them would surely have picked some quarrel against him and fought with him to have made trial of his valour.[35]

While Gerard's words perhaps should not be taken literally, the statement is largely consistent with what is known of Percy. He was older than the others, at least seven years Guy's senior, providing a big-brother type of influence on the young men, perhaps contributing to their bravery but also to their lack of judgement.

In 1591 Guy's name reappears on the records at the age of twenty-one when he finally inherited his late father's estates. As his father had died intestate, the formality of Guy receiving his inheritance was delayed, something that must have been frustrating. Guy wasted little time before leasing out the estates, possibly indicating that he was short of funds. Following the introduction of a penal law in 1581 it was required that all recusants pay £3. 10s. a year into the parish poor box on top of an extraordinarily large fine of £20 a month to the Crown. The statute further entitled the Crown legally to seize all personal property and two-thirds of the estate should the payments not be met.[36] So severe was the penalty that many recusants were forced to sell property simply to pay the fine. In October 1591, merely six months after inheriting his birthright, Guy Fawkes agreed to lease much of his property to a Christopher Lumley, a tailor from York, as cited in the following document:

> This Indenture made the 14th day of October in the
> year of the reign of our Sovereign Lady Elizabeth . . .
> the 33rd, between Guy Fawkes of Scotton in the
> county of York . . . and Christopher Lumley of the city
> of York, tailor . . . witnesses that the said Guy Fawkes
> for divers good causes and considerations him there-
> unto specially moving has demised, granted and to farm
> let . . . unto the said Christopher Lumley one barn and
> garth on the backside of the said barn . . . situate lying
> and being in Gillygate in the suburbs of the said City

of York and three acres and a half of one acre of arable
land . . . in Clifton in the said county of York, whereof
half of one acre called a pit land, and one rood of land
lying at New Close Gate . . . in the common field of
Clifton towards Rocliffe, one half acre lying in the
field called Milnefield in Clifton, one half acre lying
in the flat or field called Laires, one half acre called
Hungryland, one half acre beyond the new windmill,
and one half acre at More brotts . . . and also one acre
of meadow lying and being in the ings or meadow of
Clifton . . . to have and to hold unto the said Christopher Lumley his executors and assignees from the feast
of St Martin . . . during the term of twenty and one
years . . . yielding and paying during the said term unto
the said Guy Fawkes his heirs or assignees, forty and
two shillings of lawful English money at the feast of St
Martin the Bishop in winter and Pentecost, or within
ten days next of either of the said feasts . . . And the
said Christopher Lumley . . . shall well and sufficiently
maintain and uphold the said barn at all times during
the said term in all necessary repairs great timber only
excepted, which the said Guy Fawkes . . . covenants to
deliver upon the ground at all times as often as need
shall require during the said term . . .

Guy Fawkes. L.S

Sealed and delivered in the presence of us . . .

Dionis Bainbrigge

George Hobson

John Jackson

X (Christopher Hodgson).[37]

Evidently Christopher Lumley was well known to Guy. Some

ten years earlier a man of the same name was mentioned as having witnessed the will of Guy's Uncle Thomas. Interestingly, Lumley's wife was mentioned as having been twenty shillings in debt to Thomas, yet this was forgiven in his will.[38] Within ten months of this agreement being made, Guy is recorded as having sold his estates to a spinster named Anne Skipsey for a sum of £29. 13s. 4d., as recorded in another surviving document:

> This Indenture made the 1st day of August in the 34th year of the reign of our Sovereign Lady Elizabeth . . . Queen of England . . . Between Guy Fawkes of the City of York, gentleman . . . and Anne Skipsey of Clifton in the county of York, spinster . . . Witnesses that the said Guy Fawkes, for and in consideration of the sum of £29. 13s. 4d. of good and lawful English money . . . the said Guy Fawkes . . . hath sold unto the said Anne Skipsey, her heirs and assignees, that his messuage, tenement or farmhold, with the appurtenancies and a garth and a garden belonging to the same, lying and being in Clifton in the county of York, and two acres and a half of arable land lying in several fields in Clifton aforesaid, half an acre of meadow land lying in a close called Huntington butts, within the township and territories of Clifton aforesaid, one acre of meadow lying in Lufton Car, three ings ends, and town crofts or lees of meadow in a croft adjoining on the garth ends in Clifton aforesaid, of the east part of the said messuage; all which premises are now in the tenure and occupation of the said Anne Skipsey; and also one acre of arable land meadow lying in the town-end field of Clifton, now or late in the occupation of Richard Dickenson; and all other his lands and tenements in

Clifton aforesaid, with all commons of pasture, moor ground, turf grafts . . . demised granted and to farm let for divers years yet to come and unexpired to Christopher Lumley of the City of York . . . and also the said Guy Fawkes . . . do covenant and grant to and with the same Anne Skipsey her heirs and assignees that Edith the late wife of Edward Fawkes deceased, mother to the said Guy Fawkes, and now wife to Dionis Bainbridge, gentleman, nor any other person or persons whatsoever, which have, shall have or shall claim any lawful right or title in or to the premises or any part thereof . . .

In witness thereof the parties abovesaid unto these present Indentures . . . have set their hands and seal the day and year above said.,

Guy Fawkes. L.S.

Sealed and delivered in the presence of:

George Hobson
William Maskewe
Lancelot Bett
Thomas Heslebecke
Christopher Lumley
+ (mark of John Lamb)
John Harrison
John Calv'ley.[39]

Guy's mother was also party to the deal, agreeing to release her claim to Edward Fawkes's remaining possessions, to which she had right of dowry. The quit deed was signed jointly with her new husband on 21 October 1592.[40] The survival of these documents is thanks in no small part to the antiquarian Robert Davies, FSA, who included all three in his compilation *The Fawkes's of York in the Sixteenth Century* published in 1850.

After attributing their discovery to one John Hoggard of Clifton in 1830, Davies notes: 'on the seal appended to one of them, though the impression is nearly effaced, the figure of a bird is just discernible, apparently a falcon'. For Davies, this confirmed Guy's ancestry from the Fawkeses of Farnley, whose crest was known to be a falcon.[41] The wording on the documents also provides insight into Guy's whereabouts. At the time he leased his property to Christopher Lumley, he is mentioned as a resident of Scotton, probably living in the house of his stepfather along with his mother and two sisters. Curiously, when Guy came to sell his property he was referred to as being a citizen of York. His whereabouts when witnessing the quit deed are not given. Reading between the lines, it seems as though a feud might have taken place, resulting in Guy's decision to leave home. One thing that is certain, from 1592 Guy's life in Yorkshire was largely over.

3

COWDRAY, CALVINISM AND
A SLOW BOAT TO FLANDERS

After severing his ties with his family and the city of his birth, Guy Fawkes embarked on a period of travel. Of his activities on leaving Yorkshire, details are sparse. He spent some time in Cambridge, as stated briefly in his confession, yet no detail is given as to when, for what purpose or for how long he remained in the town.[1] While it is possible that he spent three or four years as a teenager studying, it is equally possible that he lived there briefly in 1592, perhaps for employment or as a stopgap before travelling further south. Alternatively, some recusants were known to seek refuge at distant family properties or properties of friends, often in other counties in order to avoid persecution. Among the families in the West Riding of Yorkshire, recusant members of the Arthington family from Adel often sought refuge at one of three different properties.[2]

There has been some suggestion that Guy married around this time. According to the International Genealogy Index put together by the Church of the Latter Day Saints (the Mormons), he married a Maria Pulleyn some time in 1590, and she bore him a son a year later. Maria Pulleyn is documented in the same record as having been born in May 1569, eleven months before

Guy, and the date of the birth of their son, Thomas, is given as 9 February 1591.

Connections between the Fawkes and Pulleyn families are readily found. Records exist of a marriage between Anne Pulleyn of Scotton and Nicholas Fawkes, son of John Fawkes of Farnley, Steward of Knaresborough, in 1520.[3] In addition, there are other examples of marriages that connect the two families with other Catholic families, including the Arthingtons of Castley and the Vavasours of Weston. History also records that while Edith Bainbridge was staying with her new husband at the Pulleyn-owned house Timble, they shared the house with Bainbridge's mother, a Frances Pulleyn, née Vavasour, once married to Anthony Fawkes, grandson of Nicholas, and, assuming the falcon crest on the document is correct, probably a distant relation of Guy's. Her second marriage had been to a Bainbridge and her third to a Pulleyn, thus highlighting the complicated web of marriage between Catholic families, as frequently occurred during the Elizabethan era.[4]

It is not unreasonable to believe that Guy could have married a Pulleyn. The Pulleyns of Scotton were renowned advocates of the old religion and were already well connected to his family. Nevertheless, its inclusion is suspicious. Catherine Pullein in her family history of 1915 makes no reference to this marriage, while no further proof has been found in parish records or other primary sources. In Pullein's book, a Mary Pulleyn, wife of Edward Rudd, is recorded as having been born before 1564 rather than 1569, while another Mary, daughter of Henry Tempest, married a John Pulleyn in around 1574.[5] However, there are no contemporary accounts of Guy's life that refer to him as a married man. In Oswald Tesimond's account of the Gunpowder Plot, written under the alias Greenway, Guy's former schoolfriend notes 'He was also – something decidedly rare among soldiery, although it was immediately evident to all – a very devout man, of exemplary life and commendable reticence', perhaps suggesting his piety was the kind befitting a monk.[6] As previously mentioned, it is notable that a number of the men in the Fawkes family seem to have died unmarried. Both of Guy's sisters are known to have married, Anne in 1599 and Elizabeth in 1594, proof of which can still be found among the registries of St Oswald's Church in Farnham, near Scotton. Perhaps in Guy's case a Catholic reception did take place, away from this Protestant parish and otherwise unrecorded by the state, the evidence for which has still to come to light. Certainly, it is a fact that most of his fellow conspirators in the Gunpowder Plot were fathers and husbands. If Guy had married, the ceremony would almost certainly have been clandestine. Given what we know of Guy's personality and his devotion to his cause both as a Catholic and later as a soldier, it would not be unreasonable to conclude that he would have been a committed husband and father, so his sudden decision to sell his estates within two years of his possible marriage could suggest that his life had been hit by tragedy – possibly the death in quick succession of both his wife and his son. Perhaps a tragic event of that nature made its mark on the 22-year-old, convincing him to cast off the shackles of religious repression and find refuge in another land. Although experiences of this kind might provide a logical explanation for his sudden departure and the shaping of his character, there is no evidence to support such a claim.

Later in 1592 Guy reached Sussex where he found employment in the powerful house of Cowdray, the residence of the Viscount Montague and his wife Magdalen, prominent Catholics with colourful histories. During his time there Guy worked in the household as a footman, effectively a table waiter. Although this seems a humble position, it was a reasonable move for a

Catholic gentleman. At the time it was common for young men of such status to attach themselves to the gentry or nobility in order to improve their standing and to obtain valuable experience and training. Evidently this backfired, as Montague took a dislike to Guy and dismissed him after only four months.[7] Nevertheless, as fate would have it the viscount died later that year, following which Fawkes returned to the household in the service of the viscount's eighteen-year-old grandson, Anthony-Maria. Proof of Guy's employment is found in a letter written by the 2nd Viscount to the Earl of Dorset in the aftermath of the Gunpowder Plot. According to the letter:

> he should seem to have been my servant once . . . for such a one I had even for some four months, about the time of my marriage, but was dismissed from me by my lord upon some dislike he had of him; and discontinued for a year, till some six months after my lord's death, at what time he coming to one Spencer, that was, as it were, my steward and his kinsman, the same Spencer entreated me, that for that instant (being some few days) he might wait at my table, which he did, and departed, and from that time I never had to do with him, nor scarcely thought of him.[8]

To judge by the letter, it was Montague's steward, a man named Spencer, who pleaded for Guy to be allowed to wait table at the house. Spencer, evidently, was related to Guy, described as being his kinsman, and it may well have been through his involvement that Guy had been taken on at Cowdray in the first place. In the letter the 2nd Viscount recalls that he accepted Spencer's request to re-employ Guy without much thought. With hindsight he undoubtedly regretted the decision. Following

Guy's arrest and subsequent torture, the 2nd Montague was arrested on suspicion of complicity with the Gunpowder Plot and was forced to endure a year in the Tower of London. Previous historians have speculated that Montague might even have provided a character reference for Guy when he enlisted in the English Regiment of the Spanish Army fighting in the Low Countries, yet, when it came to his knowledge of Guy, Montague remained vague on the subject.[9]

Why Guy came to serve in Montague's household is unstated. Possibly his salary was a consideration, yet it is likely that he still had most of the money from the sale of his land to Anne Skipsey at the time. Perhaps the influence of Spencer was a deciding factor, and the employment was convenient while he considered his future. Nevertheless, when examining his time at Cowdray in the context of his later years, the influence of both viscounts on Guy should not be underestimated. While serving Anthony-Maria Browne, the 2nd Viscount, Guy would have been part of a diligently run household. Several years after Guy's departure, Browne famously wrote a book on how to manage a nobleman's household, entitled *A Book of Orders and Rules*.[10] For historians, the book provides a first-hand account of the routines of life of both lords and servants and offers an intriguing insight into the daily routines that would have been in place during Guy's time in service. His time in the household of the 1st Viscount was possibly of greater significance. While no less strict in manner and style, in the 1st Viscount Guy would have had a different kind of role model. Born in November 1528, Anthony Browne became a prominent figure in the higher echelons of the society of his day. His father, another Sir Anthony, had previously held much esteem in the Court of Henry VIII, holding positions such as Henry's standard-bearer and master of the horse. At least one previous commentator described him as an unashamed Francophobe, and it was partly through his hatred of the French that Sir Anthony voiced his disapproval at Henry's divorce from Katherine of Aragon, while in 1536 he showed notable devotion to Princess Mary, coming at a time when her right to succession was still a matter of debate.[11] Following the dissolution of the monasteries the Brownes inherited the Manor of Worthing – something that would remain in their family for two centuries – although their commitment to the Roman Church remained strong. For his funeral in 1548 Sir Anthony directed that mass and dirges should be said for the good of his soul, despite the fact that the Protestant Edward VI was king. Politically he was often held as having minority views and was accused of being on the fringes of the Prebendaries Plot aimed at displacing Archbishop Thomas Cranmer.[12]

The younger Anthony Browne, later the 1st Viscount, was no less vociferous and was of the opinion throughout the reign of Edward VI that the new religion was out of place. Although, ironically, Edward was responsible at his coronation for knighting Browne, Sir Anthony was imprisoned in 1551 on the charge of hearing mass in the presence of Princess Mary. Despite being pardoned of his crime and later released, his zeal for the old religion was noteworthy, albeit that he was no longer in a position to influence matters. Nevertheless, he was fondly remembered in many quarters and described by his widow's chaplain, Richard Smith, as having possessed 'love of God's worship and religion'.[13]

Following the execution of Lady Jane Grey and the subsequent accession of Mary Tudor, Browne rallied behind the new Catholic regime. In 1554 he was elevated to the peerage, taking the new title Montague, and was sent to Rome later that year as the queen's ambassador in a bid to reconcile the Church of England with Rome. He was appointed to the Privy Council in 1555, a position that he ultimately lost on the accession of Elizabeth as a result of his unwillingness to support the new regime. Furthermore, Montague was the only temporal peer to oppose the final Elizabethan Supremacy Bill in 1559 and the dissolution of the new religious houses.[14] Yet despite his celebrated zeal, throughout his later years Montague opposed violent opposition to the state, developing a reputation as a moderate man capable of being both Catholic and a loyal subject to Elizabeth. Such a reputation was illustrated in no better way than his celebrated role in raising troops to combat the Spanish Armada in 1588, an event subsequently used to epitomize a general sense of Catholic loyalty to the Crown against any of their fellow Catholics who might invade English soil.[15]

Despite retaining some degree of favour for the majority of Elizabeth's reign, Browne was tainted by conspiracy against the monarch. After seeing out most of the 1560s without major incident, it was suggested by the Spaniard Guerea de Specs that around December 1569 both Montague and his son-in-law, the Earl of Southampton, had consulted with him on whether to join the Norfolk Conspiracy or even defect to the Duke of Alba's forces in the Spanish Netherlands.[16] Earlier in 1569 Montague was, in fact, recorded as having attempted to dissuade Leonard Dacre, son of the 3rd Baron Dacre of Gilsland, from assisting the rebels in the Northern Rising, a warning Dacre must have wished he had heeded considering its failure. Montague himself narrowly avoided implication in the later Ridolfi Plot, masterminded by Italian banker Roberto Ridolfi, an alleged agent of the Pope, who attempted to establish an invasion of 6,000 men to be led by the Duke of Alba.[17]

While the parts played by Montague in the Norfolk Conspiracy, the Northern Rising and the Ridolfi Plot were fringe at best, the complicity of several of his friends and relations called his loyalty to the Crown into question. His possible involvement may have been exaggerated by the testaments of others involved – such as William Barker, Edmund Powell and Ridolfi himself – under interrogation, all of whom claimed Montague personally approved of a marriage between Mary Stuart and Norfolk, yet other evidence that Montague favoured Mary Stuart over Elizabeth is absent.[18] The same, on the other hand, cannot be said of Montague's son, Sir George Browne, who was subsequently taken to the Tower of London for his complicity in the Ridolfi conspiracy.[19] For Montague, any minor involvement probably did little to blemish his character permanently, but this changed in 1581 after he was found offering protection to Catholics with suspected connections with Edmund Campion. Among these was Montague's wife's brother-in-law, Sir Alexander Culpeper, who was hounded by the authorities shortly after Campion's arrival in England in 1580. Culpeper is also recorded as having stated that most of the principal Catholic Sussex gentry incarcerated at the time were close to Montague.[20] This was also true of Montague's wife, Magdalen. According to her chaplain, Smith:

> She built a chapel in her house (Cowdray) . . . and there placed a very fair altar of stone . . . almost every week was a sermon made . . . such was the number of Catholics resident in her house . . . Lady Magdalen, gave it the title of Little Rome.[21]

Among the Montague's Catholic guests were several priests, including the influential Jesuit Father Robert Southwell who spent time there in the early 1590s.[22] Given this, it is not unlikely that priests and other Catholics were also being harboured at Cowdray during Guy's own time there. While involvement in support of the Catholic activism that occurred during Elizabeth's reign is something that Montague seems never to have specifically endorsed – he is not recorded as having spent time in prison during this time – it seems a notable and prudent trait of character that his adherence to the old faith was better served through private observance and secret aid rather than all-out conflict.[23]

While Montague's tendency to approach conflicts of religion with quiet stubbornness seems to have been lost on Guy, it is likely that his time in service had at least some effect on the development of his character, which was still a long way from being fully formed. The 1st Viscount Montague in particular was highly polished in all forms of military procedure and may have instilled some of these skills and values in Guy. Perhaps, too, the 1st Viscount's diplomacy would have had an influence on Guy's education, particularly viewing with hindsight his later mission to petition the Spanish King in 1603. It is also likely that it was at this time that he became familiar with the military style of discipline. While Guy would have been no stranger to strict regimes from his time at school, life in the service of both viscounts would have given him a first-hand insight into what life would be like as a soldier.[24]

Guy departed Cowdray, and England, in around 1593 when he voyaged to Flanders with his cousin Richard Collinge. It is possible that Guy embarked on a military career immediately, but there is a suggestion that he might have travelled first, most likely through France, Italy and the Low Countries. When present at the Court of Spain in 1603, Fawkes is recorded as having been asked to escort Anthony Dutton on a voyage because he could speak French, an interesting request of a soldier from Yorkshire. When questioned in the aftermath of the Gunpowder Plot, Guy answered that he learned to speak French 'first here in England', yet considering his answer came at a time when he was still concealing his true identity, his truthfulness can be called into question. Other factors that suggest he might have travelled include Guy admitting to those questioning him that his father left him a small inheritance 'which he spent'.[25] Evidence that Guy had already spent the money, in addition to his statement that he had lived in Cambridge and four other places, certainly suggests he was well travelled.[26]

In order to understand the next decade of Guy's life it is vital also to understand the world of which he was then a part. By 1593 the wars of religion had been raging for over thirty years. Collectively, the term refers to a series of wars that engulfed Europe in the sixteenth and seventeenth centuries, largely a result of the Reformation. Following the spread of Lutheranism and Calvinism throughout Europe in the sixteenth century, Europe had become divided. In France, a series of disputes between the established Catholic faith and the new Protestantism, brought about primarily by the teachings of Martin Luther in Paris, developed further, largely owing to a series of Calvinist preachers who came to France from Geneva charged with the aim of setting up secret underground congregations in opposition to the Catholic rule. Although the monarchy opposed the new wave of Protestantism, and sought to suppress the teachings of Luther, King Francis I of France and later King Henri II both offered military support to Protestant German princes in their fight against the Habsburgs – rulers both of the Holy Roman Empire and Spain. By 1562 this new wave of Calvinist reformers had created alliances with certain members of the nobility, who, rather than being possessed of any deep spiritual mission, probably saw in the new developments opportunities to enhance their own political power and influence. The most powerful of these families was the newly converted House of Bourbon, a branch of the French royal family with links to the

Capetian dynasty, who found themselves in direct civil war with the Catholic House of Guise (a cadet branch of the Duchy of Upper Lorraine), ardent supporters of the French monarchy, the House of Valois-Angoulême. A growing Calvinist influence was also apparent in both Scotland and the Netherlands, resulting in religious unrest.

In France, a series of Protestant attacks on Catholic churches in 1560, which resulted in the destruction of countless religious statues and images, exacerbated the unrest further. Later that year, Catherine de'Medici, the mother and regent of the new king, Charles IX, voiced her support for religious tolerance of the Protestant Huguenots, yet this was withdrawn following an attack on Protestant worshippers by the Guises, leading to what is historically referred to as the First War. A brief truce followed in 1563, but hopes of a peaceful solution soon faded. With unrest in the Netherlands threatening to boil over, the Protestant Huguenots failed in their attempts to persuade the French government to attack the Spanish forces *en route* to the Netherlands, and this resulted in a failed attempt to capture the French King in 1567. The Second War duly followed, again ending with an awkward truce and the Third War in 1568. As the feud continued, the Protestants' position became strengthened by the support of Elizabeth I, who had funded many of the Huguenot campaigns. By 1572 tensions between Catholics and Protestants reached melting point following the wedding of the Protestant Henri of Navarre to the Catholic Marguerite de Valois, sister of the French king, resulting in the deaths of some 10,000 in what is now dubbed the St Bartholomew's Day Massacre and culminating in further war.

In addition to this devastating blow to the Huguenot movement, the political situation in Europe took a further twist following Elizabeth's decision to sign the Treaty of Blois in 1572.

This led not only to a new trade agreement between England and France but to a military union between France and England against the Spanish. This had a profound effect on England's history – and the life of Guy Fawkes. By 1575 Henri of Anjou was crowned Henri III of France, and within a year the Catholic cause was strengthened when Henri, the 1st Duke of Guise, formed the Catholic League with support from the Papal States, the Spanish and the Jesuits. A further war, the seventh, ended in a truce in 1580, yet further tensions arose in 1584 when Henri III refused the right of succession of Henri of Navarre, who was next in line for the throne of France. By 1588 the king's own position was weakened as the Catholics of France became frustrated with his inability to suppress Calvinism. This led to the murders of Henri de Guise and Cardinal de Guise by Henri III, ironically resulting in Henri's murder but not before he named the Protestant Henri of Navarre, his cousin, as successor on the condition he converted to Catholicism in order to unify the religious divide within the nation.

While some conflict continued between 1589 and 1594, the year of the king's formal conversion and coronation, the situation in France was cooling, resulting in a decision by Henri of Navarre, now Henri IV, to declare war on Spain. Meanwhile, in the Low Countries – which roughly encompassed modern-day Belgium, the Netherlands and part of north-east France – the situation was becoming increasingly turbulent. Following the influx of Calvinist preachers in the 1560s, the Spanish-controlled Netherlands became plagued by Protestant iconoclasm, particularly in the south, in a display of discontent at Spanish rule. In 1568 this vandalism escalated when the Dutch nobleman, William the Silent of Orange, led a revolt that aimed to drive the Duke of Alba from Brussels. Various Protestant attempts to take over the Netherlands from the Spanish followed with some successes, yet total victory against the Spanish was not forthcoming, largely because of a lack of funds.

For the Spanish there was another problem. In addition to putting out fires in the Netherlands, Philip II was fighting a war against the Ottoman Turks. Conflict in the Netherlands subsided in 1570, but the Protestants recovered in 1572 when Dutch Calvinists fleeing England captured the town of Brielle. Over the next six years the rebels continued to build on their success resulting in William the Silent entering the Netherlands in 1578 with forces of over 20,000, some of which were French Huguenots. Many Dutchmen supported the rebels, not only Protestants, but also Catholics who were still prepared to fight for the rebel cause because of their opposition to Spanish rule. However, by 1579 many Dutchmen living in the south declared their loyalty to Philip after taking a dislike to the hard Calvinist stance in the north. Over the next decade Alexander Farnese, now Governor of the 'Spanish Netherlands' and later Duke of Parma, reclaimed much of Flanders and the Duchy of Brabant, restoring Catholicism to the area. By the 1590s the south retained a Catholic majority and a Spanish military presence, while two decades of consistent Calvinist rule had left the north strongly Protestant, leading to the establishment of the Dutch Republic or the United Provinces of the Netherlands.[27]

Guy Fawkes's enrolment in the forces of the Spanish most likely occurred in 1594, although it might have been as late as 1595. At that time the Spanish were still actively engaged in conflict against the Calvinist Dutch, yet military action was not restricted to those two nations. For Guy, the decision to enlist in the Spanish Army was not necessarily through any overwhelming desire for a Spanish victory, yet neither was it simply a financial decision. In the past, some historians have branded him as being a soldier of fortune, a mercenary, placing his decision to enrol down to greed. Undoubtedly, some soldiers did enlist for military service in search of financial gain, but this is unlikely to be true in Guy's case. For a man of gentleman status, particularly following his service at Cowdray, life as a soldier was a definite step up the career ladder, something that he would have the opportunity to build on throughout the coming years. For a young English Catholic this was in many ways the best career on offer at the time. What is more, operating in a Catholic nation he was no longer burdened by the harsh penalties of recusancy. Guy's decision was by no means unique. Sir Roland Yorke, a recusant from the West Riding is also recorded as being a soldier in the service of Spain.[28] Realistically, Guy never even considered fighting on the side of the Calvinist Dutch. His decision was one of conscience. In addition, although Elizabeth had offered some support to the Protestant cause, the Spanish were not at war with England, meaning Guy would never be placed in a situation where he would be engaged in direct combat against England, leaving him free to act independently of the sovereign. The reality of fighting in the wars of religion was in many ways comparable to taking part in the Crusades of the eleventh to the thirteenth centuries. As a Catholic, forced to endure a repressed existence in England, fighting abroad was the first opportunity Guy would have had to strike a blow for his cause.

4

A TRAITOR TO THE CROWN

For Guy Fawkes enrolment in the Spanish forces would not have been difficult, nor would it have been particularly unusual. Instead he became one of many Englishmen of Catholic sympathy to enter the war by association with Sir William Stanley.

Born in 1548, Stanley was the eldest son of Sir Rowland Stanley of Hooton and Storeton in Cheshire and heir to his father's title. As Catholics of noble birth, the Stanleys had endured turbulent relationships with Elizabeth, which came to a head in 1570 when William's cousins, Sir Thomas and Sir Edward Stanley, attempted to rescue Mary, Queen of Scots from Chatsworth House and lead her to safety on the Isle of Man.[1] Before the events that led up to the Stanley Plot of 1570, William himself had already spent time in the service of Sir Edward Stanley, the 3rd Earl of Derby, and was undoubtedly swayed by his Catholic sympathies. After completing his service, Stanley, like Guy, left England to embark on a military career, becoming a volunteer in the service of the Duke of Alba in 1567.[2]

Despite his Catholic leanings, Stanley changed his allegiance in 1570, choosing to fight for Elizabeth I in Ireland. After nine years of loyal service, Stanley was knighted for his gallantry, particularly his achievements in combat at Limerick against the

Earl of Desmond, while he was also instrumental in helping quash a rebellion against Elizabeth the following year. For a further five years he served with honour in Ireland, for which he received the titles Constable of Castlemain and Sheriff of Cork. Towards the end of 1584 he was severely wounded while attempting to put down a rebellion in Ulster, resulting in his return to England.

After more than fifteen years of service, which earned him a reputation as one of England's finest soldiers, Stanley was becoming frustrated. His success in Ireland had been of much benefit to Elizabeth, yet surprisingly when the Earl of Desmond was defeated and his estates divided up Stanley was unrewarded. As a man of Catholic leanings fighting for a Protestant monarch against a Catholic nation, Stanley's allegiance must certainly have come into question. In 1585, following a brief period in Ireland during which time he recruited a further thousand troops for the Protestant cause, he travelled to the United Provinces to assist the Earl of Leicester in his campaign aiding the Dutch against the Spanish.[3] However, while still in Ireland Stanley was allegedly spotted in the company of several Jesuit priests, and it was claimed that he had corresponded with the Spanish Ambassador to the King of France, Don Bernardino de Mendoza. This alleged communication with Mendoza has aroused suspicion that he may have been involved in the Babington Plot of 1586. While in Ireland it was noted that Stanley delayed his journey to the Low Countries, giving rise to a suggestion the delay was a deliberate ploy to assist the Spanish in an invasion of England in the event of Elizabeth being assassinated or the arrival of a Spanish Fleet from Cadiz. Mendoza had earlier been banned from England for operating as a spy for Philip II and for his involvement in the Throckmorton Plot. Since the death of his wife, Queen Mary I of England, in 1558 Philip had lost influence in England, and attempts to obtain favour with Elizabeth had failed. Following the failure of the Throckmorton and Parry Plots in 1583 and 1585, two Englishmen – Charles Paget and Thomas Morgan – both loyal agents of the still imprisoned Mary, Queen of Scots, were working on two separate plots to dethrone Elizabeth. In 1585 Paget attempted to consolidate both plots, one involving a Spanish invasion and the other to assassinate the queen, by securing the support of England's Catholic gentry by building on vague promises of support from the Catholic League of France. Such support was eventually found in the form of Sir Anthony Babington, a Catholic nobleman, who had been unaware that any prospect of assistance from the Catholic League had been grossly overstated or that details of the plot had fallen into the hands of Elizabeth's secret service, led by Sir Francis Walsingham, thus leading to the failure of the plot and the execution of Mary, Queen of Scots.

Stanley eventually arrived in the United Provinces in August 1586 and fought at the Battle of Zutphen. Later that year he was instrumental in the capture of the city of Deventer, after which he gained control over the entire garrison, comprised of approximately 1,200 men, mainly Irish Catholics. Then, within a year of taking the city, Stanley's life changed dramatically. Acting independently of any other command, he communicated with the Catholic Governor of Zutphen, Juan de Tassis, and surrendered the garrison at Deventer to the Spanish in January 1587, at which point he and his men defected to fight for Spain, to the delight of the Jesuits.[4]

Stanley's decision to defect was probably threefold. Although undoubtedly swayed by his commitment to Catholicism, the decision was probably also one borne out of frustration at Elizabeth for his lack of reward during his time in Ireland. Ironically, if he had waited a few months, he might have been appointed

Viceroy of Ireland.[5] Yet his frustration might, too, have been growing in other ways. On Boxing Day 1586, just over a month before his defection, he had written to Sir Francis Walsingham criticizing the conditions endured by his men. According to the letter, his captains were surviving entirely on bread and cheese, while the ordinary soldiers had only half a pound (225 grams) of cheese a day, resulting in many of them becoming sick. Stanley also lamented his lack of funds, claiming 'we have not received a month's pay since our coming into these countries, which is now almost six months'.[6] However, under Spanish control things failed to improve. As reported by an agent to the queen, Sir Ralph Sadler, within a year the troops were forced to survive simply on dry acorns.[7]

For the young Guy Fawkes, Sir William Stanley would have been quite a role model. If we consider how Guy's own reputation as a soldier developed over the subsequent years it is perhaps not unreasonable to conclude that his new commander influenced him significantly. Stanley would have been something of a father figure to the Yorkshireman, and in time he would even have become a close friend. By the mid 1590s, the time when Guy joined his service, Stanley had been officially exiled by Elizabeth for his decision to defect to the Spanish and had his own regiment in the army of the Archduke of Austria, with the rank of colonel. While Stanley's regiment is known as the English Regiment, it was composed of many nationalities, including Scots, Welsh, Italians and, notably, Irish. According to sources in Spanish records the English Regiment comprised ninety officers, mainly English Catholics, 626 soldiers who had defected to them from Deventer in addition to some two hundred refugee Catholics and other men serving under Sir Rowland Yorke. Yet by 1589 morale had fallen and numbers were down, leaving the regiment in danger of being disbanded.[8]

By 1588 Stanley had other ambitions. During that year, he was reported as having made several trips to the Court of Philip II with the intention of influencing the King's plans for an invasion of England. Despite his defection, there is reason to believe Philip did not particularly like Stanley. In addition to ignoring his ideas, Philip is reputed to have said that while he approved of Stanley handing over the city of Deventer, he did not approve of the traitor himself.[9] In hindsight he may have wished he had paid him more attention. Drawing on his knowledge of Ireland, Stanley attempted to convince Philip to abandon his plans for an invasion of the south coast of England and instead sail to Ireland and subsequently land at Milford Haven in Wales, taking advantage of Ireland's Catholic leanings to use the country both as a stop-off point and to take on extra troops. Philip, however, dismissed the idea and headed straight for England, leading to the famous defeat of the Armada. Following the defeat, Stanley left for Antwerp and spent time there planning his next move and strengthening the English Regiment. In 1590 he returned to Madrid seeking an audience with Philip, claiming he had a legion of a thousand men under his command, consisting mostly of Irishmen and Englishmen ready to assist in another armada against Elizabeth. In 1592 he was involved in the Patrick Cullen conspiracy, another Catholic plot to assassinate Elizabeth.[10] Stanley continued to strengthen his forces by accepting volunteers into his regiment, usually Catholics discontented by the iconoclasm in the Spanish Netherlands. The increased numbers in Stanley's regiment suggest conditions had improved by the mid 1590s – at the very least, Guy would have received a bed and sufficient rations to live on.

It seems from the information available that Guy did not command any notable rank in his early days of service but adapted well to his profession and served Stanley with enthusiasm.

According to his contemporaries, Guy was strong and brave and a champion of the Jesuits whenever they were attacked in the Low Countries. Another account describes him as being a tall, athletic man with brown hair and an auburn beard with a personality that was direct of purpose, simple of heart, modest, self-controlled and valiant and also skilled in the wars.[11] This compares well with the words of Father Tesimond, who described Guy as a man who had 'acquired considerable fame and name among the soldiers'.[12] When we look at Guy's service in the context of his later life it is clear that he served his profession loyally, and over the course of his time in the Spanish forces acquired many new skills through his military experience. The combination of the circumstances of the war and its location made him an indispensable member of the later Gunpowder Conspiracy. The Low Countries was a marshy area comprising wetland, canals and tributaries in close proximity to the sea, making traditional warfare almost impossible. As a result, most battles involved the invasion of fortified towns and structures rather than open field battle. Guy spent much of his time in service charged with the task of blowing up fortifications, making him an expert in the use of gunpowder. By the end of his time in service he was capable of firing a train – a trail of slow-burning powder connecting to gunpowder in a barrel – and was also highly skilled in the art of the slow match, a technique used for firing military mines using a rope soaked in a mixture of limewater and saltpetre.[13]

While details of Guy's military history remain incomplete, some scattered accounts have survived. The earliest is from 1596, when Guy is reported as being present at the Siege of Calais. Calais at the time was an important shipping port under French control, and the attack by the Spanish was to prove an unexpected and significant turning point in the war. The new governor of the Spanish Netherlands, Albert, Archduke of Austria, took the decision to march on the port, although early indications suggested his army was, in fact, heading for La Fère in Picardy.[14] Elizabeth, who was in the process of raising an army to invade Cadiz, was approached by the French King, Henri IV, to assist in combating the Spanish. According to the chronicler William Camden:

> As soon as the Queen heard by the fearful messengers of the French King that Calais was besieged, she commanded a power of men to be gathered that very day, being Sunday, while men were at divine service, to aid the French King, and, withall, provide for the safety of England. This army, hastily raised, she committed to Essex; but before they were shipped, she had certain advertisement that both the towne and castell were yielded up into the Spaniards' hands.[15]

The surprise of the siege caused great consternation, even in England, as noted by Lord Burghley in a letter to his son, the future Secretary of State, Sir Robert Cecil, stating 'this alarm of Calliss hath kept me waking all night, and hath styrred up in me many cogitations'.[16] In retrospect, Elizabeth might have wished she had deployed the fleet. If nothing else, the taking of Calais was a major morale boost for the Spanish. When Henri asked Elizabeth for assistance, the queen replied that her price was control of the town, to which Henri said: 'You must excuse me, I would rather be robbed by my enemies than by my friends.'[17]

The battle itself was an impressive victory for the Spanish. Evidence that the attack on Calais came as a surprise is clear from Henri IV's decision to reinforce his army, who were attempting to besiege the Spanish-controlled city of La Fère. Albert is recorded as having ordered supplies to be delivered to the city, including some five hundred cartloads of wheat, bread and other supplies to replenish its depleted stocks. Discovering this, Henri attempted to maintain the French advantage by ordering all his nobles to join him. However, unbeknown to Henri, Albert's force of some 5,000 troops was marching on Calais, seizing several posts of importance by Tuesday 9 April. After sending members of the light cavalry towards Montreuil (Monstreul), near Calais, to take on the threat of the enemy, Albert himself arrived with the remainder of his forces. Within two days Henri's army responded to the siege by sailing several barques into the port. In total, over one hundred French ships had reached the harbour to combat the Spanish fleet. Between 12 and 14 April the Spanish began their land assault on the city, undoubtedly involving immense quantities of gunpowder. By early the following week it became clear that some assault would be necessary by sea. By the Friday, the inability of the French forces to protect a weakened rampart on the harbour side from Spanish cannonades led to their request for a truce, which was refused by the Spanish. As a result, the city was surrendered on the condition that nothing of harm should come to any citizens wishing to evacuate. On taking the city, the archduke gave permission for its inhabitants to seek refuge in other parts of France, an offer accepted by all but two families.[18] While a late attempt by Henri IV to reinforce his army did take place, it was too late to avoid the surrender of the city, as only the citadel was still under French control. On the 23 April the Spanish sent word to the citadel, asking if it was the governor's intention to surrender it. He declined, spurred on by aid having arrived thanks to the incompetence of the Spaniards on guard. Nevertheless, the Spanish subsequently conquered the citadel on Wednesday the 24th.

The victory was a celebrated one for the Spanish not only

because of its military importance but because Calais had been so well defended. Some 1,500 soldiers, in addition to over 2,000 citizens taking refuge there, defended the citadel alone, yet the assault on the citadel was completed in less than three-quarters of an hour, concluding a siege that had lasted fourteen days, including six days given to those taking refuge in the citadel to deliberate its surrender. All in all over a thousand people were killed and many others wounded. Only nineteen Spanish died while taking the citadel, in addition to some thirteen Walloons, twenty-five 'Almains' (Germans), while a hundred or so were wounded. The Spanish were celebrated for their gallantry, as were the Walloons, while the French, too, put up a heroic resistance.[19] Guy himself was praised for his gallantry and prowess to such an extent that Stanley rewarded him with his own company of men. Spink suggests that Guy already held a post of command.[20] During the siege Guy's primary role would have been to destroy the walls of the town with gunpowder.

Guy's activities over the following four years are largely unrecorded. Most likely he continued to serve the English Regiment. Stanley is known to have been present at battles in Amiens and at Geldern against Maurice of Nassau. The Spanish invasion of Amiens took place in 1597 when the Spanish Army captured the city disguised as peasants. Henri declared his immediate goal to be to recapture the city, and this was achieved after six months.[21] Albert, Archduke of Austria, despite financial constraints, attempted to raise an army of 28,000 to relieve the city, but by the end of the year he was instead pressing for peace with Elizabeth. Following the recapture of Amiens by the French, Elizabeth asked Henri to extradite Stanley for torture along with any other English traitors at the Spanish garrison at Amiens. Stanley, however, was nowhere to be found and escaped unpunished.[22]

Successful negotiations between Henri IV of France and

Philip II of Spain brought about peace in 1598, effectively ending the wars of religion in France. The treaty, signed in May 1598 in the small town of Vervins in Picardy – and known thereafter as the Peace of Vervins – ended Philip II's involvement in the war against the French, yet Spanish conflict with the Dutch continued. The year 1598 was also the final one of Philip II's reign, and he was succeeded by his son Philip III.

Although Guy remained in service of the archduke, there is evidence to suggest he travelled to Venice in 1599, as highlighted by a letter from his cousin, Richard Collinge, to one Guilio Piccioli:

> Good Sir
>
> I pray you let me intreat your favour and friendship for my cousin german Mr Guido Fawks [*sic*] who serves Sir William Stanley as I understand he is in great want and your word in his behalf may stand him in great stead. I have not deserved any such courtesy at your hands as for my sake to help my friends but assure yourself that if there be any thing I can do for you, you may command me for the respect I bear to our friendship but also by this means you shall bind me more unto you. He hath left a pretty living here in his country which his mother being married to an unthrifty husband since his departure I think hath wasted away. Yet she and the rest of our friends are in good health. I durst not as yet go to them but this summer I mean to see them all God willing let him tell my cousin Martin Harrington that I was at his brother Henry's house at The Mount but he was not then at home he and his wife are well and have many pretty children.
>
> Things go well forward here our enemies persecute us all more than ever and are in particular fear or rather

look for somewhat more from our own malcontents.
Thus requesting your favour in my suit and remem-
brance in your best memories as you shall have mine.
I commit you to sweet Jesus his whole protection this
St. John Baptist's eve.

Yours in Christ,
Richard Collinge[23]

It seems from the letter that Guy was seeking out his cousin,
Martin Harrington, one of the Harringtons of Mount St John.
It confirms that Guy was still in the service of William Stanley
and that his reputation was a fine one. Collinge refers to Guy as
being 'in great want', while a similar fact is recalled by Father
Tesimond, who described Guy as an accomplished fighter whose
company was 'sought by all the most distinguished in the Archduke's camp for nobility and virtue'.[24] Reference to his name as
Guido demonstrates the effect of the Spanish influence, while the
letter also provides insight into the personalities of his parents,
notably his stepfather, who Collinge describes as 'unthrifty'.
Apart from its historical value the letter had little effect on Guy's
life, as it never actually reached its destination. Perhaps Guy did
make contact with Piccioli, but there is no way to prove it.
Collinge, on the other hand, is known to have spent time in Italy
throughout the 1590s. Any trip Guy might have made to Italy
would have been relatively brief, as he was recorded in the following year as having returned to military action as an ensign,
roughly equivalent to a lieutenant, under the new commander of
the English Regiment, Colonel Bostock, at the Battle of Nieuwpoort, a tragic blood-and-thunder affair between the Dutch
armies of Maurice of Nassau and Sir Francis Vere and the Spanish
force led by Albert of Austria on 2 July 1600 near the town of
Nieuwpoort in Flanders. The battle, later nicknamed the Battle

of the Dunes because of its treacherous location, was, in reality, a disaster for both sides. Despite a victory for the Dutch resulting in the loss of somewhere between 2,500 and 3,000 Spanish men, plus some 500 taken prisoner, the Dutch themselves lost some 2,000 and failed to make any significant gain.

Among the casualties was Colonel Bostock. Guy presumably fled the field largely unharmed – no known surviving record exists to suggest he was captured – yet it is equally possible that the wounds mentioned during his confession at the Tower of London five years later were sustained in this battle. For Guy, the battle would have been both energy sapping and demoralizing. In addition to having to march across mile upon mile of unstable sand without rest or refreshment, fighting on sand dunes would have been very demanding. Judging from accounts of the battle, Bostock's regiment, one of three making up the third line of attack, were successful in overcoming the Dutch cuirassiers who had earlier wiped out much of the Spanish light cavalry and inflicted significant losses. However, any advantage the Spanish had was lost in the hazardous conditions. Following the regrouping of the English support under Vere and reinforcements in the Dutch third line the Spanish were forced to retreat. Meanwhile, the Spanish third line, in which Guy was present, became bogged down, resulting in their being outnumbered by the Dutch cavalry and ravaged by gunfire from the hills.[25] For the Spanish, the result would have been almost total annihilation. Following the death of Bostock, Guy's rank would have enforced some degree of leadership on him, particularly when the scattered remnants of both his own company and those others making up the regiment had become disorganized.[26]

While the masses bled to death on the treacherous wet sand, those who survived fled in various directions. Many of those who did manage to escape sought refuge at the abandoned

Dutch garrison at Ostend. His day may have ended in defeat, yet there is little reason to believe his battle ended in disgrace. For Guy Fawkes, his future was not to be marching the boggy beaches of the Low Countries; instead what awaited him was a different task, one that, had it been successful, would have had a dramatic effect on the course of English history.

5

A RUTHLESS AND UNLOVING LAND

Despite experiencing defeat at Nieuwpoort, Guy remained in Flanders, spending some time in the service of Stanley's illegitimate brother. His activities there are unrecorded, but a short time later he returned to the employment of Sir William, this time acting as a steward.[1] By 1600 Guy would have been well known to Sir William. In addition to rewarding Guy with his own company of men after his heroics at Calais, Stanley had spent much time in Guy's company in the officer's mess, a customary privilege for any soldier of rank.

It was also around this time that Guy became acquainted with two other key Catholics, Hugh Owen, Stanley's aide-de-camp, and the controversial Jesuit, Father William Baldwin. Baldwin, an Englishman who had spent time in the Tower of London for his faith, was the senior English Jesuit resident of Flanders, and Owen was a Catholic spy operating primarily in the Low Countries. Like many Catholics in exile, Owen had a dubious past. Born in Caernarvonshire, he was in his sixties by 1600 and had been living on the Continent for some thirty years. A veteran of the wars, Owen had developed a reputation for controversy. Possessed of an intriguing nature, he was fluent in several languages other than his native English, including Latin, French,

Spanish and Italian, and he is reported to have been involved in most Catholic conspiracies that took place in England during his exile. Owen, like Stanley, supported the Spanish Armada in 1588 and had previously travelled to Madrid in Stanley's company.[2]

By 1599 Stanley had been replaced by Bostock as head of the English Regiment, after which time he turned his attention to diplomacy. Despite his failed efforts to assist Philip II with his planning of an invasion of England, another attempt, this time involving Philip III, was in the pipeline. It was also around this time that Guy Fawkes was chosen for a highly important and controversial mission to the Court of Philip III in Spain. His purpose was to seek an audience with the King of Spain to whom he would reveal the true state of England's Catholics and, in doing so, seek to obtain a guarantee of Spanish military backing in support of the Catholic cause, an event that is often referred to as the 'Spanish Treason'.

Although Guy officially remained conscripted to the Spanish Army until 1605, by 16 February 1603 he was given permission to be placed on indefinite leave.[3] According to one source, he was being considered for promotion to the rank of captain shortly after his departure.[4] With his leave granted, Guy made his way to Spain, acting as the official envoy of three unidentified senior political, religious and military officials. Although the identities of these three figures have never been uncovered in Spanish documents, when questioned by the English government following the Gunpowder Plot, Guy was forced to admit that his trip was under orders from Stanley, Owen and Baldwin.[5]

To appreciate the significance of Guy's role in the Spanish Treason it is important to understand the circumstances that preceded it. By 1598 the war with France and was over, yet the question of who would succeed the childless Queen Elizabeth to the throne of England remained unanswered. Since the execution of Mary, Queen of Scots in the aftermath of the Babington Plot, Elizabeth had no obvious successor. Henry VIII's decision to bar the descendents of Margaret Tudor, wife of James IV of Scotland, on the grounds that her offspring were foreigners, left the same question mark over James's claim as it had his mother's. According to the book *Conference About the Next Succession to the Crowne of England*, written mainly by the Jesuit Robert Persons, Princess Isabella, daughter of Philip II of Spain, had the best claim. In addition to being descended from John of Gaunt, the third son of Edward III of England and father of Henry IV, Isabella was also descended from the Duchy of Brittany on her mother's side and so had a further claim through the pledge of feudal allegiance originally put forward by William the Conqueror.[6] For England's Catholics Isabella was the preferred option, yet support for her was complicated. In addition to her not being English, as a childless, unmarried woman the status of her successor would be more difficult to resolve when she died.

By 1601 confirmation of Elizabeth's successor was still no clearer. At this time there was much movement and speculation among key members of the Privy Council. Among them was Sir Robert Cecil, son of Sir William Cecil, and Sir Robert Devereux, the 2nd Earl of Essex. Although a former favourite of the queen, Essex was then under house arrest for neglecting his duty while putting down a rebellion in Ulster the previous year. Essex had already made contact with James VI of Scotland in 1598 regarding the possibility of his becoming King of England, while Cecil did the same with both Isabella and James. By 1601 Essex attempted to weaken Cecil's position by leaking knowledge of Cecil's correspondence with Isabella to James, yet this backfired after Essex's disastrous decision to incite a rising against Elizabeth in February 1601. The rebellion failed to capture the hearts of the masses. Among those involved were several young English Catholics who saw it as an opportunity to help improve the lot of England's Catholics.[7] After failing to obtain the queen's pardon, Essex was executed on 25 February. Although his accomplices avoided this fate, most still endured a loss of status, significant fines and some period of imprisonment. Among those penalized were the prominent Catholic Lord Monteagle and future Gunpowder Plot conspirators Robert Catesby and Francis Tresham.[8]

While support in the Cecil faction centred on James, movement among the exiled Catholics in support of a Catholic heir to the English throne struggled to gather momentum. Following the accession of Philip III in 1598 in the aftermath of the Peace of Vervins, Father Joseph Creswell, the leader of the English Jesuits in Spain, attempted to convince Philip to act on military intelligence that Elizabeth was preparing an assault on Spanish territory by ordering another armada against England. Harbouring hopes that a successful invasion would not only end the political conflict with England but also finally put an end to oppressive conditions endured by England's Catholics, Creswell and his advisers offered plans for a military invasion of England and a proclamation for their victory.[9] The proclamation itself was not entirely original; the same one had been in existence for over a year, written for the king's father, for an armada in 1597. It aimed to restore 'religion and justice' to England and establish a parliament to specify the most appropriate successor to Elizabeth while allowing no violence against the queen herself. Yet their plans left a number of issues unresolved, notably any specific information regarding the rising of English Catholics to support a Spanish invasion. As a result, Philip responded coolly to the idea, choosing instead to concentrate on the domestic policy of his own kingdom.[10]

On the question of Elizabeth's successor, Philip remained neutral, at least officially. For the English Catholics this was problematic. As noted in a memorandum to the Court of Philip in 1599 by the influential Jesuit, Father Robert Persons, no decision could be made until Philip put forward his intention to be involved in the process. In many ways, this was of benefit to James, as the longer Philip remained inactive the less chance there was of a Catholic alternative. In April 1599, when Isabella married Albert of Austria, the same time as Philip himself married the Archduchess Margarita of Austria, any interest Isabella might have had in the throne of England seemed to fade. For Isabella, her new role as co-ruler of the Spanish Netherlands with Albert, albeit under Spanish sovereignty, was more important. For Creswell, the occasion provided an ideal time for Philip to make his intentions known. However, the King of Spain once more failed to respond. Questions regarding the nature of any future invasion were left to Philip's council, which also failed to make any progress. Of more imminent concern was Spain's failing military expedition to assist the Irish in their rebellion against Elizabeth, often known as the Nine Years War (1594–1603).[11] Philip had little enthusiasm for an invasion of England, particularly as the requests and promises of support were from a minority of the population, largely exiles that had been absent from England for over fifteen years.

Philip, in fact, wanted peace with England, and signs of a possible agreement came in 1600. A conference, held between representatives from England, Spain and the Spanish Netherlands in May and June, although failing to come to any definitive agreements, was a sign of things to come. Philip's reluctance to make his intentions clear with regard to Elizabeth's successor continued, although by July he did confirm to his ambassador in Rome that he had decided on a candidate before revealing in

February 1601 to the Spanish Council of State that he would support Isabella's claim. Nevertheless, the possibility of Isabella becoming Queen of England remained remote, as the continuing war in the Low Countries remained Philip's priority. In addition, Isabella herself was still to give any indication of her interest, despite continuous pleas from the English exiles. As time passed, relations between Isabella's new husband, Albert, and James became warmer. For over a year talk of an invasion of England and support for Isabella stalled, much to the annoyance of Creswell, while any sign of Pope Clement VIII or Henri IV of France offering support for an alternative candidate also remained unforthcoming.[12]

Yet by March of 1601 there were signs that the wind was beginning to change. Following the failure of Spanish military operations in Ireland, an Englishman named Thomas James travelled to Brussels from Rome with letters of introduction from both the Spanish Ambassador to Rome, the Duke of Sessa, and the Jesuit, Robert Persons, with the intention of gaining further knowledge of the state of the English Court, the English Catholics and their resources and Isabella's view on the succession of Elizabeth, knowledge of which he would later take back to England.[13] After spending several months in Brussels, he moved on to Paris where he compiled a report for Creswell, highlighting the rise of several anti-Spanish 'Appellant priests' who had travelled to France from England and who were gaining favour with Henri IV. These were a separatist group of Seminary priests that flouted the authority of the archpriest George Blackwell who had been appointed by the Pope as head of the the Catholics in England. The report claimed their intention was to diminish the public image of England in the eyes of Rome, something that undoubtedly made its mark on the Jesuit Creswell. Early in 1602 Thomas James travelled to the Court of

Philip III, where he waited for two months before presenting his case before the king to urge an invasion of England. Despite his attempts to highlight Catholic discontent in England, the proposal was not well received, largely for the same reasons as the earlier attempts by Creswell. Yet questions over Elizabeth's successor remained. While Thomas James held the view that James VI would not ascend the throne of England unopposed, Philip still refused openly to support an alternative. Yet neither did he officially support James. In the minds of Philip's council, the idea of Isabella succeeding Elizabeth could only be successful if James's claim could be weakened through both diplomacy and sufficient military backing, something the archduke clearly doubted.[14]

By July 1602 another Englishman had arrived in Spain to seek an audience with Philip. Although he travelled under the name Timothy Browne, this man was Thomas Wintour, a known Catholic and later member of the Gunpowder Plot, who would soon cross paths with Guy Fawkes. Born in around 1571, Wintour was the second son of George Wintour of Huddington Court in Worcestershire and his wife Jane Ingleby. Wintour was of knightly stock as the grandson of his mother's father, Sir William Ingleby, and he was also, as were the Wright brothers, a nephew of the executed priest Francis Ingleby.[15]

Although raised a Protestant, Wintour made the decision to convert to the old faith some time in the 1590s. Like Guy, Wintour had also served in the Low Countries, at first for the United Provinces against the Spanish. It is also likely that he fought against the Turks.[16] As a soldier he was praised, Tesimond saying of him that 'he could have become one of the most outstanding and widely talked of condottieri in that field of war'.[17] Another prominent Jesuit, Father John Gerard, also praised Wintour's military abilities as well as describing him as:

a reasonable good scholar, and able to talk in many matters of learning, but especially in philosophy or histories ... He could speak both Latin, Italian, Spanish and French ... And was of such a wit, and so fine carriage, that he was of so pleasing conversation, desired much of the better sort ... He was of mean stature, but strong and comely and very valliant ... He was very devout and zealous in his faith, and careful to come often to the Sacraments, and of very grave and discreet carriage, offensive to no man, and fit for any employment.[18]

By 1600 Wintour had ended his involvement in the war, regarding it as unjust. Following this, he travelled to Rome where he spent some time at the English College. Within a year of the Essex Rebellion in 1601 he travelled to Spain as Browne, equipped with letters of introduction from Father Henry Garnet, Superior of the Jesuits in England, acting under instruction of several English Catholics who fought alongside Essex in 1601, including Lord Monteagle and Robert Catesby. According to his confession four years later regarding his time in Spain, he came before Philip

to bestow some pensions here in England upon sundry persons, who making use of the general discontent that young gentlemen and soldiers were in by reason of my Lord of Essex's death, and the want of his purse to maintain them, might no doubt by relieving their necessities have them all at his devotion. Because in all attempts upon England the greatest difficulty was ever found to be the transportation of horse, they assured Philip of 1,000 or 1,500 against any occasion or enterprise.[19]

Despite support for Isabella waning in some quarters – the view of Robert Persons was that Isabella was no longer the appropriate candidate since her marriage and taking on her new role as ruler of the Spanish Netherlands – Wintour was greeted quite favourably. Soon after his arrival, Creswell arranged a meeting for Wintour with Philip's Secretary of the Council, Don Pedro de Franqueza, and Philip's favourite, the Duke of Lerma. Notwithstanding that Lerma was of the opinion that Philip would not take the matter further, Wintour was granted an audience with Philip at the royal palace of El Escorial near Madrid to seek pensions for the financially depleted victims of the Essex Rebellion. In response, Wintour received word from the president of Philip's treasury, the Count of Miranda, that not only would Philip commit 100,000 escudos for the cause, half to be paid within the year and the remaining half in the following spring, Philip agreed to join them 'and set foot in England'.[20]

For Wintour and England's Catholics this new development must have seemed like the answer to their prayers. Not only had Philip pledged 100,000 escudos – equivalent to approximately £25,000 at the time – but Wintour was also convinced an armada would follow in 1603. News of the widely awaited concordat was well received among England's Catholics. Creswell received several letters from English Catholics calling for the expertise of Sir William Stanley both for leading troops for the actual invasion and also in assisting the Spanish with their invasion plans.[21] Shortly after this, one of the Englishmen who had been behind Wintour's visit – most likely Catesby or Monteagle, although described only as 'the person who keeps the correspondence between the Catholics of England and Spain in secret' – wrote to Creswell recommending Stanley come to Philip's Court himself. This, as far as history recalls, never happened. Although a regular in the Court of Philip II, Stanley's previous attempts had continuously fallen on deaf ears. It seems likely that Stanley's insistence had exhausted the patience of the Spanish King, resulting in Stanley's decision to send envoys rather than speak with Philip at first hand. It cannot be ruled out entirely that Stanley was the man who sent Wintour, although more likely it was a Catholic involved in the Essex Rebellion. The author of the letter also suggested Philip's money was already being spent on preparing for the invasion, yet without any indication of where and by whom. Stanley himself was clearly aware of the situation. In a letter to Creswell, written soon after, he stated: 'For an affair such as this, I will do what the friends in England have sought by this and other messengers. I will return.'[22]

Stanley was referring to the recommendation of the English Catholics that he would assist in both the planning of the invasion and the invasion itself. In addition, he was clearly favourable to the possibility of a special commission, also suggested by the English Catholics, allowing him to return to England at the time of Elizabeth's death to lead an uprising until the Spanish came. It appears from the evidence that Stanley was well informed of events as they happened. Records tell that two Englishmen were present at El Escorial when the president of Philip's treasury, Miranda, gave promises of support and finance. Wintour was one; the other, an unnamed man, may well have been Thomas James, who was present at El Escorial around the same time as Wintour and who had also been in Rome with Wintour in 1601.[23] At least one of these men had communicated personally with Stanley. According to Creswell, word came from England of 'the arrival of one of the gentlemen who kissed your Majesty's hands the day he left El Escorial. He has heartened and encouraged them greatly with the reports he has carried. The other awaits in Flanders the response that was promised.'[24]

The first of these men was Wintour. He was back in England by Christmas of 1602, while the other man, possibly Thomas James, was in Flanders waiting for the promised money. Supposedly the money was to come via a man named Federico Spinola, who commanded a significant squadron of galleys. When Spinola sailed from Spain in August his fleet was attacked and severely depleted by an Anglo-Dutch force deployed to disrupt Spanish trade practices. Come December, the second Englishman was still waiting.[25]

By early 1603 there still seemed little sign that the promises given by Spain would come to pass. In Spain, Creswell continued to converse with the Catholics of England and the King of Spain but without progress. Despite the commitments first made by Don Franqueza and the Count of Miranda, the majority of the council did not share their views. Instead, it was concluded that an invasion of England was impossible at that time. The Spanish Council of State also rejected the idea of Stanley receiving a commission. In early 1603 Creswell attempted to persuade Philip to act by informing the king that he was still receiving enquiries about the Spanish views on Elizabeth's successor and warned him that if nothing was done they would have no option but to choose another way. After liaising by post with Wintour, Creswell corresponded with the king, asking for a 'very trustworthy person' to be appointed in the Flemish ports to act with authority when needed and also one trusted by the English Catholics, Spinola being the most likely.[26] In addition he brought up the subject of the still unpaid 100,000 escudos that the English Catholics were already spending. Finally, he again presented the question regarding Elizabeth's successor.

To this Philip remained uncommitted. Nevertheless, he was interested enough to hold another meeting of the council. The result was that the council recommended Philip release the

English Catholics from any obligation, based on their religion, to support the claim of Isabella and called on the Catholics to select their own candidate, one who would be acceptable to Spain. It also recommended they take any actions necessary to convince Pope Clement VIII and Henri IV of France to assist with any backing that ensured the successful taking of the Crown.[27] Stanley himself is recorded as being granted an audience with Henri IV, most probably for this very reason.

Still it did not end there. In March a further debate followed regarding exactly how the English Catholics were to be told to select their own successor to Elizabeth. Then, by April 1603, Elizabeth had died and there was no successor in place. After five years of planning the Spanish still had no credible plan for invasion, no money to fund such a venture or even a sufficient army in place to mount an attack.[28]

Queen Elizabeth I was in her seventieth year when she finally passed away. Signs of her declining health, originally noticed in early March when it was detected that she had been suffering from insomnia, were increasingly apparent over the following two weeks, after which time it was announced that she had become weaker. News of her slow demise was passed on to James VI of Scotland through an agent, yet definitive confirmation that he was to be Elizabeth's successor was still to come. Elizabeth finally made that long-awaited decision, when bedridden, on 23 March. Eyewitness accounts of the weakened monarch describe her as having lost the power of speech and being capable only of communicating through signs. It was by such means Elizabeth is said to have indicated that James should be her successor, leaving her feelings on the subject unknown until the last possible moment.[29]

The morning following Elizabeth's death, the key members of the Privy Council departed the queen's chamber and pro-

ceeded with the arrangements to pronounce James as Elizabeth's lawful successor as sovereign of England. Proclamation
was first made at Whitehall Gate in London at approximately
ten o'clock in the morning of the 24th followed by other read-
ings in the city and throughout the rest of the country soon
after. Prisoners at the Tower of London, many of them
Catholics, greeted the news of Elizabeth's passing with good
cheer, while news of James's confirmation as the new king
brought with it great hope to the people of England, who celebrated the event with the lighting of bonfires.[30]

In England, Catholic reaction to the proclamation of James
as king was positive. Throughout the late queen's long tenure,
penalties for Catholicism had become increasingly severe, and
individually Catholics had become figures of hate. According
to the Catholic priest William Weston, England had become a
'ruthless and unloving land' in which those of other faiths 'lay
in ambush for them, betrayed them, attacked them with violence
and without warning . . . plundered them at night, confiscated
their possessions, drove away their flocks, stole their cattle' while
lay Catholics filled every prison 'no matter how foul or dark'.[31]

Several Jesuits were quick to display their affection for the
new king. Father Henry Garnet wrote a letter to James expressing Jesuit desire to be 'dear and not unnatural subjects of the
Crown'.[32] Both Albert and Isabella greeted news of James's
accession warmly. On hearing news of James's proclamation, the
archduke released several English prisoners and sent an envoy to
James as a mark of his delight at the new situation.[33] Among
England's Catholics there was much hope and belief that the son
of the Catholic Mary Stuart would not only restore the rights and
privileges of the old religion but also convert to Catholicism himself.

Garnet typified this optimism. Writing less than a month after the King's accession, he declared 'a golden time we have of unexpected freedom . . . great hope is of toleration'.[34] James's wife, Anne of Denmark, had converted to the old faith within the preceding two years and wrote affectionately to the Pope on matters of religion, doing much to heighten rumours that the king himself might convert. In a letter to Clement VIII, Anne not only declared her fidelity to the Roman church but reassured the Pope that her children would be educated in the Catholic ways and that James might allow liberty of conscience to Catholics.

While Thomas Wintour was still in Spain, another future member of the Gunpowder Conspiracy, Thomas Percy, the former neighbour of Guy Fawkes, was also taking an active interest in the subject of Elizabeth's successor. Shortly before James's accession, Percy travelled to Scotland to seek an audience with James claiming, like Wintour, to be acting on behalf of England's Catholics. According to the Jesuit Oswald Tesimond, Percy visited the King of Scotland 'whether of his own initiation or by someone else's'.[35] Most probably he travelled under the instruction of his relative, Henry Percy, the 9th Earl of Northumberland, who was thought to have some Catholic sympathy. His ancestor, the 7th Earl, had fallen from favour with Elizabeth and later lost his life following the Northern Rising of 1569, for which he was later beatified by the Catholic Church. Thomas Percy was of ancient noble lineage as the descendent of the 4th Earl, and he served the present Earl as the constable of the family castles of Alnwick and Warkworth in Northumberland.[36] Although born a Protestant, Percy, like many others from Scotton, converted to Catholicism at some point during the 1590s. Around this time he married Martha Wright, sister of Jack and Kit Wright, thus providing him with a direct link to at least two future Gunpowder Plot conspirators.[37]

The timing of Percy's visits, three in total, coincided with the Scottish King's correspondence with other key English nobility, notably Cecil. Northumberland was intent on confirming his allegiance to the new monarch and keen to avoid the hardships that the family had previously encountered during the reign of Elizabeth, particularly after the rebellion of the 7th Earl.[38] While conversation on the matter probably did occur, Percy is described as having asked the king, on behalf of England's Catholics, to accept them as his loyal subjects, upon which they would accept him as the rightful king.[39] To this, James is reputed to have reacted positively. Percy later recalled certain promises James made, not only of religious tolerance but also to favour Catholics most actively.[40] Overjoyed by such a result Percy returned to England where he shared his news with the Catholic community.

It is understandable that England's Catholic community celebrated the new reign of James with such optimism. If such promises were to be believed, James would alleviate the heavy penalties established during the reign of Elizabeth as well as grant Catholics the same privileges already granted to Protestants. However, what exactly James promised is never stated, as no written account has survived. In his narrative, Tesimond referred to Percy having recounted the story to him in greater detail than Tesimond had recorded in writing.[41] James was quieter on the subject, yet he did give some indication. When writing to Henry Carey, 1st Baron Hunsdon, in 1584 he said that he had good relations with the Pope, and there was also a suggestion that he had refused to hand fugitive Jesuits over to Elizabeth, much to the queen's annoyance.[42] In 1592 Elizabeth again displayed her irritation with James because of her belief that he might deal too leniently with Catholic nobles.[43] In his writings to Robert Cecil before his accession, James displayed opposition to an Anglo-Spanish treaty and tolerance towards Catholics.[44] Evidently his opinions changed on the matter, as demonstrated in a later letter to Cecil:

I will never allow in my conscience that the blood of any man shall be shed for diversity of opinions in religion, but I would be sorry that Catholics should multiply as they might be able to practise their old principles upon us.[45]

Although clearly unwilling to fight a war over religious issues, James was manifestly worried about the possibility of the number of Catholics increasing. This seems at odds with Percy's recollection that the king would consider admitting Catholics to 'every kind of honour and office in the state', as stated by Tesimond.[46] Writing to the Earl of Northumberland, Thomas Percy's patron, James echoed the sentiments he had put to Cecil by stating he was unwilling to persecute Catholics who were not 'restive'.[47] In other correspondence with Northumberland he maintained that he would not persecute any Catholic 'that will be quiet' and would reward or advance any judged to have been of 'good service'.[48]

The signals James sent out seem to have been mixed. While it is possible that Thomas Percy might have exaggerated some of these promises, the timing of James's earlier letters to Cecil coincided largely with the aftermath of the Essex Rebellion and with the activities of Thomas Wintour in Spain. It seems that the Catholic factions in Spain and Brussels were either less optimistic about the promises given to Thomas Percy or, equally likely, they were largely unaware of them. Certainly there are clear indications that Catholic support for James was far from unanimous.

6

A Defence to the Innocent

Despite the official proclamation of James as Elizabeth's successor by members of the Privy Council, attempts by the English exiles to convince the King of Spain to persevere with plans for a Spanish invasion did not cease altogether. In the summer of 1603 the English Catholics put a new case to the king. Their representatives were two Englishmen: one Anthony Dutton, the other Guy Fawkes.

Dutton was the first to arrive. By the evening of 15 May 1603, less than two months after the death of Queen Elizabeth, Dutton is recorded as having made his way to Valladolid, the capital of Spain between 1601 and 1606, after travelling through France. His first port of call was the College of St Alban's where he hoped to find Father Creswell. Instead, a Jesuit priest named Manuel Velada – a native of Portugal who had been freed from prison in London and supposedly knew of the people who had sent Dutton – greeted him on his arrival.[1]

Of Anthony Dutton, nothing is known. The papers that he carried revealed nothing that could trace him. While the possibility cannot be ruled out that Anthony Dutton was a relation of Sir William Stanley's first wife, Ann Dutton, most likely the name was an alias. Thomas Wintour, as mentioned, had already been present in the Court of the King of Spain, travelling as Timothy Browne. The most likely candidate is Guy's former schoolfriend, Christopher Wright. According to Guy Fawkes's examination, dated 25 November 1605:

> Christopher Wright had been in Spain about two months before this examinate – Guy Fawkes – arrived there, who was likewise employed by Baldwin, Owen and Sir William Stanley from Brussels into Spain. This examinate's employment was to give advertisement to the King of Spain how the King of England was like to proceed rigorously with the Catholics

thus building on promises that Wintour had earlier negotiated.[2] Christopher Wright was dead by the time Guy Fawkes was being interrogated, while no example of Christopher Wright's handwriting has survived that can be compared with Dutton's. Any accusation that Guy was acting on behalf of Stanley, Owen and Baldwin is also not found until Guy's confession.[3]

The choice of Dutton as a representative is a strange one. He did not speak Spanish and instead had to rely on an interpreter, usually Creswell. What is more, there is no obvious record that he had ever been employed in the service of Spain. While in Valladolid Dutton confirmed that he was not the first person to have been selected by his comrades. He also made reference to another who brought 'some things' that he did not – presumably a reference to Guy. Dutton was clearly aware of the events that had preceded his arrival, giving firm indication that he had been in contact with Thomas Wintour. He admitted that he had been involved in the original proceedings and suggested another person, clearly known to him and in league with the same people, would be sent to visit the archduke in the hope of convincing him to offer support against James.[4] If Dutton was to be taken literally, among their resources were some 2,000 horses, an increase on Thomas Wintour's reference to between 1,000 and 1,500, with the possibility of more should funds be made available.[5] It may be that the resources were a new development, perhaps building on Creswell's claim that the Catholics were already spending the 100,000 escudos, which they still had not received. Dutton also talked of other assistance. Among others, he claimed that if Francis Stewart – 5th Earl of Bothwell and nephew to the 4th Earl, the third husband of Mary, Queen of Scots – were to be sent back to Scotland (he had been absent since 1594) he could raise support from some Scottish lords, although Dutton failed to name them. Dutton also informed Philip that the English Catholics would be ready to rise if aid was forthcoming. Many would not make themselves known, however, until they witnessed the sight of Spanish soldiers landing on England's beaches.[6]

Not for the first time, the specific details remained undecided, making the planning of any realistic invasion strategy unlikely at this stage. Nevertheless, Dutton's plans were not dismissed out of hand. In addition, Dutton presented an ultimatum to the king by insisting that if Philip would not support their cause they would turn instead to Henri IV, who had pledged assistance because he did not want to see 'the Scot be king in two realms'. There is reason here to suspect that the Catholics who had sent Dutton were themselves living on borrowed time, as suggested in his statement to Philip that if neither he nor Henri would assist they would be forced to 'drive the Scots from England, or lose everything'.[7] Evidence of this is also reinforced in another statement, confirming:

This is the last embassy that the Catholics can send to Spain. They wish only for the response from his Majesty

... whether he can assist with the aid promised for this spring... Upon a reliable report about what they can expect from here hangs the decision to do or to leave undone many important things.[8]

Dutton did at least proceed to provide Creswell with a more detailed plan for an invasion. Consisting of thirty-three points, he highlighted details of one fleet to be sent from Flanders and perhaps a second from Spain to places that remained a secret – later identified as either Milford Haven or Kent.[9] As with the views put forward through Thomas Wintour the previous year, Stanley was designated as a commander; Spinola was identified as being responsible for the boarding of supplies and personnel, while Hugh Owen, Thomas James and some other exiles were put forward as subordinates.[10] Despite this, Dutton's ideas failed to find favour with the Spanish King or his council. By 5 June the council had made a list of eleven objections, six of which centred on Dutton's assertion that James I would not favour alliance with Spain. This ties in, more or less, with James's own correspondence with Cecil, but it is unlikely that Dutton was actually aware of this.[11] Dutton made light of James's assurances to the Pope about tolerating Catholics – correctly as history would tell – and used the matter to convince Philip that the longer James ruled unopposed the less effective Spain would be as a force in Europe. Dutton also remained unconcerned by Spanish fears that any invasion and subsequent war would be a costly one. When questioned on the amount of cost and risk involved, Dutton declared that 300 resolute men would be sufficient – a similar number took part in the crushed Essex Rebellion – and that 'with work, speed, secrecy and good weather' overthrow of the English government could be achieved within 'six days'.[12]

Talk of an invasion subsided over the next few weeks as Spanish domestic affairs took precedence, and over the summer the chances of the invasion taking place receded. Spinola was killed in May, thus removing one of Dutton's key men, while a Catholic, Lord Buckhurst and 1st Earl of Dorset, had travelled to Rome where he liaised with Philip's Ambassador to Rome, the Duke of Sessa, on the subject of an invasion. Attempting to convince Philip to proceed with an invasion, Sessa remarked:

> It is of the greatest importance that . . . at the moment of the Queen's death Colonel Stanley should cross over to England . . . This will encourage the councillors greatly to make a decision and the Catholics to be united in their defence. The arrival of the colonel with such a small force will not cause much unrest, yet it will clear the way for all the rest.[13]

This letter was written in March, before Elizabeth's death. The possibility of a commission for Stanley had, as mentioned, already been rejected. Although continuing to assure the English Catholics of Spain's concern, Philip replied to Sessa, who was now aware of James's accession, that there was little at present that could be done.

By July 1603 any hopes the Catholic community still had of an invasion looked more remote than ever. It was at this time that the last of England's Catholic envoys made his way to the Spanish Court. Guy Fawkes arrived in mid July, two months after Dutton, coming at a time when the Spanish Council of State was still deliberating Dutton's proposal. Guy brought with him letters of introduction from Baldwin to Creswell and up-to-date information on the political condition of England.[14] It is likely that this information was that which had been promised by Dutton earlier to be delivered by another person. Regarding his purpose, Guy simply announced that he had been sent by an Englishman who had recently been present in the Low Countries but was unwilling to travel further into Spain.[15] This presumably referred to Baldwin, or else Stanley or Owen. The person who sent Guy did not identify himself officially in any of the letters, but they did confirm that he had first travelled to the Court of Albert, Archduke of Austria, to enlighten him of the true conditions endured by England's Catholics. Seeing that the Archduke was 'desirous of peace', he concentrated his attempts on the Marquis Ambrosio Spinola, brother of the recently deceased Federico, yet also without success. Following his failed attempts, he sent Fawkes south from Brussels around 16 June.[16]

Unlike Dutton, Guy was a skilled linguist, fluent in French and Spanish. This was undoubtedly a factor in determining his suitability for the mission, the purpose of which was an extension of Dutton's, and also further to emphasize the untrustworthiness of James. In Guy's possession was a written plea to the Spanish Court to ask the assistance of the Pope in excommunicating James and to have the Papal text published in time for the invasion.[17] How much of this Guy personally agreed with is impossible to determine. He had never met King James in person and had been absent from England for over a decade. In addition, Guy also carried news that 'all the friends are well' – that is, those who had sent them – and were awaiting Dutton's return.[18]

In addition to Guy's letters, he brought with him two documents. One was a copy of a petition written in Spanish, originally presented to James by the Catholic priest Father Thomas Hill on the behalf of England's Catholics while the king was in York in April. The aim of this petition was to have the harsh laws against Catholics left over from Elizabeth's reign repealed. It failed, probably in no small part because of its manner in comparing the plight of the Catholics with the Israelites in the time of King Jeroboam, who flouted the king's authority because of his tyrannical rule. Far from seeing his petition progress, Hill was imprisoned for his behaviour. The condition of his treatment was put forward by Guy to Creswell as a sign of James's villainy, while also claiming that any future action against the king was justifiable on the basis that it was for the 'security of their faith'.[19]

The second paper Guy carried was a letter, written by him, based on a verbal message from the man who had sent him from Brussels. Its content comprised approximately five pages of text telling of the general antipathy Londoners felt for the new king, highlighting their hatred for Scots and James's lack of wealth as reasons for their dislike. Not for the first time, stories of discontent failed to make any impression on Philip.[20] Nevertheless, the Jesuit Robert Persons was more interested in the rumours from London. Writing to a friend in Flanders, known simply as A. Rivers, Persons claimed:

> Catholics must take heed least upon passion, some break out . . . now it may be that some of our friends in England or Spain or elsewhere, seeing my fear in this behalf, have thought it best not to make me privy of any such treaty during the Queen's life, for so it is that for this 2 or 3 last years I have known no particulars at all, neither concerning Timothy [Browne, the alias of Thomas Wintour] his journey nor his companion nor any such thing.[21]

Browne's companion was most likely Thomas James.

Soon after this occurred, Philip's Ambassador to Rome, Sessa, wrote to the king regarding news that the Pope favoured the possibility of a peace agreement with England rather than war and encouraged the Catholics to do likewise. Soon afterwards the Spanish Council of State reached a decision on the evidence put forward by Dutton, Fawkes, their accomplice in the Low Countries and the previous attempts by Creswell, James and Wintour. The greatest concern was that Spain did not have the capital to support an invasion of such magnitude while the promises of military assistance given by Dutton and Guy could not be authenticated. Philip's key consultant on English affairs, Juan de Idiáquez, recommended that the king refrain from any form of violence, according to the wishes of the Pope, and that England's Catholics follow the pontiff's wishes and remain patient and peaceful until every alternative had been tried. At that time there had been no threat of violence from James himself, leaving Philip with huge risk if he were to invade.[22]

Back in Brussels, the Englishman responsible for Guy's journey to Spain managed to gain an audience with the archduke, although only by posing, falsely, as the messenger of the archduke's contact in London, a Dr Robert Taylor, who was there to gather information as a prelude to later peace talks. On 26 July the Spanish Council of State reviewed the information put forward by the Englishman, which was little more than a collection of anti-James propaganda in keeping with that put forward by Guy. His writings provided proof of his contacts with Guy and Wintour while manipulating the views of Garnet and the Jesuits, who at the time welcomed James. However, Taylor, on hearing of the affair, dismissed the messenger's spurious pedigree.[23]

The council, many of whom viewed these Catholics as untrustworthy, were quick to dismiss the Englishman's writings. Overall, the Spanish verdict displayed little willingness to help unless the English Catholics declared themselves, something that many of the key members of the council doubted would happen.[24] On 31 July, a meeting of the council was set up to decide the final outcome. While the possibility of an invasion was well and truly shelved, two days before the meeting Creswell wrote to the king asking for 'these men, whom I keep here almost by force, to be sent away'. During the meeting the council agreed that any error on the part of Spain would be severely costly to any chance of peace. However, they did agree in principle to honour the pledge of 100,000 escudos and recommended that a letter be sent to Spinola on behalf of Guy confirming this. Discussion of Dutton's safe passage back to England also took place, but this changed over the coming week when it was suggested that Guy's and Dutton's return to England might compromise the peace mission of Philip's ambassador, Juan de Tassis.[25]

Although ordered to remain under the supervision of Creswell, neither Guy nor Dutton were actually imprisoned. While in Creswell's care, they continued to receive correspondence from England and took advantage of their status to establish more petitions and appeals concerning the plight of England's Catholics. Although these initiatives contained little that the Spanish council had not already heard, new proposals made by Dutton were rather more original than hitherto and included newly drafted proclamations for the deposition of King James should an invasion be successful. Following on from this, the two men concentrated their efforts on the legal case against James's claim for the throne of England. Although their work was incomplete, it did at least offer a new opportunity for further discussion. Dutton and Guy proceeded to pick apart the circumstances of James's accession, arguing that the decision of his rightful succession by Elizabeth had occurred 'without sufficient means' on the part of the Privy Council in addition to fears on behalf of the magistrates of a rumoured invasion leaving the commoners and peers of England with little choice but to follow.[26] Dutton's proclamation also centred on claims that the mother of the king, Mary, Queen of Scots, had been convicted of treason, while arguing that James, as a foreigner, was excluded from taking the Crown by the laws of the land as previously highlighted by Henry VIII's decision to exclude any descendent of Margaret Tudor on the grounds that they were not English. The circumstances of James's birth were also challenged as being contentious to his right of succession. James was the product of Mary Stuart's second marriage, his father being Henry Stuart, Lord Darnley who, as first cousin to Mary, also descended from King Henry VII of England through his grandmother, Margaret Tudor.

According to the work of Dutton and Guy Fawkes the new king had been born of an invalid marriage. However, unlike the marriage between Henry VIII and Anne Boleyn, Darnley married Mary after the death of Mary's first husband, Francis II of France. Dutton and Guy then went further by claiming James's right to the throne on his mother's side was subject to his fulfilling relevant criteria, notably upholding the Catholic faith, as specified in his mother's last will. While Mary had been a devout Catholic, James had shown no inclination to convert to the faith.[27] Guy and Dutton even went as far as to highlight James's lack of help and support to his mother during the events that led to her death as an act of matricide and consequently included in their proclamation a decree that he would be barred from England as punishment.

Certainly James's attitude to his mother was far from straightforward. Apart from the first year of his life, his mother had been in prison, so he would have had no conscious memory of her – he never visited her after that time, but he did correspond with her. In the early 1580s, he wrote to her on the subject of a joint rule but later lost interest in such an arrangement.[28] In 1584 James wrote to Sir William Cecil confirming his willingness to abandon his mother in order to cement an alliance with Elizabeth.[29] Following the Babington Plot, James wrote to Sir Robert Dudley protesting his innocence of any involvement, although requesting mercy for Mary, and condemned the plot.[30] His timing was crucial, as Parliament was intent on prohibiting the offspring of the traitor from succeeding to the throne, something Guy and Dutton were also attempting to do seventeen years later. More than likely they would not have been aware of the exact correspondence between James and William Cecil. James made a few weak attempts to save his mother's life, but following her execution he decided not to take action. Instead, he made a scapegoat of Lord Gray, a political schemer and James's Ambassador to England, who had been sent by James to negotiate on behalf of Mary without success.[31]

Further to those points that would bar James from the throne, the proclamation also ordered his return to Scotland, with the possibility of future penalties as punishment for his 'illegitimate acts'. Despite this, they were willing to be lenient to those who supported the new monarch, whoever they might be, and forgive past offences in exchange for present loyalty and acceptance of the restoration of the Catholic faith as England's primary religion, while any other outstanding issues would be dealt with by the new Parliament.[32] Once completed, the proclamation was placed in the hands of Creswell, leaving Guy and Dutton free to draft another one, this time to be printed in English. According to this proclamation:

> Since God, nature, and both human and divine law, grant a defence to the innocent who are unreasonably oppressed to resist unjust violence by the lawful use of arms when no other remedy is offered

the people of England are required:

> to live and die in the defence of our honour and the
> liberty of our homeland against all illegitimate usurpers
> of an office which does not belong to them.[33]

The possibility of religious tolerance for all Englishmen, despite official restoration of the new Catholic faith, depicts the work of Dutton and Guy more as religious idealists than Catholic fanatics and traitors. Finally, the proclamation targeted responsibilities of the new Parliament, including freedom of conscience in England and peace with European monarchs, an end to domestic grievances, monopolies to be withdrawn and recently introduced heavy taxes and subsidies for minority worship to be repealed. In addition, the proclamation would also serve as a warrant for payments to repair damages as a result of fighting in England during the period of enforcement of the proclamation. Not for the first time, the decision of the Spanish Council of State was negative in terms of an invasion, yet they did voice their support to the aims of the proclamation, claiming they could not condemn what was being sought.[34]

Although James was at that time unaware of the events that were taking place in Spain, during the first summer of the king's reign a new threat had emerged closer to home. Spurred on by failed promises regarding instant tolerance of England's Catholics, a group of rogue priests devised a plot with the intention of kidnapping the king and holding him prisoner until he agreed to a series of demands.

The plot's main conspirator was Father William Watson, a prominent Appellant priest. Among his accomplices were Father William Clarke and several laymen. Watson had earlier met

James while still in Scotland and, like Thomas Percy, had been given assurances of religious tolerance. Back in England, Watson declared that James had made such promises, something he later admitted under questioning, perhaps under duress, that he had exaggerated.[35] Less than three months after the coronation of the king the seeds of conspiracy had been sown. Later dubbed the Conspiracy of the Bye, or the Bye Plot, the plan was to hold James prisoner in the Tower until his early promises had been fulfilled. In addition, Watson also demanded the removal of James's anti-Catholic advisers, particularly Robert Cecil.[36]

Those responsible were arrested in July 1603 and held in the Tower until the autumn. Under interrogation one of Watson's laymen accomplices, Sir George Brooke, revealed another plot against the king, the so-called Main Plot, this time conspired by English Protestants and led by Brooke's brother, Lord Cobham, and the Puritan Lord Grey de Wilton, involving the raising of a regiment to march on London and take over the government. Cobham was to obtain financial support from the Spanish government, with Charles de Ligne, the 2nd Prince of Aremberg, a military commander in the Spanish Army, acting as an intermediary. Unlike the failed Bye Plot, however, this was to be no simple kidnap. Instead, the plan was to kill James, his wife and his children and replace them with the next in line for the throne, Lady Arbella Stuart.[37]

The trial of those involved in both conspiracies took place in early autumn. Lord Cobham and his brother, Sir George Brooke, were condemned to death, but a late reprieve saved Cobham. Sir Walter Raleigh was also sentenced to death for his alleged role in the Main Plot, yet he, too, was saved following a change of heart from the king. Watson and Clarke, on the other hand, were both executed. Nevertheless, the overwhelming reaction to the plots was astonishment and condemnation by the Catholic community at large, particularly Garnet, who referred to the Bye Plot as a 'piece of impudent folly', which was not only badly planned but also, as the following two years would show, badly timed.[38]

After the collapse of the Main Plot, Thomas Wintour resumed correspondence with Father Creswell. In a letter dated 30 August 1603 he lamented the lack of cooperation they were receiving from Philip for action against James, while explaining to Creswell that his 'friends' could not 'be restrained much longer'. He assured Creswell that he would gladly speak with Philip's Ambassador to England, Juan de Tassis, on the Spaniard's arrival in England, but he doubted whether any attempts by Tassis to speak to James about peace, including generous terms for England's Catholics, would have the desired effect, outlining present discontent as 'so violent and so general among everyone'. In addition, Wintour highlighted the difficulty of meeting Tassis because 'there will be spies about him'.[39] A meeting did, however, take place in Oxford two weeks later, where Tassis was introduced to the proceedings for the first time. Although he seems to have taken quite kindly to Wintour, referring to him in a letter to Philip in September as 'An Englishman . . . who, I was convinced, was not a fraud or a liar since he gave me the countersign of the English confidant in Brussels', he saw no genuine possibility in Wintour's plans, and declared to Philip that any Spanish invasion, if one were to occur, should be sent without expectation of useful backing from England.[40] While Tassis continued with his attempts, on Philip's orders, to investigate everything he could with regard to reports of Catholic unrest, by the end of September he wrote to the king declaring that he was now even less convinced of the chances of a successful Catholic uprising. Among his observations he confessed his doubt that the Catholics would take up arms unless convinced of likely success, a view similar to that of Philip's, while of Wintour and his accomplices he stated to the king that he did not trust their guarantees of support, despite being convinced of their dedication to Catholicism.[41]

In Valladolid, Guy and Dutton remained under observation. While there Dutton's frustration with Philip continued to grow. A memorandum written by him at that time revealed that he continued to harbour aggressive feelings towards James and also clear anger at Philip's stance in favour of peace. In his writings, later translated and toned down by Creswell, Dutton highlighted peace with England as being pointless, as war in the Low Countries was still ongoing, with forces of the United Provinces continuing to have support from England's Protestants. He also explained how the people who had sent him had been most patient in waiting for an answer and throughout that time continued to align with Philip, while Philip, by embarking on peace with James, was placing his trust in a new friendship with someone who, being a Protestant, was fundamentally his enemy as opposed to trusting those who were already his friends, the Catholics. Despite Dutton's persistence and supreme confidence in his proposals, Philip continued to focus on the idea of a peace treaty with England and ordered that surveillance of both Dutton and Guy should continue. Creswell, when writing to Philip, suggested that keeping Dutton under surveillance at that time was having an unproductive effect on the Englishman. Creswell also predicted that 'the longer he is detained, the more it shall be through violence'. In addition, he informed the king that both Dutton and Guy were still in direct correspondence with England and were, by late November, under instructions to return.[42] Writing to Creswell at around the same time, Dutton stated: 'If your health will not serve you to travel, let me go myself or send Mr Faux [sic] to let his majesty and the council know the peremptory which I have to return presently.'[43]

Meanwhile, Dutton continued his written attacks, particularly of the Catholics Tassis was investigating in London, referring to them as 'counterfeit Catholics', who would make Tassis believe that 'the moon is of green cheese', while blasting Philip for believing naïve promises, labelling him a victim of 'fair words'.[44] With regard to his departure, whenever that would be, he asked Creswell that Guy should be allowed to travel with him, citing his ability to speak French as the reason, and that all evidence of the mission in Spain, including the earlier trips of Wintour and James, be destroyed, stating 'our friends will not be satisfied till they know they be broken'.[45]

Tired of Dutton's consistent complaints about his incarceration, Creswell wrote to Juan de Idiáquez, Philip's consultant on English affairs, in the hope of obtaining passports for him and Guy. Of Dutton, Creswell wrote that he was 'bound in honour' to return to England, as to stay in Spain was to violate the orders of the people who sent him.[46] The council, on the other hand, were not to be swayed. Rather than agree to his safe passage they maintained their stance that nothing was to upset the peace process, something the unmonitored activities of Dutton might jeopardize. Another worrying factor for the Spanish Council of State was that the 100,000 escudos promised to the English Catholics back in 1602 had still to be handed over. By February 1604 the council had become so fearful that talks of an invasion could compromise the peace process that payment of the promised funds was, once again, deferred. This was even worse news for the Catholics, as back in England money was still being spent. According to correspondence between Creswell and Wintour, or those in league with Wintour, the amount spent was already over three times the amount promised by Philip.[47]

By the middle of February 1604 discussions regarding the Spanish Treason came to an end. Although Philip's commitment to payment of the money remained, there is reason to believe that around February or March Guy and Dutton were at last given permission to leave Spain. In a statement written by Philip in March, he maintained his insistence that the events of the past two years remain secret while, of Dutton, ordering that he be 'informed that he has to assure them [the English Catholics] above everything else that I will look after them as I have promised'.[48]

7

A DESPERATE DISEASE

From March 1604 the activities of Guy and Dutton are undocumented. The absence of any further letters from them to the Spanish Council of State through Creswell suggests they had probably left Spain by then. Thereafter, all reference to Dutton ceased entirely, underlining the possibility that the name was an alias for Christopher Wright. Considering Dutton's earlier letter to Creswell, it is likely that he travelled with Guy through France to Brussels and remained there for a time to report back to Stanley, Owen and Baldwin.

While the outcome of the Spanish Treason was perhaps not altogether unexpected, back in England many of those who had been behind the visit of Thomas Wintour had lost patience and resolved to take direct action. In January 1604 King James I, in his new role as head of the Church of England, presided over an ecclesiastical conference at Hampton Court that aimed, through theological debate, to resolve doctrinal differences with the Puritans. Even at this early stage signs of James's true feelings towards Catholics were beginning to show. According to the testimonies of Father Tesimond, while the conference proceedings were a victory for the Protestant bishops over the learned representatives of the Puritan faith, in order to appease the disconsolate Puritans, James hardened his stance against the Catholics. Tesimond states: 'He flayed us beyond measure, and in words so full of bitterness that they would scarcely be believed by any who read them.' While Tesimond did not say what these words were, citing their bitterness and 'other reasons' for not giving them, he summarized that James's loathing of the Catholic religion was so great that no one in attendance was left in any doubt regarding his stance on religious tolerance and that James himself claimed that he would take it as an insult if anyone suggested anything different. Finally Tesimond quotes of James: 'I know that some scoundrels to my shame wish to make me out as one who favours the papists'.[1]

While Tesimond's reference can perhaps be taken as a slight exaggeration, James's position was clear. On 19 February 1604 the new king declared publicly his 'utter detestation' of the 'superstitious' Catholic religion. On 22 February he went even further by announcing a proclamation banning Catholic clergy from England.[2] Although undoubtedly this was in part a reaction to the role of Watson and Clarke in the Bye Plot of the previous summer, Catholic loathing towards the monarch was compounded by confirmation that the penal codes that had been in place during the reign of Elizabeth would be reintroduced during the reign of the new king.

Among the English Catholics involved in the Spanish Treason who had already lost patience with the new king was Robert Catesby. Born in Warwickshire in 1573, Robert was the only surviving son of Sir William Catesby of Lapworth and Anne Throckmorton, daughter of Sir Robert Throckmorton of Coughton Court, near Alcester, whose relation Sir Francis Throckmorton had earlier been executed in 1584 for plotting against Elizabeth. On his father's death, Robert was left an income of some £3,000 per annum, something that served him well, particularly as he also received rent from leasing out his lands, although according to Father John Gerard he wasted much of it in his wild youth.[3] On his father's side, Catesby was of even nobler lineage. Dating back to the fifteenth century, Robert was sixth descendent of another Sir William Catesby, a councillor of Richard III, whose legacy was celebrated as the cat in the famous rhyme of Colyngbourne: 'The Cat, the Rat and Lovel our Dog / Rule all England under a Hog'.

His mother came from a long line of recusant Catholics, as did his father. Gerard recalls a story that one of Catesby's ancestors received a visitation by an angel, later depicted in a painting at the church in Ashby, that correctly forewarned him of his death.[4] Robert's father was also a renowned adherent of the old faith and is known to have suffered for it. At the age of eight Robert witnessed his father being arrested for harbouring Edmund Campion, along with other notorious Catholics – Lord Vaux, father of the Vaux sisters, Anne and Eleanor, who themselves later harboured Jesuits, and Sir Thomas Tresham, father of Francis Tresham, who was fined heavily for his involvement in the Essex Rebellion and a later co-conspirator in both the Spanish Treason and the Gunpowder Plot.[5] Through his mother, Robert was related to several prominent Catholic families, including the Vaux family, the Treshams, Throckmortons and Parkers.

Robert Catesby was held in the highest esteem by his family and friends, including several priests, particularly Jesuits. Robert's cousin William Parker, Lord Monteagle, referred to him as 'my loving kinsman . . . the only sun that must ripen our harvest'.[6] Thomas Wintour, who was also Catesby's cousin, held him in equally high regard. Tesimond, writing after the Gunpowder Plot, still referred to Catesby in a positive light, depicting him as a man who inspired love and delivered generosity and sweetness. Physically his appearance was pleasing, reaching over six feet (1.8 metres) in height – very impressive for his time. He was grave in manner, but he was rugged and handsome with a formidable physique and was celebrated as one of the most dashing and skilled horsemen in England.[7] He was well educated, having spent at least two years at Gloucester Hall, now Worcester College, at Oxford University in 1586 and 1587, but like many Catholics at the time Catesby did not receive his degree, because he refused to take the Oath of Supremacy.[8] Following his days at university, he may have spent time at the English College at Douai in the Spanish Netherlands (now in France). The university at Douai had been established by Philip II as part of Spain's consolidation of the Low Countries in the early 1560s, becoming an important institution specializing in theology, canon and civil law, art and medicine. As well as being of Catholic origin, it possessed a strong English influence, notably from recusant professors who had taught at Oxford during the reign of Mary Tudor. In 1569 Father William Allen – an English exile who later assisted Philip II in the planning of the Spanish Armada – founded an English seminary college so exiled Catholic priests could continue their studies, thus establishing an English Catholic community in the Low Countries. It was mainly from Douai that Seminary Priests ventured back to England, at least half of whom were eventually executed.

Catesby married while still only nineteen and fathered two children, one of whom died in infancy. His wife, Catherine Leigh from Stoneleigh in Warwickshire, was a Protestant from a respectable family and brought Robert a handsome dowry of some £2,000 per year. Catherine died in 1598, the same year as Robert's father, after only six years together. Previous commentators have often linked this event with Robert's reversion to the old faith and his later zealous defence of the religion.[9] Although this theory could have some validity, Catesby had, in fact, remained devoted to the Church throughout his marriage. In 1594 he is recorded as having sheltered the Jesuit Henry Garnet at his home in Uxbridge, while the prominent Father Gerard also fled there following his audacious escape from the Tower of London in 1597.[10] Speaking of his regard for the Catholic faith, Tesimond referred to Robert as being seen nowhere without his priest and mentions that his ability to convert Protestants was greater than that of most priests.[11] Tesimond goes on to state that by both 'example' and 'persuasion' his views often resulted in conversions, including Londoners and those at Court.[12]

Like his father, Catesby is known to have suffered for his faith. In 1598 he was arrested along with Francis Tresham and the Wright brothers as a precautionary measure when Queen Elizabeth was suffering from an illness, and he was not released until the queen's health had returned, an event later known as the Poisoned Pommel Affair – an assassination attempt on Elizabeth led by Edward Squire involving poisoning the pommel of the queen's saddle. Within the circles in which he moved, he became well known to Robert Devereux, the 2nd Earl of Essex, leading to his participation in the doomed Essex Rebellion of 1601. While Catesby himself may have seen the rebellion as an opportunity to push aside members of the Cecil faction – certainly Essex was far more sympathetic to Catholics than Cecil – the outcome of his involvement was personally damaging. Although he escaped imprisonment and execution, he was fined 4,000 marks, roughly £3,000, forcing him to sell his property at Chastleton. From then on he spent much of his time living with his widowed mother at Ashby St Ledgers in Northamptonshire, a property he was due to inherit on her death.[13] Despite the rebellion Robert escaped with his reputation largely intact. According to Father Gerard:

In that business, though it was weakly performed by those that had the chief carriage, especially that Earl of Essex, yet did Mr Catesby show such valour and fought so long and stoutly, as divers afterwards of those swordsmen did exceedingly esteem him and follow him in regard thereof . . . as well for their performance, as for the hurts they received.[14]

Around February 1604 Catesby sent a letter to his friend, cousin and recent ally in the Spanish Treason, Thomas Wintour, requesting his company at Catesby's property in Lambeth. At the time Thomas was staying at the family home of Huddington Court near Droitwich in Worcestershire with his elder brother, Robert, himself later entangled with the Gunpowder Plot. Evidently Thomas was unwell at the time and did not take up the offer until a second messenger arrived some time later. According to a copy of Thomas Wintour's declaration in the aftermath of the Gunpowder Plot, recorded on 23 November 1605 by Cecil's private secretary, Wintour made the journey to Lambeth at the second time of asking, where he met Catesby and Jack Wright:

> I remained with my brother in the country for Allhollantide [All Saints' Day] in the year of our Lord 1603, the first of the King's reign, about which time, Mr Catesby sent thither, entreating me to come to London, where he and other friends would be glad to see me. I desired him to excuse me, for I found not myself very well disposed, and (which had happened never to me before) returned the messenger without my company. Shortly I received another letter, in any wise to come. At the second summons I presently came up and found him with

> Mr John Wright at Lambeth, where he brake with
> me how necessary it was not to forsake my country
> (for he knew I had then a resolution to go over),
> but to deliver her from the servitude in which she
> remained, or at least to assist her with our utter-
> most endeavours.[15]

At the time Wintour was unaware of the reason behind
Catesby's request. The reference to not forsaking his country and
his resolution to go over refers to Wintour's willingness to live
abroad. By 1604 he had already spent time fighting in the Low
Countries as well as having spent time in Spain. More important
is the reference 'to deliver her from the servitude in which she
remained, or at least to assist her with our uttermost endeavours',
referring to a plan by Catesby to aid the situation of England's
Catholics. Wintour agreed early on that he was willing to aid
Catesby for the good of the Catholic religion but was at the time
doubtful that there was any way to succeed. He was already
familiar with the events that had taken place in Spain and he had
since spent at least one fruitless meeting with Juan de Tassis on
the subject of tolerance.[16]

Catesby, however, believed that there was a way to succeed.
According to Wintour's statement:

> He [Catesby] said that he had bethought him of a
> way at one instant to deliver us from all our bonds,
> and without any foreign help to replant again the
> Catholic religion, and withal told me in a word it
> was to blow up the Parliament House with gun-
> powder; for, said he, in that place have they done us
> all the mischief, and perchance God hath designed
> that place for their punishment.[17]

At first, Wintour's reaction was one of caution. In his confession he stated that he questioned the 'strangeness of the conceit' while also fearing that failure of the plot would result in widescale condemnation from both their enemies and friends. To this Catesby replied that 'the nature of the disease required so sharp a remedy', and on asking whether Wintour would agree to be involved he replied: 'Yes, in this or what else soever, if he resolved upon it, I would venture my life.'[18]

Father Tesimond also included a detailed account of the conversation between Catesby and Wintour, which was similar, although not identical, to the account in Wintour's declaration on 23 November 1605. Over the years Wintour's declaration has itself been subject to certain scrutiny over its authenticity. According to Tesimond, Wintour was alone when discussions took place with Catesby and, when asked of the enterprise, responded that he would willingly 'expose body and life to every danger' if he were convinced that the scheme was 'lawful, tended to the service of God, and was moreover likely to succeed'. Yet he did highlight two things that troubled him. First, he referred to the cruelty of the scheme, in particular the large number of deaths involved and also the hatred they would receive from both enemies and relatives of Catholics who had been killed, something that more or less echoes the statement in his confession. Second, Wintour highlighted more practical details, such as finding an appropriate location to carry out the task and also labour and capital. After proceeding to question who else could be involved, he ended by considering the problem of buying such large quantities of gunpowder and the difficulty of working underground without being overheard.[19]

In his confession Wintour highlights similar problems: 'I proposed many difficulties, as want of a house, and of one to carry the mine; noise in the working, and such like.'[20] In the confession, Catesby's reply was quite casual, simply stating: 'Let us give an attempt, and where it faileth, pass no further.' In Tesimond's narrative Robert seems to have been far more thoughtful, having wrestled at length with his conscience. Regarding whether the scheme was lawful or offensive to God, he stated that he would rely on his own conscience rather than the advice of others and presently saw the scheme as being entirely for the Catholic good rather than through hatred or self-benefit. With regard to Wintour's view about the infamy that would result, Catesby replied that it was insignificant when compared with the good that would follow.[21]

Robert then proceeded to summarize the plight of his fellow Catholics with an intelligent and eloquent speech, which he ended by asking of Wintour only his usual commitment. According to Wintour's declaration he had still not entirely given up hope of a peaceful solution being reached. After showing enthusiasm for the plot, Catesby then asked of Wintour:

> because we will leave no peaceable and quiet way untried, you shall go over and inform the Constable [of Castile] of the state of the Catholics here in England, intreating him to solicit his Majesty at his coming hither that the penal laws may be recalled, and we admitted into the rank of his other subjects.[22]

Shortly after this meeting had taken place Wintour did indeed visit the constable. Around early April 1604 he made the crossing to Flanders where he was granted his audience.[23] The constable, Juan de Velasco, was due in London to conclude the peace treaty between Philip and James, which was by then a virtual formality following the early efforts of Juan de Tassis. All that remained was for Velasco to ratify the agreement on Philip's behalf. Although Tassis had attempted to secure some rights and liberties for England's Catholics, in reality this was unlikely to happen.[24] Any assurances James did give were vague ones, perhaps not dissimilar to those given to Percy and Watson.

Not for the first time Wintour argued the case for support of the Catholic cause in England, emphasizing the faith English Catholics had previously placed in Philip as a defender of their religion and the harsh, intolerant treatment that they were continuing to receive. Velasco responded kindly, explaining that he had already been aware to some degree of the condition endured by England's Catholics but was better informed after hearing it directly from Wintour. It is likely that the two had met before while Wintour was in Spain. He assured Wintour that he would do everything possible to aid their cause, but Wintour was firmly of the belief that Philip's desire for peace would make Velasco's assurances, albeit perhaps given with good intentions, ineffective.[25] Catesby was clearly of the same opinion. When speaking with Wintour back in Lambeth, Catesby instructed Wintour to carry out another task before returning to England. 'Withal, you may bring over some confidant gentleman such as you shall understand best able for this business, and named unto me Mr Fawkes.'[26]

8

TO SHAKE THE THRONES
OF PRINCES

Hugh Owen had been the first of the English exiles to greet
Thomas Wintour on his arrival in Flanders and it was through
his connections that Wintour was granted an audience with
Velasco. After leaving Velasco's Court at Bergen, Wintour made
the short journey to Dunkirk in Owen's company, during which
time they spoke at length about the political climate. Owen was
doubtful that any tangible benefit would result from Wintour's
recent audience with Velasco, whom he felt was motivated only
by self-interest and held little regard for England's Catholics.
There is no indication at this stage that Wintour divulged any
information about Catesby's plan to destroy Parliament with
gunpowder, but he did disclose 'that there were many gentlemen
in England, who would not forsake their country until they had
tried the uttermost, and rather venture their lives than forsake
her in this misery', to which there is no evidence that Owen found
any objection. Wintour went on to say that they were looking to
add another man – Wintour refers to this person as a 'fit man'
– both for 'counsel and execution of whatsoever we should
resolve', highlighting 'Mr Fawkes' of whom he had 'heard good
commendations'.[1] Judging from Wintour's choice of words,
Catesby was well aware of Guy Fawkes, perhaps through an

acquaintance, but had probably not met him at this stage. If Anthony Dutton and Christopher Wright were the same man, then Guy's background would have been relatively well known to Wright through their time at school together and their recent mission in Spain. Kit Wright's brother, Jack, would also have remembered Guy from school. Guy, as previously stated, was also well known to Owen. In answer to Wintour's statement that he had heard good commendations of Guy, Owen replied that 'the gentleman deserved no less'. According to Owen, Guy was in Brussels at the time, yet he did not expand on his activities. Owen did, however, assure Wintour that if he did not meet Guy while still in Flanders then Owen would send him to England soon after.[2]

Shortly after these discussions Wintour proceeded to Ostend where, within two days of his arrival, he was joined by Sir William Stanley. According to Wintour's declaration, he remained in Stanley's company for three or four days where they, too, spoke at length of the situation in England. Stanley, like Owen, poured cold water on the likelihood of obtaining foreign help and highlighted the archduke's desire for peace with James as a major stumbling block. This probably indicates that Stanley was, or at the very least was aware of, the person referred to in Spanish documents only as 'el caballero inglés', who received an audience with the archduke while Guy and Dutton were still in Spain.[3] Back in Ostend talk between Wintour and Stanley moved on to other matters before Wintour brought up the subject of Guy, 'whose company [he] wished over into England'. When asked of Guy's ability in the wars, Stanley also gave good recommendations. There is some suggestion that Guy had been present at the Siege of Ostend, which could explain the gaps in his history between his appearance at the Battle of Nieuwpoort in 1600 and his mission to Spain in 1603. The siege, which had begun in July 1601, was still taking place at the time of Wintour's journey and did not come to an end until September 1604. Often dubbed the Carnival of Death because of its reputation as the bloodiest battle of the Eighty Years War for Dutch independence the siege eventually resulted in a crucial but long-drawn-out victory for the Spanish. At least one account described it as the 'assailing of the unassailable'. It was under the leadership of Don Ambrosio Spinola that the Spanish destroyed the heavily fortified defences, chiefly through the prolonged and consistent use of gunpowder, eventually forcing the Dutch to surrender. Of the siege, Stanley is said to have reported that entire companies were often blown into the air and that Guy had been involved in this.[4] What is less clear is whether he was at the siege before his journey to Spain or after. After taking leave of Philip, probably no later than March 1604, Guy almost certainly travelled through France, most likely with Dutton, before making his way to Brussels to inform Stanley, Owen and Baldwin of his activities in Spain. Bearing this in mind it seems most likely that if Guy was at the Siege of Ostend it would have been before his journey to Spain rather than after his return.

Following four days or so in Stanley's company, Guy arrived in Ostend after making the journey from Brussels. Most likely he had received word of Thomas Wintour's request for him to return to England from Hugh Owen. At the time Wintour was preparing to journey to Nieuwpoort to find a ship to take him home. On his arrival, Guy greeted Wintour and Stanley with a salute before being introduced to Wintour by Stanley. Wintour's recollection of the event is curious. The wording of his declar-ation reads: 'This is the gentleman, said Sir William, that you wished for, and so we embraced again.'[5] Two things spring to mind here. First, although Wintour was reasonably direct with Stanley about his hopes for religious tolerance, he did not inform Stanley of the plot itself. Second, Stanley's introduction suggests that Wintour and Guy had never met, yet Wintour's wording 'embraced again' suggests that they already knew one another. While Wintour and Guy do not appear to have been in Spain at the same time, it stands to reason that all of the key players of the Spanish Treason would have been known to one another. In addition, Wintour might have been known to Guy through his relation to the Wrights. According to Spink: 'in the days of their joyous youth these two gifted men may have many a time and oft played and sported together in Nidderdale' in Yorkshire.[6] Unfortunately neither Wintour nor Guy elaborated any further.

Wintour evidently took kindly to Guy. In his narrative Tesimond refers to Guy's character as 'pleasant of approach and cheerful of manner . . . liked by everyone and loyal to his friends'.[7] After their greeting Wintour informed Guy that 'some good friends of his wished his company in England; and that if he pleased to come to Dunkirk, we would have further conference'.[8] Wintour did not, however, disclose the identities of these friends in front of Stanley, nor did he give Guy any idea of the purpose of the visit. The reference to them as 'friends' was probably one relating to their strict devotion to the Catholic cause rather than being people Guy knew personally, although the latter was perhaps true in the case of Jack Wright. It is certainly possible that Wintour may have mentioned Jack Wright's name to Guy in order to help convince him to make the journey.

Wintour departed Ostend within a day of his discussions with Guy and made his way back to Dunkirk. Guy joined him two days later, presumably on leave from his post as an ensign in the Spanish Army. Alternatively, he might still have been on the indefinite leave granted to him before his mission to Spain. It is uncertain how much detail Wintour went into while at Dunkirk, only that his 'friends' were intent on restoring the liberties of the old faith in England with or without foreign help. Although Wintour was clearly resigned to carrying out the attack on the king and the House of Lords without aid from abroad, he remained cautious, as ratification of the peace treaty was still to be settled; Velasco himself did not come to England to conclude the treaty until August. Conversation continued as Guy and Wintour made their way to Gravelines where they waited for a fair wind to take them back to England.[9] Within a few days the wind changed, and together they sailed to London. There is no indication that Guy was made fully aware of the Gunpowder Conspiracy before arriving in England, although it is possible that Wintour gave him some insight. In Guy's deposition, recorded on 17 November 1605, he stated that the plot 'was first propounded unto me about Easter last was twelvemonth, beyond the seas, in the Low Countries of the Archduke's obeisance, by Thomas Wintour, who came thereupon with me into England.'[10]

Wintour and Fawkes landed in England around 25 April 1604.[11] According to Wintour's declaration, they journeyed to Greenwich in one passage before making their way by longboat to Catesby's lodgings in London. For Guy, this would have been the first time he had set foot in England for over a decade. London had recovered from the misery of the mid 1590s when bad harvests, poor weather, food shortages and scattered outbursts of plague had resulted in countless deaths and regular outbursts of violence by angry mobs. Despite its hardships, Guy would have witnessed a city whose population had doubled to some 200,000 in the final years of the late queen's reign, many of whom were enjoying a successful living thanks to the city's flourishing commerce and dynamic banking system.[12] Yet, scattered between London's new opulent buildings, luxury shops and churches marked with Gothic spires, were reminders of the city's former self. Lining its ancient streets, buildings that had once served as monasteries, priories, nunneries and convents lay empty or, in some cases, had been taken over for use by adherents of the new religion or by the custodians of one of the city's several new businesses or enterprises. It is tempting to conclude that the sight of London's new wealth was not lost on Guy, who, despite having been born over thirty years after the dissolution of the monasteries, still found meaning in the sites of the old faith, furthering his desire to see Catholicism restored to its former dominance.

Together, Thomas Wintour and Guy Fawkes visited Catesby, to whom Wintour introduced Guy as the man for whom he had sent. After exchanging pleasantries, Catesby asked Wintour about his audience with the Constable of Castile. Wintour replied that Velasco had said 'good words' but remained unconvinced that the mission would have the desired outcome. This was hardly a surprise to Catesby. He had already encountered much of the same lack of enthusiasm for direct action throughout the course of the Spanish Treason, while his earlier conversation with Wintour demonstrated that he viewed the possibility of the Gunpowder Plot as a practical and effective option. Evidently nothing had occurred in Wintour's absence to put Catesby off the idea. If anything, the opposite was true. Catesby was undoubtedly aware of developments that had occurred just days earlier on 22 April 1604 following James's request to introduce a bill to the House of Commons labelling all Catholics as excommunicates. For England's Catholics conditions were now even worse than under Elizabeth. Tesimond writes that, by that time, Catholics were no longer able to make their wills or dispose of their goods . . . There was no longer any obligation to pay them their debts or rents for land held from them. They could not now go to law or have the law's protection. They could seek no remedy for ills and injuries received. In a word, they were considered and treated as professed enemies of the state.[13]

Guy's first meeting with Catesby was probably relatively informal. While discussion of Wintour's meeting with Velasco clearly took place, it seems that Catesby did not reveal any details of the plot at this point. For Catesby the meeting was probably a chance to judge for himself whether Guy was up to the task and whether he could be relied on to keep the matter a secret. Conversation may well have centred on Guy's career in the Low Countries, his time in Spain and matters of faith in general. Catesby clearly approved of Guy, and in return Guy also found Catesby's charismatic personality and devotion to Catholicism most welcome.

Guy lived quietly in a lodging in London over the following weeks before being invited to a second meeting with Catesby. This took place around 20 May 1604 at a quiet house located in the fields behind St Clement's Inn just off the Strand area of London.[14] Also in attendance with Catesby, Wintour and Guy was Jack Wright – who already knew much of the plot from the earlier meeting with Catesby – and Thomas Percy. Percy's involvement was hardly surprising. He was suffering something of a diminished reputation as a result of James's broken promises and was known for his tendency for direct action. On his arrival Percy greeted the four with the soon to be infamous words: 'Shall we always, gentlemen, talk and never do anything?'

Catesby undoubtedly viewed Percy's thirst for action as an asset and revealed to him all details of the plot. According to Tesimond, Percy's reaction when told of the plot was one of disbelief at the audacity of Catesby's scheme, yet this did not prevent him from agreeing both to keep all knowledge of the plot secret and to assist in any way possible. Percy was the oldest of the conspirators, in his mid-forties with white hair, but attractive in manner, strong of stature, tall in height and serious of expression. At the time of the plot he still held a position of authority in the service of the Earl of Northumberland and was known for his enthusiasm, great energy and total commitment to the Catholic cause.[15]

On that day all five present agreed to carry out what is now known as the Gunpowder Plot. Before Guy and Percy were told of the plot, each man demonstrated his allegiance by swearing an oath of secrecy. In an otherwise deserted room, they kneeled in turn before all present and, with prayer book in hand, made the vow:

> You shall swear by the Blessed Trinity, and by the Sacrament you now propose to receive, never to disclose directly or indirectly, by word or by circumstance, the matter that shall be proposed to you to keep secret; nor desist from the execution thereof till the rest shall give you leave.[16]

As the day was a Sunday, the conspirators celebrated mass and received Holy Communion.[17] Based on confessions given by Guy and Wintour after their arrest, the priest who took the mass had been the notorious Jesuit Father John Gerard. Gerard was well known to Catesby, and the pair had been friends for many years. Nevertheless, despite the testimonies of Wintour and Guy,

Gerard denied having been present that day. Although this denial could have been untrue, inspired both by the priest's desire to escape retribution for disobeying the recent proclamation by James, which made his very presence in England illegal, and also to avoid implication in the plot, no other account exists to suggest Gerard was the man in question. In his own narrative of the events, Father Gerard remains adamant that Wintour and Guy were mistaken; furthermore, there seems little reason for Gerard to have falsely denied his presence, as he was overseas at the time and free from fear of persecution.[18]

Following the mass, in the privacy of a quiet room, Guy and Percy learned what the other three already knew. In order to carry out the plot it was necessary for a mine to be dug underneath the House of Lords. Because of the knowledge and experience Guy had gained in the Low Countries, it was agreed that he would supervise this work. Once the mine had been completed the area would be filled with gunpowder, which would be set off at the reopening of Parliament with the aim of killing all present, including the king, the queen and the Prince of Wales, who were viewed by the conspirators as the arch-enemies of Catholicism.

With this, the seeds of conspiracy were sown. The next task was to find an appropriate location from which to make the necessary preparations. Evidently Catesby had already given the matter considerable thought. In Wintour's absence Catesby had identified a small dwelling in the confines of Westminster. During the early seventeenth century the Palace of Westminster was made up of several buildings that surrounded Parliament, very different from what we see today. The buildings had originally belonged to the defunct College of St Stephen's, which had been occupied by monks before the dissolution of the monasteries. Following the Reformation in England, the Commons met in what had once been the Chapel of St Stephen's, while the other buildings that surrounded Parliament were in the possession of the Crown. At the time of the plot, various houses surrounding the Lords and Commons were in the possession of clerks of the exchequer, government officials and other gentlemen, many of whom sub-let them as business ventures. Some of these houses were sub-let a second time, usually to tradesmen who used them to store their produce.[19] It seems Catesby was well acquainted with the Westminster area and had a particular house in mind when working out the logistics of the plot. In May 1604 this house belonged to a Mr John Whynniard, who was employed as Keeper of the King's Wardrobe. At the time Whynniard was sub-letting the house to Henry Ferris, a lawyer and antiquarian. Ferris, ironically, was also the owner of Baddesley Clinton in Warwickshire, a lower-gentry mansion located in close proximity to Lapworth where Catesby had been born and lived much of his life. Anne Vaux, who had connections to both the Jesuits and the conspirators as the daughter of Lord Vaux of Harrowden, had rented Baddesley from Ferris during the 1590s.[20]

Over the next month Percy's luck continued to change for the better. Thanks largely to his connections with the Earl of Northumberland, Percy became employed as a gentleman pensioner, a special assembly of fifty bodyguards operating under Northumberland's leadership charged with the responsibility of protecting the king. Some previous commentators have highlighted this event as the key outcome in Percy being able to acquire the premises he sought from John Whynniard, but this assertion is unconvincing, as it is likely the conspirators had already secured occupation of the house on 24 March (other accounts suggest it was May) at the rent of £12 a year, so before Percy's promotion in June. Curiously, the March date also predates Wintour's journey to Flanders. Equally unconvincing is

the account given by most previous commentators that Ferris
was evicted from Whynniard's house because of Percy's
powerful connections. Surely Ferris could not have failed to be
aware that Vaux had employed the services of the Jesuit
Nicholas Owen to fill his house at Baddesley with hiding-holes
for priests and that Vaux had entertained Jesuits there.[21] Ferris
was himself a Catholic and, although he was probably unaware
of the Gunpowder Plot, would probably have favoured any enterprise that would improve the lot of the Catholics in England. In
his declaration Wintour states that Percy's letting of the house
encountered some difficulties. However, there is no evidence that
this was as a result of Ferris being forced to vacate the building.
Ferris revealed no sign of being under duress when he signed the
agreement.

> Memorandum that it is concluded between Thomas
> Percy of London Esquire and Henry Ferrers of Bor-
> desley Clinton in the County of Warwick Gentleman
> the xxiiii day of March in the second year of our
> Sovereign Lord King James.
>
> That the said Henry hath granted to the said
> Thomas to enjoy his house in Westminster belonging
> to the Parliament House, the said Thomas getting the
> consent of Mr Whynniard, and satisfying me, the said
> Henry, for my charges bestowed thereupon, as shall be
> thought fit by two indifferent men chosen between us.
>
> And that he shall also have the other house that
> Gideon Gibbons dwelleth in, with an assignment of a
> lease from Mr Whynniard thereof, satisfying me as
> aforesaid, and using the now tenant well.
>
> And the said Thomas hath lent unto me the said
> Henry twenty pounds, to be allowed upon reckoning

or to be repaid again at the will of the said Thomas.

    Henry Ferrers

    Sealed and delivered in the presence of

        Jo: White and Christopher Symons.[22]

Ferris was probably well known to Catesby and certainly to Father Garnet and Anne Vaux. Furthermore, the memorandum states that Percy gave Ferris a £20 loan to clinch the deal. Whynniard himself clearly had no idea of the reasons behind Percy's renting of the house. Whynniard, ironically, is recorded as having died, supposedly of shock, merely hours after Guy was arrested. When the inquisitors came round to investigate the change of sub-tenancy, the only person available to question was Whynniard's widow. It is written in her official statement that

> Mr Percy began to labour very earnestly with this examinate and her husband to have the lodging by the parliament house, which one Mr Henry Ferris, of Warwickshire, had long held before, and having obtained the said Mr Ferris's good will to part from it after long suit by himself and the great entreaty of Mr Carleton, Mr Epsley, and other gentlemen belonging to the Earl of Northumberland, affirming him to be a very honest gentleman, and that they could not have a better tenant, her husband and she were contented to let him have the said lodging at the same rent Mr Ferris paid for it.[23]

While the suggestion that Percy manipulated his connections stretches a point, his recent appointment did give him a good excuse for needing the house, as it was within easy reach of Whitehall, convenient for Percy when carrying out duties as a gentleman pensioner. Once in possession of the house, Guy was installed as 'caretaker', adopting the alias John Johnson, Thomas Percy's servant and house-sitter – a perfect cover through which to divert attention from the actual work being carried out.

Previous commentators have often questioned why Guy should have used an alias when the others did not. A few things spring to mind here. Guy was the only conspirator who had spent the majority of the last decade out of England and was largely unknown to the authorities at the time while the others were well known. Catesby had previously been arrested as a precaution in the wake of the Poisoned Pommel Affair and was also implicated in the Essex Rebellion. Wintour was often the target of Cecil's spies when venturing abroad. Percy's links with Northumberland also gave him recognizable status, while Jack Wright was also well known as a Catholic with a tendency for troublemaking. For Guy, it served a purpose that he should remain as anonymous as possible. The words of Thomas Wintour seem to back this, as he is recorded as saying: 'Mr Fawkes underwent the name of Mr Percy's man, calling himself Johnson, because his face was the most unknown.'[24] Another point is that Wintour and possibly Christopher Wright, too, had used aliases in Spain where their identity was less known, whereas Guy on that occasion did not. If word had got out that Guy Fawkes, a recent envoy to Spain on behalf of known English exiles and troublemakers, was presently living in Westminster it would undoubtedly have raised suspicion. In addition, Guy was still officially in the employment of the Spanish Army at this stage, as demonstrated by his inclusion in a list compiled in autumn of 1605, among the Lord Arundel's company in Spain, as 'Mr Faukes of Yorkshier'.[25]

Over the following months the conspirators' desire for action continued to grow. Between the meeting on 20 May and the official adjournment of Parliament on 7 July 1604 anti-Catholic legislation continued to be rolled out. On the final day of Parliament the king gave royal consent to a new, more repressive, recusancy act.[26] By August priests were dying for their faith. In September James issued a commission to Lord Ellesmere to lead a committee of privy councillors charged with the task of eradicating the Jesuits from England in addition to all other priests and 'divers other corrupt persons employed under the colour of religion', who attempted to convert Englishmen to the old faith. Later that year recusant fines were reintroduced, resulting in accusations of severity from even the most established recusant families. By August, when Velasco finally made his voyage from Flanders to England to conclude the peace treaty, all hope of tolerance had been extinguished. Although Velasco acted in good faith and argued the case for the lot of England's Catholics, the English government left no room for manoeuvre and concluded the peace talks safe in the knowledge that such tolerance was not a vital clause of any agreement.[27]

With Parliament adjourned until 7 February 1605 the conspirators had several months to plan their task. Some time after the adjournment in July they went their separate ways, agreeing to return to London at the beginning of Michaelmas term, the start of the legal year (Michaelmas lasted from 9 October to 28 November in 1604). Of their activities during that period, there is little information. Wintour's declaration suggests they simply departed for the country. Presumably Guy did the same, although his exact movements cannot be traced. Perhaps he used the opportunity to return to Yorkshire for the first time in over a decade to renew acquaintance with his mother and her husband.[28] Whatever the movements and activities of Guy and his fellow conspirators during this period, news of the recent peace treaty with Spain, proclaimed by herald across the country on

19 August, would have further intensified their frustration and opposition to the Stuart rule. The executions of several priests in the north of England, including Father John Sugar and his servant in Lancaster, could not have gone unnoticed.[29] Perhaps news had also reached them that a recusant by the name of Thomas Pound had been arrested, fined £1,000 and placed in the stocks in both London and Lancaster as punishment for placing before the king a petition expressing opposition and concern about the verdicts of various judges who had condoned the execution of recusants in Wiltshire, the Midlands and the north.[30] For the conspirators, the penalties of the new Recusancy Act of July 1604 would have had a restrictive effect on their finances.

Catesby almost certainly passed the summer months deliberating the next steps of the plan. As penalties meted out to Catholics continued to harden, the plight of the old religion had reached a new low. The king's failed promises had escalated into insult to those who had believed them while endangering the lives of those who disobeyed him. Spain's awkward peace agreement not only ended all hopes the Catholics had of salvation from abroad but for Thomas James, Thomas Wintour, Anthony Dutton, Guy Fawkes and those behind their visits to Spain, it was a bitter and frustrating conclusion to more than two years of intensive effort to seek support for the Catholic cause in England. Philip III's requests that the Catholics exercise patience until the peace talks were finalized had been honoured, but any hopes of a peaceful solution had passed. What was evident now, and history would confirm, was that tolerance would never come as long as James remained on the throne of England. With all hope of foreign assistance and diplomacy gone, the fate of England's recusants rested in the hands of five men set on shaking 'the thrones of Princes'.

9

THREE SCORE BARRELS OF POWDER BELOW

Following their summer in the countryside, the conspirators returned to London. By now it was October 1604, which left them with less than four months to make their preparations in time for the reopening of Parliament.

Over the last two centuries a number of writers have attempted to pinpoint the exact location of the Westminster house. Writing in 1897 the writer and historian Father John Gerard, namesake of the Jesuit alive at the time of the plot, maintained:

> That the lodging hired by Percy stood near the south-east corner of the old House of Lords (i.e. nearer to the river than that building, and adjacent to, if not adjoining the Prince's Chamber) is shown by the following arguments:–
>
> 1. John Shepherd, servant to Whynniard, gave evidence as to having on a certain occasion seen from the river 'a boat lie close to the pale of Sir Thomas Parry's garden, and men going to and from the water through the back door that leadeth into Mr Percy, his lodging.
>
> 2. Fawkes, in his examination of November 5, 1605, speaks of the window in his chamber near the

Parliament House towards the water-side.

    3. It is said that when digging their mine the conspirators were troubled by the influx of water from the river, which would be impossible if they were working at the opposite side of the Parliament House.[1]

Writing within a year of Gerard, the historian Samuel Rawson Gardiner shared Gerard's view. The location of the house was ideal in many respects, as it was situated in such close proximity to Parliament, almost certainly abutting the hall used as the meeting place for the Lords; also, at that time the houses had small gardens that offered easy access to the river by narrow passageways.[2]

For the conspirators, river access to the house was also essential. Before returning from the country it was decided that another house would be needed to store the gunpowder and the wood required for assembling the mine, which would then be transported to Whynniard's house at a later date. The declaration of Thomas Wintour states that no house was more appropriate than the one owned by Robert Catesby in Lambeth, which had already served as a meeting place for the conspirators. There it was agreed that at the appropriate time the gunpowder would be taken from Catesby's house, transported by boat under the cover of darkness to a mooring place outside Whynniard's house and subsequently taken through the garden into the cellar.

Exactly how the conspirators acquired so much gunpowder is unrecorded. It is written in the official account that thirty-six barrels were discovered, yet no explanation was ever given as to where it had come from. At the time the supply of gunpowder was a government monopoly, which has convinced some previous commentators that the powder was acquired through corrupt officials. This is possible, but the conspirators could also have acquired it from a member of the nobility who maintained his own stock, a frequent practice at the time.[3] Others have speculated that Hugh Owen, and perhaps Stanley, supplied the powder.[4] Gunpowder of such quantity could certainly have been obtained on the black market abroad. Quite possibly one of the conspirators acquired it from a merchant operating on the Continent and transported the cargo to London by a merchant ship.

Although the acquisition of powder was seemingly achieved without undue difficulty – there is certainly no indication that the conspirators were suspected or questioned over their activities at this point – a new problem had arisen. While they were working on the excavation of the mine, another person would be needed to look after the gunpowder and other items at the house in Lambeth. It was agreed, therefore, that a sixth conspirator should be added to their number.

The man in question was Robert Keyes, a committed Catholic who was initiated into the plot some time between June and October 1604. As with Guy and Percy, the conspirators were cautious in approaching Keyes, who was also obliged to swear an oath followed by the taking of Holy Communion on agreeing to pledge his allegiance to the conspiracy. Keyes was the son of the Protestant clergyman Edward Keyes, once Rector of Stavely in Derbyshire, and of noble blood on his mother's side as the grandson of Sir Robert Tyrwhitt of Kettleby in Lincolnshire. Although Keyes's official conversion to Catholicism was as a result of the Jesuit mission, he already possessed strong Catholic connections on his mother's side, giving him family links with, among others, the Wintours and the Wrights.[5]

Keyes was about forty when he was initiated into the plot and is described as being tall with a red beard. At the time he was in the employment of the Catholic Lord Mordaunt, while his wife Christiana was governess to Mordaunt's children. Keyes was evidently not particularly wealthy and saw the plot as an opportunity to improve his personal circumstances in an England free from recusancy penalties. Nevertheless, his character witnesses were impressive. Tesimond refers to him as 'magnanimous and fearless',[6] while Father Gerard paints a similar picture, describing Keyes as 'a grave and sober man, and of great wit and sufficiency . . . His virtue and valour were the chiefest things wherein they could expect assistance from him; for otherwise, his means were not great, but in those two, by report, he had great measure.'[7]

Around this time, plans were in place to begin the construction of the mine. Thomas Wintour's declaration confirms that Thomas and Guy visited Catesby at his property, Moorcrofts in Uxbridge, at the beginning of the Michaelmas term, where it was agreed that work would begin immediately. Later that day Guy travelled to London to make preparations at the Whynniard house. The following day he sent for Wintour, who joined him at the house only to discover, to his surprise and alarm, that it had been repossessed by the Crown.[8]

It was at this time that James was attempting to finalize a political union between England and Scotland. As the properties close to the Parliament buildings belonged to the Crown, the government had the right to requisition them for state business. Consequently, the Whynniard house and all others around it had become the temporary homes of the Scottish lords negotiating the union. This was potentially disastrous for the conspirators. Although the house offered no evidence to incriminate them, a more pressing concern was that there was no official deadline for the talks to end. As far as the conspirators were concerned the house might not be available to them for several years. The possibility cannot be ruled out that at this time they attempted, unsuccessfully, to find alternative premises. Presumably Guy was also required to find alternative lodgings. As stated in the lease agreement between Ferris and Percy, Percy had, in fact, leased two houses from Whynniard (see page 133). Percy and Guy may have had access to the other house, although that may also have been requisitioned. The alternatives for Guy would have been temporary lodgings in London – Catesby's house in Lambeth or perhaps White Webbs, a house near Barnet. White Webbs was known to have a number of priest-holes, and at the time of the conspiracy it was in the possession of Anne Vaux, who lived there with her sister Eleanor Brooksby, her sister's husband Edward and Anne Vaux's long-time friend and confessor Father Garnet. Guy and the other conspirators are recorded as having stayed as guests there from time to time. For the conspirators, its isolated location provided an ideal refuge, while Vaux herself was well prepared for entertaining Catholic guests eager to avoid detection. Undoubtedly, Guy Fawkes and his co-conspirators spent several hours in the company of Garnet during their visits and would have celebrated mass and received confession and Holy Communion. Vaux herself was interrogated in the aftermath of the plot, largely because of her connections with Garnet, and was forced to admit that she had hosted Guy at least as far back as Easter 1605.[9]

Luckily for the conspirators, the delay was a relatively short one. Based on the account given in Thomas Wintour's declaration, it lasted no more than a couple of months. In it he states: 'This hindered our beginning until a fortnight before Christmas.' After receiving permission to return to the house they resumed preparations for the mine. One of the first tasks to be carried out was a thorough investigation of the cellar. By the early seventeenth century the cellar was already aged and decrepit. Its walls, constructed from brick, measured some 9 feet (2.75 metres) in width and the same in height, while reaching a length no less than 20 feet (6 metres).[10] Meanwhile, at Catesby's home in Lambeth, another cellar was being used to store materials. This house was described as secretive. Located in an isolated spot on the banks of the river, its windows were protected by shutters, its doors could be firmly bolted against intrusion, while a flat stone concealed the stairway to the vaults. The vaults themselves were described as high and arched, with thick stone preventing water from the river from causing the cellar air to become damp, an essential requirement when storing gunpowder.[11]

Work on the mine began around 11 December, by which time Thomas Percy and Jack Wright had returned to London. Catesby had already successfully obtained a large quantity of gunpowder, which was then being guarded by Keyes at Lambeth, while Wintour, Guy, Catesby, Wright and Percy began work.

The preparations were well planned. Each man was equipped with appropriate tools and brought with them supplies of 'baked meats' so they did not need to leave the cellar. Guy was charged with acting as sentinel, or watchman, and directing the actions of his fellow conspirators.[12] Wintour states that the neighbours never saw any of the conspirators with the exception of Guy posing as Percy's servant. They limited their comings and goings to late at night after carrying out the work in the daytime. The debris was removed from the cellar via an outhouse that they had constructed and placed just outside the cellar in their garden, while other rubble may have been disposed of in the nearby river. Tesimond is quick to praise the efforts of the men in the mine, describing their commitment as 'remarkable' considering they were not used to this type of work. Guy refers to all involved in the mine as 'gentlemen of name and blood'.[13] Tesimond also highlights that several hours of labour in such a cramped area, devoid of air and light, left its mark on some of the plotters,

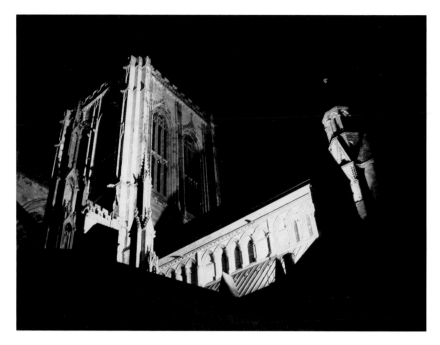

York Minster at night (Photograph: Mike Davis)

The Shambles, York, at night (Photograph: Mike Davis)

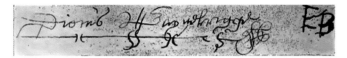

Signatures of Denis and Edith Bainbridge (From
Catherine Pullein's *The Pulleyns of Yorkshire*, 1915)

Coats of arms of the Pulleyn families of Scotton,
Blubberhouse and Timble (From Pullein)

View of Mickelgate Bar in York (From William Hargrove's *History and
Description of the Ancient City of York*, 1818)

Percy House in Scotton, Yorkshire, once the residence of Guy Fawkes following his mother's marriage to Denis Bainbridge and the Percy family, kinsmen to Thomas Percy (From a reconstruction of an old photograph published in Pullein)

Right: A Huguenot attack on a Catholic church in France (From James Thompson's *The Wars of Religion in France 1559–1576*, 1909)

Below: *The Massacre of St Bartholomew in 1572* by Francois du Bois of Amiens in 1584 (From Thompson)

The Buck Hall at Cowdray House. During Fawkes's time at Cowdray this room was considered to be one of the finest in England. The house is now a ruin, having been gutted by fire in 1793. (From *Sussex Archaeological Collections*, Vol. 20, 1868)

The `Jesuit Father Robert Persons (From James Caulfield's *The History of the Gunpowder Plot*, 1804)

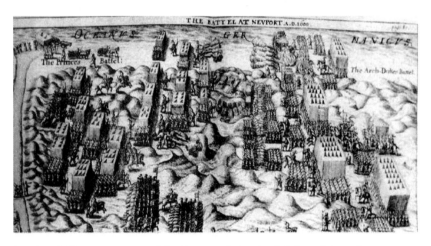

Battle of Nieuport, 1600. The forces of the Archduke of Austria appear on the right. (From Francis Vere's *Commentaries of the Divers Pieces of Services*, 1657)

Thomas Wintour (From
Philip Sidney's *History of the
Gunpowder Plot*, 1905)

Guy Fawkes (From Sidney)

The Gunpowder conspirators as depicted by Crispijn van de Passe. Keyes,
Grant, Tresham, Rookwood and Digby are all missing. (From Sidney)

Above left: A painting in St Stephen's Chapel, used as a meeting place for the Commons and which was near Guy Fawkes's house (From John Timb's *Mirror of Literature, Amusement, and Instruction*, Vol. 24, 1834).

Above right: Thomas Percy (From Sidney)

Alnwick Castle (Photograph: Mike Davis)

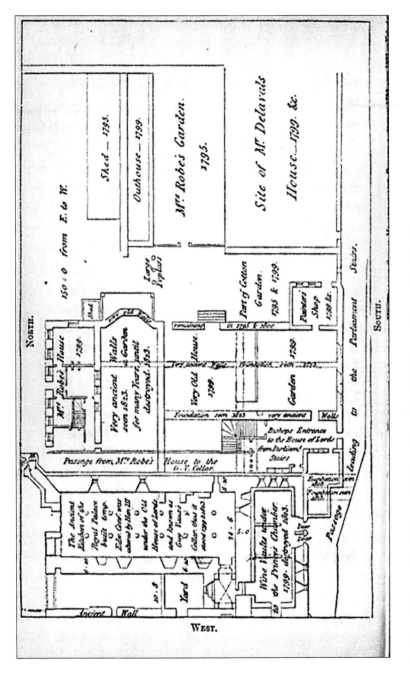

A plan of the ancient Palace of Westminster by W. Capon (From Gardiner)

Sir Edward Coke (From Sir
Edward Coke's *Three Law Tracts*,
1764)

Sir Robert Cecil, 1st Earl of
Salisbury (From Sidney)

Sir Henry Howard, the Earl of
Northampton (From Horatio
Walpole's *A Catalogue of the
Royal and Noble Authors of
England, Scotland and Ireland*,
1812)

Sir Thomas Howard, the Earl of
Suffolk (From Walpole)

Guy Fawkes laying the powder
(From Ainsworth)

Guy Fawkes under interrogation
(From Ainsworth)

Guy Fawkes's arrest
(From Ainsworth)

The accident at Holbeach
(From Ainsworth)

Top: The east side of the House of Lords (From Samuel Gardiner's *What the Gunpowder Plot Was*, 1897)

Above: The Powder Cellar (From Sidney)

Left: Guy Fawkes's Lantern (From Sidney)

Left: King James's entry into London in 1603 (From Sir James Mackintosh's *The History of England*, Vol. 4, 1835)

Below left: King James I (From Sidney)

Below; Prince Henry Frederick (From Lucy Aiken's *Memoirs of the Court of James the First*, 1823)

Queen Elizabeth of Bohemia, eldest daughter of James I. Had the plot been successful, Elizabeth would have been proclaimed Queen of England. (From Elizabeth Benger's *Memoirs of Elizabeth Stuart, Queen of Bohemia*, 1825)

Guy Fawkes and the conspirators working in the mine (From William Ainsworth's *Guy Fawkes: or, the Gunpowder Treason*, 1857)

Guy Fawkes and Robert Catesby transporting the gunpowder from Lambeth to John Whynniard's house (From Ainsworth)

The house at Lambeth (From Sidney)

Above: The Tower of London
(Photograph: Mike Davis)

Left: Guy Fawkes's Dungeon,
'Little Ease'

Above: The Council Chamber in Governor's House, identified as the
location where Guy Fawkes was interrogated and tortured
(From Lord de Ros's *Memorials of the Tower of London*, 1866)

The execution of the conspirators (From Sidney)

The execution of Guy Fawkes
(From Ainsworth)

The death of Catesby
(From Ainsworth)

Bonfire Night in Britain (Photograph: Mike Davis)

Left: Firework display on Bonfire Night (Photograph: Mike Davis)

Below: An anarchist poster of Guy Fawkes, twentieth century (Artist unknown)

VOTE FOR GUY FAWKES
THE ONLY MAN EVER TO ENTER PARLIAMENT WITH HONEST INTENTIONS

forcing them to take frequent rests. The construction of the mine also required large amounts of wood to support the excavation. Supplies of wood were bought in large quantities and brought over from the Lambeth house when required.[14]

By Christmas Eve the plotters had made some progress but were still to disturb the wall below the Parliament building. During the two weeks in which they had laboured, discussion had centred primarily on the immediate business in hand, but some consideration had also been given to plans for action after the attack had been carried out.[15] Reminiscent of the Spanish Treason, elimination of the Protestant heirs to the throne was central to their plans. Prince Henry, the eldest son of James I, would be present in Parliament on the night and a victim of the planned explosion. Second in line was Prince Charles, the Duke of York (later King Charles I), who was unlikely to attend Parliament. It was suggested by Thomas Percy that through an acquaintance he would be able to enter the young prince's chamber at his residence in London without suspicion and abduct him unharmed. Alternatively, if Charles were present at Parliament, the problem would be solved.[16] The next concern was James's daughter, Lady Elizabeth, a far easier target, who was under the guardianship of Sir John Harrington at Coombe Abbey in Warwickshire.

The possibility of obtaining the aid of foreign princes was also debated. Thomas Wintour dismissed the idea of seeking help from the Spanish king, describing him as 'too slow in his preparations to hope any good from in the first extremities'.[17] Similarly, France was regarded as being 'too near and too dangerous'. After much discussion, the conspirators agreed that no foreign monarch should be made aware of the conspiracy in advance and forced to swear the secrecy oath. This, in part, arose from the possibility that those who sympathized with their plight might not necessarily agree with their methods. With this in mind, it was decided that if any foreign aid were to come it would have to be after the event. Philip III's reluctance to support the Spanish Treason had already left its mark on those conspirators involved – although, if the earlier reports of Juan de Tassis are considered, Spain might have acted with more enthusiasm regarding an invasion if an uprising by English Catholics had been guaranteed.

Further attention was focused on the finance and horses that would be needed for the uprising that was to follow the destruction of Parliament. In time this would mean recruiting several new conspirators to assist in the planned rebellion. Thomas Wintour's declaration confirms that some discussion also took place as to whether some of the Catholic lords should be forewarned of the event to avoid their being killed in the explosion. This was both vital and fatal to the success of the strategy, as any uprising would be quickly crushed without support from members of the nobility, but the more people who were aware of the conspiracy the less chance there was of keeping it a secret. Thus it was agreed that as many would be saved as possible without compromising the mission, yet without any firm indication of how this could be achieved.[18]

Shortly before Christmas the conspirators faced another setback with the news that the reopening of Parliament was to be delayed to 3 October 1605 because of renewed fears of the plague. In many ways such a delay should have been advantageous to the conspirators, as by Christmas construction of the mine was still a long way from completion. Realistically, any chance of being able to carry out their task in February was optimistic. The delay not only gave them more time to finish the mining work, it allowed Catesby to spend more time to consider the aftermath should the plot succeed.

It was around this time that Catesby added two more accomplices. One of these was his servant, Thomas Bates. It is probable, although not definite, that Bates was already aware of some elements of the plot, which may, at least in part, have influenced Catesby's decision to involve him. Even if not fully informed he could not have failed to notice his master behaving more secretively than normal. When questioned regarding his initiation while in the Tower of London, Bates confessed that he was inducted into the conspiracy around December.[19] As a servant, he was the only participant born of lower social status, yet his life was not without privilege. Like Catesby he was born in Lapworth and was employed by Catesby at Ashby St Ledgers, where he lived in quarters in the grounds with his wife Martha. Bates was entitled to his own servant and also his own armour.[20] Tesimond suggests that Bates had been in Catesby's service for quite some time and had proved his loyalty on countless occasions, carrying out with secrecy and obedience every command placed upon him. In keeping with his fellow plotters, he had suffered persecution and hardship for his Catholicism, but he did so unwaveringly.[21] Gerard portrays him in a similar light, stating Catesby's high opinion of Bates 'for his long tried fidelity towards him, which the poor fellow continued even until he saw his master dead'.[22]

The next newcomer was Christopher Wright, who was sworn in some time between Christmas 1604 and Easter 1605. In his narrative Tesimond, probably mistakenly, suggests that Wright was the first of the conspirators to be added to the original five.[23] His involvement is no big surprise, as his brother Jack was one of the founder members. At the time of the plot Wright was about thirty-five years of age, the same as Guy Fawkes, and was tall in height and strong in stature. He had pleasing facial features and a full head of blond hair. Renowned for his bravery, he was skilled with the sword and on horseback. According to

Tesimond he matched his brother in 'valour and gallantry' and was a close friend of Catesby's. The Jesuit also refers to Wright as being little spoken and describes his life following his conversion to Catholicism as 'exemplary'.[24] Gerard offers similar praise, referring to Wright as being unlike his brother in face, yet he was 'very like to the other in conditions and qualities, and both esteemed and tried to be as stout a man as England had and withal a zealous Catholic and trusty and secret in any business as could be wished'.[25]

Of Wright's activities before joining the plot little is known. If Guy's examination of 25 November 1605 is to be believed, Christopher Wright had been deeply involved in the Spanish Treason.[26] Such a suggestion certainly makes sense of theories linking him with the enigmatic Anthony Dutton.[27] Should this be the case, it is somewhat surprising that Wright had not been included from the start, a possibility that cannot be ruled out entirely. If Wright, as we can assume from our knowledge of Dutton, was reasonably experienced in operating in Europe, it seems that he was as well placed as any of the conspirators to be charged with travelling abroad to obtain gunpowder. Such a theory would also explain his absence up to this time.

Work on the mine ceased briefly for Christmas, during which time the conspirators separated, forsaking their mission to celebrate the holiday season with their families.[28] The only exception was Guy. With progress on the mine at such a delicate stage he was chosen to watch over the rented house to ensure their endeavours were not discovered. Being recognizable to the locals of Westminster through posing as Percy's servant, Guy was the least likely to arouse suspicion. Perhaps, also, spending Christmas among family meant less to him than it did to the others. For the past eleven years he had celebrated Christmas in the company of his fellow soldiers, men of similar ideals, whom he both trusted and respected – a far cry from the Christmases of his earlier life, which had been spent in the company of his sisters, his mother, his father and, in his earliest years, his grandmother. Guy's relationship with his family may have soured somewhat by this point, as previously suggested. In addition, as a committed Catholic – particularly one forced to endure the harsh circumstances of warfare at a time when Calvinist iconoclasm had destroyed many traditional religious images – it seems likely that the changes in how the feast was celebrated did not sit well with Guy. The growing custom of celebration through dancing, singing, over-indulging in food and other similar festivities may well have been something the conspirators despised. Less than two years after the Gunpowder Plot, King James I continued to develop the celebrations, insisting that the event be honoured with a play on Christmas night and that festivities and games be played by the ladies and gentlemen of the Court.[29]

Evidently Guy did not spend the Christmas period in complete solitude. On 28 December he is recorded as having been present in Whitehall to witness the wedding of the niece of Robert Cecil to the Earl of Montgomery. With hindsight, Cecil might have been somewhat worried about the attendance of the inconspicuous man now notorious for attempting to kill many of those who had been present – including the king. It is easy to reflect on the irony of the event, imagining Guy standing quietly at the back, still relatively close to the king, dressed smartly in his black cloak, equipped with the usual elegant white ruff and matching black, plumed steeple hat, a sword by his side. Nevertheless, Guy was clearly not there to cause trouble. When later questioned about his presence, he replied that he attended 'with no evil intent'[30] – yet it would be interesting to speculate exactly what thoughts went through his mind as he stood in the company of some of the very people he intended to kill.

Work on the mine resumed shortly after Christmas. Based on the testimony of Thomas Wintour it continued throughout January before the conspirators decided the time was right to move the supplies of gunpowder already acquired from Catesby's lodgings in Lambeth to the cellar of the Whynniard house. Wintour states that this occurred at Candlemas, the feast of the presentation of Jesus at the Temple, placing the time period somewhere between 28 January and 3 February. The transporting of the powder was made under the cover of night when the citizens of Lambeth and Guy's neighbours in Westminster would be unaware that anything of significance was taking place. Despite Whynniard's servant John Shepherd later confessing to being roused one night by sounds outside his window, after which, on investigation, he witnessed seeing a boat close to the wall of 'Sir Thomas Parry's garden' and men travelling to and from the boat, the sleepy servant saw no reason to question the transporting of cargo undertaken by Percy and his accomplices as being anything suspicious. Considering that thirty-six barrels were discovered, the powder was probably transported over a series of trips. During these journeys it would have been loaded on to a long boat at Catesby's home and covered with tarpaulin and straw to protect it from damp. From there the boat would have been rowed towards the rented house and secured on arrival, leaving the conspirators free to offload the barrels to the cellar. There is some indication that Guy had installed a door by this time in order to take the barrels directly into the cellar from outside.[31]

Kit Wright and Thomas Bates were initiated before the gunpowder was transported and were probably both involved in the task. Wintour also suggests that Kit Wright assisted in the digging of the mine some two weeks after Candlemas. Keyes was undoubtedly also present once the gunpowder had been moved from Lambeth. By this time the determination of the conspirators was relentless. By February they had reached the main foundations of the Parliament house, which was some 9 or 10 feet (up to 3 metres) thick.[32] Because of the increased difficulty of knocking through the wall, the noise of their endeavours became louder, resulting in constant orders from Guy for the conspirators to cease their work. This was not the only difficulty. As the tunnel extended closer to the river, water began to seep in. In his narrative, Tesimond affirms that the conspirators were forced to spend at least one night carrying several barrels of water from the mine.[33] The effects of this could have been disastrous. Not only would a significant influx of water severely hinder their work but the dampness could render the gunpowder useless. Father Francis Edwards, commentating in his own investigation of the Gunpowder Plot, suggested exposure to such conditions would have made the gunpowder unusable after just a few days.[34]

As progress continued to be hindered, the plotters must have wondered whether fate was against them. In no way was this better displayed than in a strange story recited by Tesimond that some time during March work on the mine was halted suddenly when they heard what sounded like a ringing bell. As the conspirators listened, the sound became clearer and more distinctive. Yet, despite their best efforts the source could not be identified. Guy was called from his sentinel position and asked to investigate. Although he listened earnestly, he, too, was unable to explain the sound. In the minds of the conspirators the sound was an omen of evil spirits intent on ruining their endeavour. A short time later holy water was brought in and splashed against the wall. The sound faded briefly but resumed almost immediately before fading once more when the holy water was reapplied. The ringing continued for several days before finally disappearing, never to be heard in that location again – and no explanation as to where it came from was ever found.[35]

Later in March an equally unexpected but positive occurrence changed the prospects for the plot. When busy working on the mine, the conspirators heard another noise, this time described as being reminiscent of the shuffling of coal. Fearing that the plot had been uncovered, Guy was detailed to investigate. Returning shortly afterwards, he revealed that the sounds came from a vault located directly beneath the House of Lords. The vault in question had been let out to a coal merchant who was presently removing the remaining stock. Having had the opportunity to survey the cellar Guy advised his co-conspirators that not only was the cellar perfectly located for their purpose but also it was available to rent. Faced with the difficulty of progressing further with their work on the mine, Percy was dispatched immediately to lease it.[36]

The cellar, like the house, was the property of John Whynniard. An entry in the *King's Book*, written shortly after the discovery of the plot, states that there was 'some stuff of the King's which lay in part of a cellar under these rooms', the rooms in question being the House of Lords. There is another reference that states that 'Whynniard had let out some part of a room directly under the Parliament chamber to one that used it for a cellar'.[37] The one that used it as a cellar was a coal merchant, Mrs Ellen Skinner, presently widowed, but soon to be married to a Mr Bright. When questioned in the aftermath of the plot, Mrs Whynniard affirmed that Percy laboured 'very earnestly' to obtain the cellar. Mrs Whynniard also remarked when summoned before the Privy Council that Skinner was at the time unwilling to part with it but did so under continuous pressure from Percy. One way or another Percy secured the lease for £4 a year, with Mrs Skinner receiving £2 for agreeing to part with her lease.[38]

It is surprising that the conspirators were not aware of the cellar beforehand. Agreement of the lease was signed on Lady

Day 1605, 25 March, after which time the conspirators took over from the soon-to-be Mrs Bright as Whynniard's new tenants. The reason given by Percy for requiring the cellar – ironically, true in part – was that he needed the extra space to store firewood. When the powder was later transported into the cellar from the Whynniard house Guy was given the order to cover the powder with wood. Wintour cites 'a thousand of billets and five hundred of faggots' in order to ensure 'we might have the house free to suffer anyone to enter that would'. Guy's examination on 5 November confirms that twenty barrels of gunpowder were brought in at first with more following on 20 July. Guy also revealed that hogsheads, barrels and firkins were used to transport the powder, with firkins being used to help carry the powder into the cellar.[39]

The cellar was practically perfect for what they intended. Although located at ground level rather than underground, its roof was constructed from the rafters and boards that formed the floor of the Lords' chamber. It was spacious, estimated at some 73 by 24 feet (22.25 by 7.3 metres), and was probably divided into partitions rather than being one long room.[40] It has often been suggested that the vault had over a century earlier been part of the kitchen of the old palace. Over the years its condition had deteriorated significantly, and it was dirty, and for the conspirators this was a further benefit: the less interesting the cellar appeared, the less likely it was to attract attention.[41]

Following Percy's successful leasing of the cellar, the next task was to transfer the gunpowder from the cellar of the Whynniard house into the vault beneath Parliament. For this purpose Guy created a door from Whynniard's house to the vault. From his survey of the cellar where the mine was being created, Guy would have already been aware that a passage connecting the Whynniard House to the new vault existed. At the time, the passage was hidden behind an iron grille. Based on his later answers to questioning, particularly given in the examination of 'John Johnsonne' – that is, Guy Fawkes – on 6 November, he was charged with creating a door some time during Lent. Although it is possible he was lying, construction of the door would have had to have been completed before he travelled to the Low Countries after Easter (see Chapter 10). When asked about the gunpowder, Guy replied that it was transported from Percy's house some three or four days after the door was created.[42] Making a new door was something he achieved with remarkable ease thanks largely to the existence of the grille. The logic behind the new door was simple. By replacing the iron grille with a wooden door, delivery of the materials to the newly rented vault could be achieved from the cellar of the house itself. In terms of transportation this was a wise move – if nothing else, it reduced the chances of being caught. If the examination of 'Johnsonne' is to be believed, Guy carried out the task himself, although he may have said this to protect his fellow conspirators who were on the run at that time.

But where one problem disappeared another arose. With the powder safely deposited in the nearby cellar there was no longer any need to continue with the mine, so it was abandoned, although not before it was successfully hidden from view in case the house was once more requisitioned for official business or broken into by any person who might stumble upon their recent activity. Most accounts of the plot state that the mine was sealed, possibly with an iron grille. In his investigation of the Gunpowder Plot Samuel Gardiner suggests this could have been achieved with a couple of flagstones.[43] Within a few months of the abandonment of the mine, Percy is recorded as having employed a carpenter by the name of York to carry out work on the Whynniard house. Presumably, by this time all traces of the mine had been hidden from view.[44] The absence of any evidence has led some to speculate whether it ever existed or whether it was a fictional concoction by the government to embellish the case against the conspirators. The confessions of Guy and Wintour remain the only evidence that the mine ever existed, yet even this has failed to clarify either its exact location or how the conspirators concealed its existence.

For Robert Catesby the leasing of the cellar under the Lords offered two benefits. Not only did it provide the perfect location to fire the gunpowder but also it allowed him to concentrate on planning the events that would occur directly after the explosion. It was principally for this reason that he decided to acquaint more people with the plot. Evidently Catesby was also short of funds at this stage, as highlighted in Thomas Wintour's declaration:

> the charge of maintaining us all so long together,
> besides the number of several houses which for several
> uses had been hired, and buying of powder, &c., had
> lain heavy on Mr Catesby alone to support, it was nec-
> essary for to call in some others to ease his charge.[45]

It was around this time that Catesby added Robert Wintour and John Grant to his group of loyal men.

As the brother of Thomas Wintour and a relation of other conspirators, notably the Wrights, through both blood and marriage, Robert Wintour was already well known to them. He was the eldest son and therefore heir to his father's estate at Huddington Court in Worcestershire, which passed to him following his father's death in 1594. In addition to Huddington he inherited several hop yards and twenty-five salt-evaporating pans near Droitwich famous for producing fine salt, which was a major source of income for the family. His wife Gertrude was the daughter of Sir John Talbot, regarded at the time as one of the wealthiest landowners in the Midlands, who had spent over twenty years in prison on recusancy charges. Robert was also a firm Catholic, and at the time of the plot Huddington had at least two priest-holes, almost certainly the work of the Jesuit Nicholas Owen.[46]

Robert Wintour was a generous character who used his fortune for good. Tesimond relates that he was short but possessed good physique with a manner described as 'discreet and judicious, devout and sincere . . . courteous and generous, and endowed with intrepid courage'.[47] Gerard delivers a similar verdict, stating that he was 'an earnest Catholic, though not as yet generally known to be so. He was a wise man and of grave and sober carriage and very stout, as all of that name have been esteemed.'[48]

Although renowned for his talent with a sword, his commitment to Catholicism and his ability to keep a secret, it was largely the fact that Robert could contribute financially that convinced Catesby to initiate him into the plot. Once accepted, Robert would be charged with the responsibility of collecting weapons and preparing horses for the uprising once the explosion had taken place. For this task he was to be joined by his sister's husband, John Grant.

Grant was the eldest son of Thomas Grant and Alice Ruding, both of whom came from families of ancient lineage. John Grant inherited the family home of Norbrook, near the village of Snitterfield, some five miles (8 kilometres) from Stratford-upon-Avon, one of a number of Catholic households located in the Warwickshire area. It was largely for this reason, and that he lived in such close proximity to Robert Wintour, that he was chosen for his specific task in the uprising, which was to prepare weapons and horses for the rebellion and be personally responsible for the kidnapping of Princess Elizabeth. Tesimond records that Grant kept his horses in stables close by – which was also used by Baron Harrington, guardian to Princess Elizabeth.

Tesimond describes Grant as being about forty at the time of the plot, taciturn by nature and also 'inclined to melancholy'. He also remarks that he was 'intelligent and discreet', able to speak several languages and describes his way of life as 'admirable'. He celebrates Grant's bravery, stating 'his courage was inferior to none in that company', which he demonstrated when facing the King's pursuivants when they came to search his house for priests.[49] Gerard, too, speaks well of Grant's personality and status, saying he 'lived well in his country' but suggests he was unable to contribute financially to the plot.[50]

Wintour and Grant were sworn in together around January or February 1605, at a time when the original conspirators were still hard at work on the mine. Grant and Robert Wintour were contacted by Robert Catesby and asked to join him and Robert's brother Thomas at an inn called the Catherine Wheel in Oxford. Once there, both were required to take the same oath as the other conspirators before they were introduced into the plot. Grant seems to have made no objection. Wintour was less willing to agree but later changed his mind.[51] Not for the first time, the persuasiveness of Robert Catesby would prove decisive in obtaining the allegiance of men whose lives up to that point had been worthy of so much praise. In the words of Father Gerard: 'More was the pity that such men, so worthy to be esteemed, should lose themselves in such a labyrinth of erring courses.'[52]

10

SPIES, SOLDIERS AND
'STIR THIS PARLIAMENT'

Around Easter 1605 Guy Fawkes was presented with a new mission. With work on the mine no longer necessary, coupled with Catesby's intention that Guy should remain as inconspicuous as possible in the run-up to the reopening of Parliament, Guy and two or three other plotters were charged with the task of travelling throughout England to identify locations where fortifications could be built should it be necessary in the aftermath. Evidence of this is provided once more by Tesimond, who states in his narrative: 'I got this from someone who was with these gentlemen after the plot was discovered, and when speech was free as to what had happened.'[1] It seems that Guy ran into difficulties with the mission, which could not be solved without the help of people skilled in the art of fortification. Following this, it was decided that Guy would return to the Low Countries where he would also pass on news of the plot to Stanley and Owen.

The best surviving account of this journey can be found in his examination of 5 November 1605 shortly after his arrest and while still posing as John Johnson. Assuming his answers to be truthful, he left London around Easter and journeyed to Dover. When asked what ship he took he said could not remember, only that the ship landed in Calais.[2] By 1605 Calais, which Guy had helped conquer for the Spanish in 1596, had returned to French control, a condition of the Franco-Spanish treaty at the Peace of Vervins. In addition, since ratification of the Anglo-Spanish treaty had been achieved in the summer of 1604 it was no longer illegal for an Englishman to enrol in the Spanish Army. For Guy this was a helpful development. Although there is no indication that his trip was connected to any official business with the English Regiment, the recent peace would have made the journey less noteworthy. Some have suggested that an important companion travelled with Guy to the Continent to acquire more gunpowder.[3] This is not impossible, but it is unlikely that two Catholics involved in the plot would travel to the Low Countries together, as Catesby was reluctant for any of them to do anything that might arouse suspicion.

After arriving in Calais Guy travelled to Saint-Omer and spent some time at the college there. The college had been established twelve years earlier, at Artois in the Spanish Netherlands about 24 miles (38 kilometres) from Calais, by the Jesuit Father Robert Persons. Persons had earlier been instrumental in the foundation of the Jesuit College in Valladolid, supported by Philip II, but wanted to establish a second college, this time for laymen. Proximity to England was an important consideration in choosing the location, and Saint-Omer was relatively convenient for Englishmen.

Following a brief stay at Saint-Omer, Guy headed for Brussels where he renewed acquaintance with several of his former colleagues, notably Hugh Owen.[4] During his three-week stay Guy discussed many things with Owen, in particular Catesby's intention to notify Stanley, Baldwin and Owen of the plot. Catesby also wished to obtain a commission in the cavalry regiment under the leadership of Sir Charles Percy, kinsman to Thomas Percy, who was to raise 2,000 men for the army of the

Archduke of Austria, which Catesby had in mind to use as part of the planned uprising in the aftermath of the plot. Catesby also hoped that Owen could use his influence to obtain further help from abroad.[5]

While Owen was pleased by the fact that the Catholic powers in England were finally doing something to improve their circumstances, for Guy the trip was ill timed. At the time of his arrival Stanley was in Spain on one of his diplomatic missions. Owen also informed Guy that Stanley was unlikely to support the conspiracy as he was presently attempting to gain a pardon from James so he could return to England. More encouraging was Owen's promise that he would send the envoy Sir Edmund Baynham to the Vatican to gain favour with the Pope should the plot succeed. Guy's answers to examination on 9 January 1606 imply that this had been Catesby's intention all along. In addition, Owen agreed that he would relay the message to Stanley once he had returned.[6]

For Guy the result was probably unexpected, as Stanley had always encouraged the possibility of an uprising. After leaving Brussels, Guy is recorded as having travelled to the camp of Ambrosio Spinola in Ostend, presumably to negotiate with him about the possibility of obtaining Catesby's commission.[7] It is stated in 'Johnson's' examination of 5 November that Guy did not receive any pay during his three-week stay, yet the fact that his name appeared on a list of members of the Lord Arundel's company in the late autumn confirms he was still officially in service. While at Ostend the possiblity cannot be ruled out that Guy attempted to rouse interest in the cause from Spinola's troops, but, if so, nothing materialized.

After leaving Ostend Guy travelled to the English College at Douai.[8] Guy's activities while at the college are unrecorded, and he did not give any reason for being there. Based on the available evidence his stay was little more than a stopgap and an opportunity to liaise with other Catholics before returning to Brussels. The length of his stay is also unrecorded. He returned to Brussels in July, at which point he resumed talks with Owen. According to the 'Johnson' examination, Guy saw Stanley, Owen, Tesimond and some other Englishmen during this second stay, which lasted about a month.[9] However, Guy did not offer any insight into any discussion with Stanley. Assuming the 'Johnson' examination of 5 November is accurate, Stanley had returned from Spain but was unwilling to participate, as Owen had predicted. Further discussions with Stanley and Owen may have taken place, but it is also possible that Guy may have simply used the opportunity to extend his stay. In his examination Guy says he saw Father Tesimond in Brussels, yet Tesimond does not mention this in his own testament.[10] Nevertheless, in his translation of Tesimond's narrative, Gunpowder Plot commentator Father Edwards draws attention to Tesimond's account, highlighting Catesby's requirement for knowledge about fortifications as the chief reason for Guy's visit, something Tesimond mentions in more detail than any other contemporary account, which might suggest that Tesimond was present when Guy spoke to Owen in Brussels.[11]

While in Brussels, Guy is also reported to have met some other Englishmen, one of whom was Robert Spiller, a messenger who had earlier accompanied Stanley, Owen and Baldwin to a meeting with Juan de Tassis.[12] Spiller had already been accused of assisting Jesuits, and it had also been propounded that members of Spiller's family had been harbouring priests, including Father Garnet. Around the spring of 1605, probably during Guy's first visit to Brussels, a spy is said to have witnessed Guy and Spiller in one another's company. This, if true, may shed light on the identity of Guy's important companion. It has been suggested that Spiller was Garnet's courier, but there is no evidence to substantiate this, and another report has Spiller in London at the time.[13]

One way or another, Guy's trip did not go unnoticed. At some point during his time in Flanders his presence came to the attention of Sir Robert Cecil. Cecil, now the Earl of Salisbury, employed a vast network of spies throughout Europe, especially in Flanders, Spain, Italy and Ireland, successfully building on the great Elizabethan network established by Sir Francis Walsingham.[14] Among his spies was a man named Captain William Turner. Although dismissed as 'light and dissolute' by the English Ambassador to Brussels, Sir Thomas Edmondes, Turner was an experienced soldier with over fourteen years of service in France, Ireland and the Low Countries. Since 1598 he had been an active observer of the Jesuit mission, and he had already gained the confidence of Hugh Owen by posing as an agent on the side of the exiles. Owen had questioned Turner, whose brother was in service in the Protestant forces of Maurice of Nassau, and delved deeply into his background, but he had stood up to all enquiries well enough to earn Owen's trust. So impressed was Owen that the Welshman entrusted £100 to Turner and sent him on an errand to Maurice to recruit his brother into the service of the archduke and 'withal to render some town of importance'. Turner must have complied with Owen's request, as he is recorded as having returned to Owen after meeting Maurice, carrying a gift from the Dutch.[15]

In May 1605 Turner allegedly met Guy and accompanied him to Ostend. While there, Turner spoke with Spinola about his recent activities in the Spanish Netherlands. After returning to Brussels Turner was welcomed into the Catholic Church by Baldwin, and he also held lengthy discussions with Owen over an invasion of England. At the time of their discussions a force of some 1,500 able men was being assembled at Dover for the

service of Spain, awaiting deployment to the Spanish Netherlands – another recent Spanish privilege that had come into
effect following the Treaty of London. Owen may have had it in
mind to use this force in any forthcoming invasion, along with
any additional support Catesby could muster back in England
and backed by the regiment in which Catesby was seeking to
become a lieutenant. Once back in Dover, Turner was asked to
wait for the return of Father Tesimond, who was travelling from
Brussels with prayer books and fresh letters and would subsequently be introduced to Catesby.[16] At some point Turner filed
a report to Cecil that Hugh Owen was part of a planned invasion by the English exiles, supported by the Spanish, to take
place in July. Details of an invasion were clearly erroneous, but
included in Turner's report was intelligence that one Guido
Fawkes, known in government circles as a mercenary operating
in Flanders and Brabant, was preparing to travel to England with
the aid of Father Tesimond. Once in England he was to be presented to Robert Catesby, himself a marked man, who would, in
turn, put Fawkes in contact with 'honourable friends of the
nobility and others who would have arms and horses in readi-
ness'.[17] Reference to Guy was in connection with the alleged
invasion rather than the Gunpowder Plot, of which Turner
seems to have been unaware. Had he known of it he would
surely have relayed everything he knew to Cecil. Turner was also
unaware that Guy had been present in England for well over
a year. At that time no one other than the conspirators had
recognized the connection between Guy Fawkes and John
Johnson, the servant to Thomas Percy who had lived peacefully,
albeit busily, at the house of John Whynniard for more than a
year. If a connection had been made it would undoubtedly have
raised suspicion. When told of Turner's intelligence, the ambassador, Sir Thomas Edmondes, dismissed it. Nevertheless, Cecil

was now aware of Guy for the first time, something that may have led to Guy's own activities being monitored more closely.

Guy's final port of call before returning to England was a pilgrimage to the shrine of Our Lady of Montague in Brabant. Guy referred to the pilgrimage as his chief reason for being in the Low Countries in the first place.[18] By the end of August Guy was back in Calais ready to return by ship to Dover before travelling on to London. There he rented a room for a time at the house of a Mrs Herbert, located in close proximity to St Clement Danes Church, but was evicted soon after for his fraternizing with Catholics.[19] Meanwhile, the house rented from Whynniard remained in the care of Percy.

Earlier, around the middle of August, Thomas Percy had met up with Catesby in Bath to discuss the logistics of the rising to take place in the Midlands in the aftermath of the plot. It was at about this time that the conspirators had become aware that Parliament had again been prorogued, this time from 3 October to 5 November, because evidence of plague had been found in some of the houses around the Parliamentary buildings. The delay may also have taken into account the custom that people often returned to London around All Hallows.[20] For Catesby, success in the aftermath of the blowing up of Parliament ultimately rested on the conspirators' ability to rouse the support of England's Catholics. Furthermore, the conspirators still lacked funds and other resources. For this reason it was agreed that more should be enlisted.

In total a further three were initiated. The first of these was a fiery young Catholic named Ambrose Rookwood. Aged twenty-seven at the time of plot, Ambrose was the eldest son of Robert Rookwood of Stanningfield in Suffolk and his second wife Dorothea. Since the reign of Edward I the Rookwood family had lived distinguished lives in the Manor of Stanningfield. They had suffered for their Catholicism during the reign of Elizabeth I and often spent time in prison. In his youth Ambrose and his brothers had been educated at the college in Saint-Omer. Their safe crossing to Saint-Omer is generally attributed to the assistance of Father Gerard, while their sister, also named Dorothea, attended the girls' school of St Ursula's at Louvain-la-Neuve.

Ambrose was married to Elizabeth Tyrwhitt, daughter of Sir William – a union that gave him family connections with the Wrights, the Wintours and Robert Keyes – and they had two children. Following the death of his father in 1600, Ambrose, as the heir to his father's estate, inherited the family home at Coldham Hall, a location frequently used to hide priests.[21] Rookwood was known to have suffered for his faith. Although he was sensible enough to have avoided participation in the doomed Essex Rebellion, he had been convicted of recusancy in February 1605. It has also been suggested that he was responsible for providing Catesby, his close friend, with large amounts of gunpowder in the autumn of the previous year under the impression the powder was for the aid of the English Regiment in the Spanish Netherlands, an action that had been legalized following the Treaty of London in August 1604.[22] It is possible, therefore, that Rookwood may have been initiated at an earlier date. Some accounts have suggested his involvement began as early as March 1605, while others state it was as late as Michaelmas. Rookwood's reaction on hearing of the plot is said to have been one of horror, but his enthusiasm grew after learning that key Catholic allies were to be informed of the event in advance to avoid their being killed by the explosion. After pledging his involvement, Rookwood was made responsible for delivering news of the outcome of the attack to Catesby at Dunchurch, Warwickshire, the proposed starting point of the Midlands Rising. In addition, Rookwood pledged both horses and finance, which would have been invaluable once the gunpowder had been set off. In around September he rented a house, Clopton House, near Stratford-upon-Avon to be used as base in the uprising.

As he does for most of the conspirators, Tesimond paints a reasonably pleasing picture of the man, saying Rookwood was good-looking and well built although shorter than most. He was easy and pleasant in manner and courteous in nature. Tesimond highlights his learning at St-Omer, describing him as a 'well-lettered man' who was also of strong faith. Tesimond also goes so far as to point out that men of such conviction should not have agreed to participate in the event if they were not so convinced both of its chances of success and its lawfulness.[23] Gerard's account is similar, confirming Rockwood's lineage and describing him as a 'very devout' Catholic from infancy as well as being 'known to be of great virtue and no less valour and very secret'. Gerard also criticizes his decision to take part in the plot, stating 'whereby I do gather, they made a great account of this business, in respect thereof, it seems, they made account of nothing'.[24]

The twelfth member of the conspiracy was Sir Everard Digby. His father, also Everard, hailed from Stoke Dry in Rutland, while his mother, Maria, was daughter of a Francis Neale from Key-thorpe in Leicestershire. In common with many of the conspirators, he was descended from ancient lineage and of noble pedigree. Gerard states that his

> ancestors were a great help to the suppressing of Richard III . . . and the bringing and setting up of Henry VII . . . whereupon King Henry did make knights in the field seven brothers of his house at one time, from whom descended divers houses of that name, which live all in good reputation in their several countries. But this Sir Everard Digby was the heir of the eldest and chiefest house.[25]

Despite possessing Catholic leanings Digby was not brought up in the faith. Following the death of his Catholic father while he was still a child Everard grew up in a Protestant household. As a result, his early life passed by largely without incident. Nevertheless, Tesimond speaks highly of both child and parents, highlighting their 'goodness and religious sincerity', which Everard inherited 'along with their possessions and income'.[26] In 1596 he married Mary Mulsho, heiress to the Mulsho estate of Gayhurst, with whom he lived happily, fathering two children. Like Percy, Digby became a gentleman pensioner and was often present at Court. In later years he officially converted to Catholicism, which placed restrictions on his progress at Court, yet Tesimond highlights his 'rare' qualities that he should prefer to suffer alongside his fellow Catholics than be swayed by worldly goods. He was approximately 6 feet (1.8 metres) tall, slightly shorter than Catesby but better built. Tesimond goes as far as to suggest nowhere in England were there two more evenly matched men. In appearance, Digby was handsome and in manner courteous. He is described as being courageous and of having proven so on many occasions, yet he went to great lengths to avoid causing offence. As with Catesby, Digby was much liked. Gerard says of Digby: 'for indeed to do him right, he was as complete a man in all things that deserved estimation or might win affection, as one should see in a kingdom', sentiments also echoed by Tesimond.[27] It was undoubtedly these characteristics that commended him to Catesby. Digby was also a skilled horseman; in fact, Gerard described him as being skilled 'in all things that belonged unto a gentleman'. He also kept a stable of horses.[28]

Tesimond dates Digby's initiation to around a month before the explosion was due to take place. If this was so, it probably occurred while he was riding with Catesby from Harrowden to Gayhurst and his wife was taking a pilgrimage to St Winifred's

Well in Flintshire in the company of Father Garnet, Anne Vaux and several other of the conspirators' wives. It was certainly no earlier than late August. Tesimond states in his narrative that only Catesby, Thomas Wintour and Guy were aware of Digby's involvement. When informing Digby of the conspiracy, Tesimond suggests that Catesby referred to it in general terms. Seeing that Digby was satisfied, Catesby explained that he would go into greater detail over the coming days. Soon after, Thomas Wintour unveiled the entire conspiracy.[29] On hearing this, Digby was dumbfounded but agreed to commit under the impression that the Jesuits approved of it. Following the explosion, Digby was to lead a rising of Catholic gentry at Dunsmore Heath, initially under the guise of a hunt – he was well known for his love of hunting and hawking and was celebrated as a skilled marksman. Once the gunpowder had been fired, Digby would then be responsible for leading the hunt into a full-scale rebellion. For Catesby, Digby's charisma and likeability would prove a deciding factor in his ability to gain the allegiance of his fellow Catholics. In preparation for the task Digby joined Rookwood, Robert Wintour and Grant in the Midlands, setting up base at Coughton Court near Alcester, which he rented from the Throckmorton family and was said to have pledged £1,500 to support the cause.[30]

Another person with the ability to contribute financially was Catesby's cousin, Francis Tresham. Tresham was the eldest offspring of Sir Thomas Tresham of Rushton, Northamptonshire, and his wife, Muriel Throckmorton of Coughton Court, and was thus heir to his father's vast estates. Tresham was yet another conspirator of noble stock, raised by parents ardently committed to Catholicism. On his father's side, Tresham's great-grandfather, Sir Thomas Tresham, served Queen Elizabeth with distinction as Prior of the Order of St John of Jerusalem, while his relation on his mother's side, Sir Francis Throckmorton, lost his life for his part in the Throckmorton Plot of 1583. Francis Tresham was educated at Cambridge, attending either Gloucester Hall or St John's College – accounts vary – but was prohibited from graduating after refusing to swear the Oath of Supremacy. Tresham took after his father in this respect, as in 1581 Sir Thomas was arrested and tried – along with his equally committed Catholic in-laws Lord Vaux of Harrowden, the father of the Vaux sisters, and Sir William Catesby – for harbouring Edmund Campion. As a result of his involvement, Tresham served seven years in prison and was gaoled again in 1597 and 1599 for failing to pay his recusancy fines.[31]

It has been suggested that in the absence of parental control Francis grew up to be something of a black sheep. In 1586 he was already known to consult with other Catholics, while in 1591 he was arrested for 'the abusing of the authority of a warrant from their Lordships' after replacing the warrant issued for the arrest of a clothier with one of Tresham's tenants who was severely in his debt. It was written in one account that Tresham and some others later ransacked the house of his tenant and assaulted his pregnant daughter.[32] While Tresham was later released, his lifestyle was condemned as wild and reckless, significantly depleting his father's wealth. In 1593 he married, Anne, daughter of Sir John Tufton of Hothfield in Kent, and with her fathered three children, one of whom died in infancy. Throughout his life he remained ardently opposed to Elizabeth's Protestant government and was arrested as a precaution in the light of the Poisoned Pommel Affair. Alongside Catesby, he had been arrested for his part in the Essex Rebellion and participated actively in the Spanish Treason.

Tesimond and Gerard were heavily critical of Tresham, in contrast to their generally favourable reports of the other conspirators. Tesimond says of Tresham that he was untrustworthy and was more interested in his own well-being than in the good of the Catholic community despite always having been a Catholic.[33] Gerard painted a similar picture, stating that that Tresham 'had been wild in his youth, and even till his end was not known to be of so good example as the rest, though, towards his later years, much reclaimed and good hope conceived of him by divers of good judgement'. Gerard added weight to the belief that Catesby's principal reason for adding him to the conspiracy was financial. Tresham joined the plot on around 14 October, merely a month after the death of his father. As his father's eldest surviving son he inherited most of his father's estates, including an annuity of some £3,000 to £4,000 a year from various properties. Gerard dismissed any possibility that Tresham was truly committed to any cause, claiming, 'Tresham had not that zeal for the advancement of the Catholics' cause in respect of itself, as the others had.'[34]

In the weeks leading up to the reopening of Parliament the conspirators remained actively engaged in making their final preparations. Digby had agreed to pledge £1,500, while Thomas Percy was preparing to return to Alnwick Castle to collect tithes for the Earl of Northumberland, which he intended to use to aid the conspirators' cause, and also to provide ten horses. Meanwhile, following a brief stay with Digby at Rutland, Guy and Thomas Wintour acquired fresh gunpowder to be placed in the cellar amid the original stock that had started to separate.[35] Throughout October a series of meetings took place in various taverns to iron out the details of the plot. It was agreed that Guy would be charged with the task of lighting the powder before escaping by boat along the Thames and obtaining a safe passage, funded by Tresham, to Flanders, where he would spread news of the explosion among the exiles.[36] Meanwhile, the remaining conspirators would lead a rising in the Midlands, culminating in the abduction of the infant Princess Elizabeth, who would then be proclaimed queen under Catholic supervision and regency. Several of these meetings took place, many of them simple dinner parties attended by a number of other guests. Meetings of this kind had taken place periodically after the mine had been abandoned.

On one occasion, shortly after Guy returned to the Low Countries, Catesby dined with, among others, Sir Edmund Baynham – the man nominated to deliver news of the successful plot to the Pope on Hugh Owen's orders – and Thomas Wintour at a tavern called the Horns in Carter Lane in London.[37] Another gathering that merits attention occurred around the beginning of Michaelmas, at a tavern in the Strand called the Irish Boy, a regular haunt of Robert Catesby. Catesby enjoyed dinner with Lord Mordaunt, Sir Jocelyn Percy, Thomas Wintour, John Ashfield, the famous playwright Ben Jonson and another unnamed guest, perhaps one of the other conspirators. What was said at these meetings remains unknown – it may be that they were simply convivial gatherings, but the predominance of Catholic guests might suggest that they had a different purpose. Cecil may also have taken this view. In a letter to Sir Charles Cornwallis, the English Ambassador to Spain, shortly after the failure of the plot, Cecil wrote: 'I had sufficient advertisements that most of those that are now fled (being all notorious recusants) with many others of that kind had a practice in hand for some stir this Parliament.'[38]

Another important meeting took place on 14 October. While returning from Yorkshire, where he had been visiting his mother, Guy stopped off at the Bell Inn in Daventry where Thomas Wintour, Kit Wright and Thomas Bates joined him for dinner. There have been long-standing claims that Guy slept at the Wrights' home at Plowland Hall before making his way to Daventry, which is feasible.[39] Jack Wright was also due to attend, but he failed to arrive until the next morning. His attendance was deemed to have been of such importance that the village blacksmith was sent on horseback to collect him. Upon his arrival, he was taken by Thomas Wintour to the inn garden to discuss the contents of a letter from Catesby. The subject matter of the letter is lost from history, but it has been suggested it was little more than a note to inform them that Tresham had joined the plot.[40] Following a convivial breakfast Guy and Wintour journeyed south together towards London.

Also in October the conspirators met at White Webbs, where the possibility of giving some kind of warning to Catholic Lords due to be present at Parliament was discussed. Guy, evidently, still held Montague in high esteem from his employment at Cowdray some twelve years earlier and is recorded as having spoken up for the viscount. Catesby is reported as having crossed paths with Montague, either on 15 or 22 October, at which time he offered Montague a hint that something was being planned. On meeting Montague in the Savoy off the Strand, the pair exchanged pleasantries before Catesby asked: 'The Parliament, I think, brings your Lordship up now?' To this Montague replied that he would be visiting his aunt, Lady Southampton, but would attend Parliament in a few weeks, that is, on 5 November, unless he received permission to be absent. Catesby's reply was: 'I think your Lordship takes no pleasure to be there.' This was a statement rather than a question. Montague had recently suffered a short spell in prison for speaking out against anti-Papist legislation and expected further trouble when the subject of additional penalties was brought up at the next Parliament.[41]

On 23 October John Grant, Jack Wright and Thomas Wintour were all mentioned as being together at the same inn. Also in their company was a man in the employment of Robert Wintour. The following day Catesby was recorded as having attended dinner at the Mitre Inn in Bread Street, London, in the company of several other recusants, one of whom was an admiral. On the 26th Guy, Wintour and Catesby were reported to have lodged once again with Anne Vaux at White Webbs. A problem had arisen with news that Prince Henry Frederick, the heir to the throne, would not be present at Parliament on the 5th. To this Catesby replied that arrangements must be changed to ensure the successful capture of the prince, and that Prince Charles would instead be unharmed.[42]

In the days leading up to the reopening of Parliament many of those due to be present started to gather in London. Among them were men of title, the bishops and men who had been elected to the Commons.[43] One man who had recently returned to London was William Parker, Lord Monteagle. Monteagle was a friend of some of the conspirators and possessed family connections to most through his wife, Elizabeth, who was Francis Tresham's sister. Furthermore, Thomas Wintour had spent several years in his employment. Monteagle's adherence to the Catholic cause was by no means clear cut. While he was one of many men of Catholic sympathy who offered his services in the Essex Rebellion, in addition to some degree of cooperation alongside Catesby in the Spanish Treason, a letter to the king in 1604 implied that he had converted to Protestantism. At the very least, Monteagle had taken the Oath of Supremacy.[44]

On the very day that Monteagle returned to London a strange thing happened. At around seven in the evening on 26 October, ten days before the reopening of Parliament, he received a visit from a man whose identity remains a mystery. According to the account given in the *King's Book*, Monteagle was staying at his house at Hoxton, just north of the City of London, which he had acquired as part of his wife's dowry. While Monteagle sat quietly eating his dinner the visitor remained outside, communicating with a page in Monteagle's employment. On approaching the page, the unknown man asked whether Monteagle was at home and if he could speak to him. The page replied that the baron had recently arrived home and was presently having supper. On hearing this, the stranger asked the page to deliver a letter on his behalf with the strict instruction it be given directly to Monteagle. After entrusting the letter to the page, the stranger departed while the page informed his master of what had happened and delivered the letter. Monteagle first attempted to read it for himself but found it difficult to decipher. He then called on one of his servants to read it. It read:

> My Lord, out of love I bear to some of your friends, I
> have a care of your preservation. Therefore, I would
> advise you as you tender your life to devise some excuse
> to shift off your attendance at this parliament. For
> God and man have concurred to punish the wickedness
> of this time. And think not slightly of this advertise-
> ment, but retire yourself into your country where you
> may expect the event in safety. For though there be no
> appearance of any stir, yet I say they shall receive a
> terrible blow this parliament. And yet they shall not
> see who hurts them. This counsel is not to be con-
> temned because it may do you good, and can do you
> no harm: for the danger is past as soon as you have
> burnt the letter. And I hope God will give you the grace
> to make good use of it: to whose Holy protection I
> commend you.[45]

On hearing it read to him by the servant he struggled at first to decide whether to take it seriously or not. The letter was not signed nor was there any clue of where it had come from. Following some deliberation, Monteagle decided to take no chances. Despite the late hour, he saddled his horse and rode for Sir Robert Cecil's house at Whitehall.

Cecil was having his supper in the company of several other key figures, including the Earl of Suffolk (the Lord Chamberlain), the Earl of Nottingham (the Lord High Admiral), the Earl of Northampton and the Earl of Worcester. Once inside, Cecil took Monteagle to an anteroom where he examined the letter. Tesimond's account suggests that the means by which Monteagle had come by the letter did not interest him, and instead he was more concerned with acknowledging Monteagle's trustworthiness. Cecil did take the matter seriously, however, and decided that the threat might be genuine. After discussing it with Monteagle, Cecil entrusted news of the letter to the others present. The Earl of Suffolk suggested to Cecil that the letter might convey proof of recent intelligence that certain recusants were planning some sort of rebellion – probably that given by Captain Turner to Sir Thomas Edmondes. The Earls of Nottingham, Worcester and Northampton, on the other hand, were less convinced by the letter's authenticity. Even so, it was agreed that the king should be informed once he returned to London from Royston, Hertfordshire, where he was on a hunting trip. Incredibly, it has been suggested that Catesby actually spoke to Anne Vaux at White Webbs about joining James on this same hunt. Rather than bother the king, Cecil saw it fit to investigate further and so began his attempts to uncover the hidden meaning behind the obscure threats in the letter.[46]

Within a day of the delivery of the letter the conspirators became aware of the leak. There are two accounts of how they came to learn of the deceit. Tesimond stated that the very man who had read the letter to Monteagle, Thomas Ward, relayed the information to Thomas Wintour the following day.[47] Some have suggested that Ward was a Catholic spy, yet there is no proof of this. Wintour and Ward were well known to each other, both being servants of Monteagle. An alternative account suggested that while Monteagle was visiting Cecil, Ward delivered a message to Catesby at White Webbs through his family connections to the Wright brothers – Kit Wright's wife Margaret, it has been asserted, was Thomas Ward's sister.[48] It is unclear whether Ward was ever aware of the plot. If he did send a message to Catesby it seems unbelievable that he had no knowledge of it. More likely Wintour heard the news from Ward in general conversation. Going by the traditional account, Wintour took the information directly to Catesby, while the remainder of the plotters had gone their separate ways into the countryside. Catesby, understandably, was distressed by the news. After a hurried conversation with Wintour it was agreed that news of the letter be kept secret. Instead it was decided that they would use their best devices to discover who wrote it, for if they could do so they could identify whether the plot was beyond all hope. Realistically, Catesby probably had no plans to abandon the action anyway. For him the situation was simple: succeed or die trying.[49]

WITH A DARK LANTERN AND A BURNING MATCH

Suspicion as to the authorship of the letter fell primarily on Tresham. Following Catesby's desperate conversation with Thomas Wintour at White Webbs, Tresham was summoned to join them at a hunt at Enfield Chase where they planned to interrogate him. Should Tresham have offered any hint of guilt then they would have hanged him without delay. Tresham and Monteagle were brothers-in-law, and the fact that Tresham had only recently been initiated into the group of conspirators also added to any doubts that Catesby and Wintour might already have had about his loyalty.

When questioned on the matter Tresham pleaded his innocence convincingly. Still no closer to knowing for sure whether the game was up, Catesby and Wintour reasoned that if the Privy Council had become aware of the conspiracy, a thorough search of the cellars would have been ordered. Careful not to draw attention to the situation, and without giving any explanation, Catesby summoned Guy Fawkes to White Webbs, following which he gave instructions that Guy should investigate the cellar. Four days after Monteagle had received the letter, Wednesday 30 October, Guy returned to the cellar where the gunpowder was hidden. After checking carefully he concluded that the marks that they had made on the door and entrance of the cellar confirmed that no one had entered the vaults since the latest stock of powder had been added. When Guy reported back to Catesby confirming that everything was as it should be, Catesby and Wintour, perhaps somewhat apologetically, explained to him the true reason for the further inspection. Although Guy had been put into a position of grave personal danger he responded constructively, stating that he would have investigated the vault even if he had known that the plot had been discovered, and over the next few days he continued to keep watch over the cellar for any sign of interest.[1]

The king returned from his hunting trip on 31 October 1605, still unaware of what had transpired in recent days. Some time in the afternoon of the following day, Cecil visited James at his palace at Whitehall at which time he revealed the letter to the king. After reading it the king paused to take in the information before reading it through once more. Strangely, Cecil dismissed the letter's importance, claiming it must have been written by a 'fool', yet the official account given in the *King's Book* states that this was a deliberate move by Cecil to see the king's true reaction. Cecil also described the circumstances in which the letter was received and the reactions of his fellow lords when Monteagle revealed it to them. On reading the words 'a terrible blow this Parliament' coupled with 'the danger is past as soon as you have burnt the letter', James expressed the view that this implied that there would be an explosion using gunpowder.[2]

The fact that James reacted in this way is perhaps unsurprising. In addition to having witnessed several plots against Elizabeth before the execution of his mother, James had lost his father following an attempt on his life by setting off some gunpowder. On 10 February 1567 Henry Stuart was found murdered, alongside his servant, in the grounds of Kirk O' Field, Edinburgh, a victim of what was believed to be a coup by James Hepburn, the Earl of Bothwell. While Henry had survived the attempted gunpowder assassination he was murdered while attempting to escape the scene.

During the short time he had spent on the English throne thus far James had already been the target of conspiracy. The foiled Bye and Main Plots of 1603 highlighted discontent in certain quarters, and these were warnings that James was unwilling to ignore. Throughout his life he was known to have had a dislike of conflict, which undoubtedly heightened his desire to ensure that the possibility of any action against him was thoroughly investigated. Immediately after seeing the Monteagle letter he ordered a thorough search of the cellars beneath Parliament.[3] At the time, neither the king nor the Privy Council were aware of the intelligence Cecil had concerning a possible Catholic uprising. Based on the account in the *King's Book* Cecil did not inform the king at this stage. Cecil approved of the king's request, however, and preparations were made for the cellars to be searched.[4]

The decision to investigate was taken on Saturday 2 November. Throughout the day discussions had taken place among members of the Privy Council, many of whom appeared before the king. There was concern about the manner in which the search should be carried out, since it was agreed that it was important not to do anything that would arouse public suspicion or reveal their awareness of the plot. It was decided that the Earl of Suffolk would visit the cellar. By the Sunday evening, the 3rd, Percy had returned to London – there is some suggestion that Guy had been sent from London to collect him – where he had a meeting with Catesby and Wintour, and he was informed about the letter. Over the past few days Tresham had attempted to convince Catesby to flee, yet to Catesby this was not an option. Like Catesby, Percy was steadfastly unwilling to abandon the project, even if it were to lead to the 'uttermost trial'.[5] Meanwhile, at Coughton Court Sir Everard Digby made preparations for the hunt that was due to take place following the explosion. The following day, Monday 4th, Digby departed for Dunchurch, taking up residence at the Red Lion Inn, the designated meeting point for the hunt. Over the course of the day several others joined him, including his uncle Sir Robert, the Littleton brothers, John Wintour (half-brother of Robert and Thomas), John Grant and his friend Henry Morgan, who had also been sworn to secrecy.[6]

Back in London, Percy visited his patron, the Earl of Northumberland, at Sion House in an attempt to discover if any news of the Monteagle letter had reached him. To his relief Percy discovered nothing was known. His next stop was Northumberland's London home, Essex House, where he visited the Earl's nephew, Sir Jocelyn Percy. Later that evening he met Thomas Wintour, Jack Wright and Robert Keyes, whom he assured with confidence that all was well. While Percy returned to his lodgings at Gray's Inn Road, Catesby set off for the Midlands in the company of Jack Wright and Thomas Bates.[7]

Guy continued to watch the cellar. On Monday 4 November the Earl of Suffolk in the company of others, including Monteagle, searched the vault. Although meaningful in purpose, Suffolk attempted to remain casual in manner in order not to arouse suspicion. While investigating the cellar, Suffolk and Monteagle came across a tall man of rough features and unsavoury in nature in one of the vaults. After ordering a thorough search they discovered, by the dim light of a solitary lantern, that the vault contained a large quantity of firewood. When asked his identity, Guy replied that he was Johnson, servant to one Thomas Percy esquire who had lease of the cellar for some eighteen months to store firewood for his house next door.

It is recorded in the *King's Book* that Suffolk, on entering the vault, 'perceived a fellow standing in the corner'. Despite Guy being described as 'a very tall and desperate fellow', for Suffolk and Monteagle his explanation was good enough. For Guy the encounter seemed to pass safely, but soon after leaving the vault Monteagle, who knew Thomas Percy well and was aware that he rarely stayed in London, expressed surprise that he would require so much firewood. On returning to the king, Suffolk and Monteagle announced their findings and speculated that Percy may have been the author of the letter. For Monteagle and Suffolk there was at least something to report, yet for the Privy Council, the possible involvement of Percy, the cousin of the Earl of Northumberland, commander of the Gentlemen Pensioners and fellow member of the Privy Council, did not bode well. Left with little alternative, James commanded a second search of the cellar on the night of 4 November under the leadership of Sir Thomas Knyvett, a member of the King's Privy Chamber and a Justice of the Peace for Westminster.[8]

Unaware of what was transpiring above him, Guy was visited by Robert Keyes at approximately ten in the evening when final preparations were made for the lighting of the fuse. During their meeting Keyes handed Guy a pocket-watch which had been given to him by Percy to pass on to Guy so that he could time the charging of the fuse exactly and give himself an opportunity to escape. Guy returned to his post, there to pass the remaining hours of nightfall before lighting the train at the reopening of Parliament the following morning. While he waited, so did the remaining conspirators. At that same time Ambrose Rookwood was preparing for his role in the proceedings. At approximately an hour before midnight he received a fine sword from a cutler in the Strand named John Craddock, engraved with a depiction of the passion of Christ.[9]

As midnight approached, Knyvett and his posse advanced on

the cellar. As they did so, Guy Fawkes waited in silence, whiling away the time in the poor light of his now famous lantern. Once inside the vault, Knyvett's search party came across a tall man, the same man seen by Monteagle and Suffolk in their earlier inspection, wearing a dark hat and cloak. Equipped with boots and spurs, it was clear that the man was ready to depart at a moment's notice. Without further ado Guy Fawkes was arrested.

There are conflicting reports on where Guy was arrested. Three possibilities exist: the cellar, outside it or in the Whynniard house. Judging by the account in both the *King's Book* and that given by Tesimond he was outside the cellar in the street.[10] Samuel Gardiner suggested there was probably a door to the passage outside the cellar and one to the Whynniard house, while Spink also referred to the cellar having at least two doors.[11] Tesimond states that Guy was outside to complete preparations for the explosion. With no signs of trouble, Guy might have used the opportunity to take a breath of fresh air after enduring the musty atmosphere of the vault. In the *King's Book* it says that Edmund Doubleday, one of Knyvett's men, apprehended him while in the passage. The account in the *King's Book* reads as follows:

> And upon the hearing of some noise Sir T. Knyvet [*sic*] required Master Edmond [*sic*] Doubleday, Esq. to go up into the chamber to understand the cause thereof, the which he did, and had there some speech of Fawkes, being therewithal very desirous to search and see what books or instruments Fawkes had about him; but Fawkes being wondrous unwilling to be searched, very violently griped Master Doubleday by his fingers of the left hand, through pain thereof Master Doubleday offered to draw his dagger to have stabbed Fawkes, but suddenly better bethought himself and did not; yet in

that heat he struck up the traitor's heels and therewithal
fell upon him and searched him, and in his pocket found
his garters, wherewith Master Doubleday and others
that assisted they bound him. There was also found in
his pocket a piece of touchwood, and a tinder box to
light the touchwood and a watch which Percy and
Fawkes had bought the day before, to try conclusions
for the long or short burning of the touchwood, which
he had prepared to give fire to the train of powder.[12]

Following the arrest, Knyvett led an investigation of the
vault. Seizing Guy's keys he carried out a thorough search,
during which he removed the firewood that covered the barrels
of gunpowder, some of which were larger than others, and discovered that some had been pierced open with a broaching tool,
and gunpowder spread in a train and ready to be lit. Guy's immediate reaction to his arrest suggests that its timing was fortuitous
for the search party. If he had become aware a little earlier of
their presence, and the certainty of his being taken, he may well
have lit the fuse, killing himself and perhaps the members of the
search party in the explosion.[13]

News of Guy's arrest reached the members of the Court
quickly. Even before dawn, certain members of Parliament were
making their way to the House of Lords, unaware how close they
had been to being killed that morning. Some members of the
council living in the palace and nearby were roused, despite the
early hour, while the king was also made aware that a prisoner
had been apprehended. Shortly after this, Guy was moved from
the cellar to the king's bedchamber and interrogated. By now the
time was little later than four in the morning. With the council
assembled, an order was put out that the gates of the palace
should be closed until the prisoner had been questioned.

On coming face to face with the king, Guy's demeanour was calm. When faced with the early questions he withstood with iron resolve. When asked his name, he replied, as he had previously done to the Earl of Suffolk, that he was Johnson, servant of Thomas Percy. When questioned about his intentions, he answered without hesitation that his plan was to destroy the Houses of Parliament and all within when Parliament reopened later that morning. When asked of his accomplices, he at first claimed that 'he could not resolve to accuse any'. He admitted to being a Catholic and highlighted James's treatment of his Catholic subjects as the catalyst behind his intention. Furthermore, Guy highlighted that the Pope had excommunicated James. When asked to elaborate, Guy responded that every Maundy Thursday the Pope sends out a Papal Bull that all who are not of the Catholic faith be excommunicated, making James a heretic.[14] James's response is, sadly, unrecorded. When Guy was asked how he could carry out such a heinous crime against the royal family, he replied that it was a desperate disease which required a desperate remedy. Throughout the interrogation he remained calm and collected. At one stage he even relayed to the Scottish members of the council how it was his intention to blow them back to the Scottish mountains.[15] From time to time he also smiled sombrely at the lords and claimed they had no authority to question him.[16]

Guy's demeanour was so unwavering that it was remarked on by those in attendance. Of his unshakeable bravery, it was commented that the councillors held before them 'some new Mucius Scaevola born in England'. Gaius Mucius Scaevola was a – probably mythological – Roman spy who entered the camp of the Etruscan Lars Porsenna, an enemy of Rome. Despite slaying the wrong man, resulting in threats of torture, his heroism was celebrated for his holding his hand over a fire in front of the king to demonstrate that he did not fear torture. For Scaevola, the gesture worked so well that the King of the Etruscans set him free. For Guy, there was no such good fortune. Instead he was taken to the Tower of London where he would await further examination.

An arrest warrant was quickly issued for Thomas Percy. At the time, he was the only other member of the plot known to the king's authorities, although there was no clear understanding of his part in it, only that he was 'privy to one of the most horrible treasons that ever was contrived'. For this reason the government decreed that Percy should be kept alive in order to obtain more information.[17] He was sought at Essex House, although he was at his lodgings at Gray's Inn Road. Meanwhile, Kit Wright learned first hand that the conspiracy had failed after overhearing the Earl of Worcester summoning Monteagle. When he heard the news Wright's immediate response was to seek out Thomas Wintour, who was lodging at the Duck and Drake Inn. On rousing Wintour, Wright stated that the matter was discovered. Wintour, meanwhile, remained calm. He told Kit Wright to investigate further to make sure all really was lost. When news was gathered that Percy was being sought at Essex House, Wright's suspicions were confirmed. He returned to the Duck and Drake to be instructed by Wintour to find Percy at his lodgings, while he would 'stay and see the uttermost'.[18]

Wright located Percy soon after, by which time haste had given way to panic. Both conspirators took flight immediately, with Percy declaring to a passing servant, 'I am undone.' Keyes also departed at sunrise, followed shortly after by Ambrose Rookwood. Rookwood's horsemanship was legendary, and he took to his journey with rapid flight. On reaching Highgate he had already caught up with Keyes, while at Little Brickhill in Bedfordshire he also caught up with Percy and Kit Wright. After passing them, he eventually caught up with Catesby, Jack Wright and Bates, who were still to be told of the recent events. On reaching them, Rookwood informed them of Guy's capture, but how Catesby reacted to this is unrecorded. What is clear is that all but Keyes continued to Dunchurch, using horses that had been sent out by Digby as part of the planned uprising.[19] Only Thomas Wintour was still in London. So calm was he under pressure that he wandered down to Westminster to investigate thoroughly. On reaching King Street he was checked by a guard and prohibited from venturing any further. While there he overheard someone say: 'There is a treason discovered in which the king and the lords shall have been blown up.' To this Wintour describes in his declaration: 'I was fully satisfied that all was known, and went to the stable where my gelding stood, and rode into the country.'[20] Following this, he left London and headed north. Given the lateness of his departure, Wintour dismissed the possibility of meeting up with Catesby and company at Dunchurch. Instead, he headed straight to the home of his brother Robert at Huddington Court, taking a brief detour by Norbrook, the home of his sister and her husband John Grant.

Robert Wintour had already departed Huddington by the time his brother arrived, as by the evening of 5 November Robert is recorded as being present at Ashby St Ledgers, the home of Catesby's mother. By around six o'clock that evening Catesby, the Wrights, Bates, Rookwood and Percy reached Ashby on their way to Dunchurch. On arriving there Catesby sent a message to Robert Wintour, instructing him to meet them in the fields outside of town and not to reveal his whereabouts to Catesby's mother. They met and Wintour was told: 'Mr Fawkes was taken and the whole plot discovered.'[21]

Catesby and company continued to Dunchurch where they met Everard Digby, and Catesby apprised Digby of what had happened. It has been suggested by some that this may have been the first time Digby learned the true nature of the plot, but this seems unlikely. Digby did not despair on hearing the news. Instead, he rallied around Catesby, who continued to talk of success. His plan of action was to travel to Warwick and break into the castle stables to steal horses for their cause. By nightfall, the total number involved, including those who had turned up for the hunt, was, according to Gerard, no more than eighty.[22] On hearing that Catesby had proclaimed, falsely, that the king and Cecil were dead and 'if true Catholics would now stir, he doubted not that they might procure to themselves good conditions', many of the party fled immediately, unwilling to taint themselves with such a dubious endeavour. For those who remained, they thundered through the cold night air to Warwick.[23]

Despite the scare, Parliament met briefly on the afternoon of the 5th, and the Commons journal includes this reference in the margin:

> This last Night the Upper House of Parliament was searched by Sir Thomas Knevett [sic]; and one Johnson, Servant to Mr Thomas Percy was there apprehended; who had placed 36 barrels of Gunpowder in the Vault under the House with a purpose to blow the King, and the whole company, when they should there assemble.
>
> Afterwards divers other gentlemen were discovered to be of the Plot.

Unsurprisingly, Parliament was prorogued again as a result of the scare – although arguably this was an excuse rather than a genuine scare.

Outside Parliament, London was alive with activity. It was stated by one contemporary observer 'the common people muttered and imagined many things', most of which were inaccurate. In keeping with tradition, the population celebrated the deliverance of their monarch from death with the lighting of bonfires, thus marking the first recorded 'Bonfire Night' on 5 November, despite not knowing the facts behind the conspiracy.[24] Within the walls of Westminster Palace the Privy Council met to discuss the situation on the morning of the 5th, with Northumberland present among their number. While Northumberland was not implicated in the plot at this time, his position had certainly been compromised through the activities of his kinsmen.

Back in the Tower, Guy was held in solitary confinement. Sir John Popham, the Lord Chief Justice to the king, led the early investigations, yet he failed to discover anything concrete. Writing to Cecil, Popham had 'pregnant suspicion' of Catesby, Rookwood, Keyes, Thomas Wintour, both Wrights and Grant, but Digby, Tresham, Bates and Robert Wintour were all absent from his list at this stage.[25] Exactly how this 'pregnant suspicion' came about is a matter of conjecture. Lady Antonia Fraser considers the possibility that Tresham had given the game away.[26] Popham was either receiving information from some unidentified source or, as a committed anti-Catholic, was merely reviewing a list of influential supporters of the Catholic cause one by one. If the words of Sir William Waad, the Lieutenant of the Tower, are anything to go by, the conspirators' guilt was perhaps given away by their decision to leave London following Guy's arrest.[27]

The king drew up a list of questions in a bid to discover Guy's true identity, and these were subsequently used during an investigation on the 6th:

1   As what he is, for I can never yet hear of any man that

knows him.

2 Where was he born?

3 What were his Parents' Names?

4 What Age he is of?

5 Where he hath lived?

6 How he hath lived, and by what trade of life?

7 How he received those wounds in his breast?

8 If he was ever in service with any other before Percy; and what they were; and how long?

9 How came he in Percy's service; by what means and at what time?

10 What time was this House hired by his Master?

11 And how soon after the possessing of it, did he begin to his devilish preparations?

12 When and where learned he to speak French?

13 What Gentlewoman's Letter it was, that was found upon him?

14 And wherefore doth she give him another name in it, than he gives to himself?

15 If he was ever a Papist; and, if so, who brought him up in it?

16 If otherwise, how was he converted, where, when, and by whom?[28]

When asked about his identity, Guy continued to answer that he was John Johnson from Netherdale in Yorkshire. His father was Thomas Johnson, and his mother Edith Jackson – which may actually have been his mother's real name. When asked his age he replied that he was thirty-six (baptismal records suggest he was thirty-five), and when asked the nature of various scars on his body, presumably from injuries suffered in the Low Countries, he replied that they were caused by inflammation of the pleura.

While none of the other answers Guy gave to the interrogators offered any real insight into his true identity, further clues were found in a letter among his possessions, addressed to Guido Fawkes from a woman named Bostock, presumably the wife or another relation of Colonel Bostock under whom he had fought at the Battle of Nieuwpoort. The contents have never been revealed, and certainly no suggestion exists that it was amorous in nature; most likely it confirmed his identity as a soldier in the army of the archduke.

At some time on 6 November the decision was taken that Guy should be tortured. In 1605 the use of torture was fairly routine, yet it was not strictly allowed – in fact, the *Magna Carta* expressly forbade it. For torture to be implemented, the authority of either the king or the Privy Council had to be sought, and it was James himself who made the decision. Since the reign of Henry VII torture in matters of treason had been reasonably common, and throughout the 1580s and 1590s many Catholics, too, had suffered in the Tower, including Sir Francis Throckmorton in 1583. Father John Gerard and Father Nicholas Owen, the Jesuit priest who had constructed so many priest-holes, had suffered torture during the 1590s.[29]

In the case of Guy Fawkes the instruction was quite specific. A letter, signed by the king, decreed that 'if he will not otherwise confess, the gentler Tortures are to be first used unto him and so by degrees proceeding to the worst'.[30] The 'gentler Tortures' referred to being shackled to the wall using iron gauntlets, while 'the worst' meant the rack. Guy would have been secured to the wall with manacles, which were gradually tightened as time passed, while wooden supports that kept the feet in place were removed, leaving the prisoner dangling in mid air. In the 1590s this type of torture was the most common of its type in England, largely because it was effective, the tools were inexpensive and it was easy to do. There was no time limit on its use, which often resulted in prisoners being forced to endure hours of pain in one session. This frequently had damaging effects on the victim, many of whom were permanently mutilated by the stress of their body-weight pulling against the iron. Records at the time confirm that Guy was tortured all day using the manacles yet, incredibly, disclosed nothing to the inquisitors.

William Waad was a renowned anti-Catholic with a cruel streak. In his official capacity he was always present when torture was being implemented. It is stated in his own account, given to Cecil on the 6th, that Guy remained in good spirits despite the pain. During the course of that evening Waad questioned Guy at length. He told Waad that 'since he undertook that action he did every day pray to God he might perform that which might be for the advancement of the Catholic faith and the saving of his own soul'. He also admitted to taking an oath of secrecy to his cause, although the unnamed priest who performed the mass that day was unaware of any deeper significance.[31] When Waad attempted to entice Guy to name his comrades by claiming their flight from London made them known anyway, Guy responded 'if that be so it would be superfluous for me to declare them'. According to Waad, Guy slept peacefully on the night of the 6th as though 'void of all trouble of mind'. After a frustrating day in which nothing new was learned, Waad informed Guy that if 'his resolution of mind to be so silent' remained unflinching, he must 'prepare himself' for what was to come, a firm indication that the rack was to be used.[32]

As long as Guy remained uncommunicative, his inquisitors continued to have no information regarding the identities of his accomplices. Whatever 'pregnant suspicion' Popham might have harboured for Catesby and the others at this stage was still a long way from proof of their guilt. No warrants had been issued for any other person in connection with the conspiracy except Thomas Percy. Back in Warwickshire, Catesby and his party successfully mounted a raid on Warwick Castle, stealing several warhorses. The theft, recorded as having occurred at around three o'clock on the morning of Wednesday 6 November, was successful at least in furthering the cause of their rebellion, but the event did not go unnoticed. The following day a proclamation was issued for the arrests of Catesby, Rookwood, both Wrights, an Edward Grant, a Robert Ashfield and Thomas Wintour. Whether the government were acting on new information, possibly from the recent theft at Warwick, or a combination of evidence from both that and Popham's 'pregnant suspicion' is difficult to clarify. Robert Wintour refused to take any part in stealing horses, probably recognizing the unnecessary risks involved. Evidently, he still did not appear on the government's list of suspects at that time. Rookwood, having plenty of horses of his own, was also not involved, yet he was now a wanted man. Thomas Wintour was named despite the fact that he was still to join the party, while Edward Grant and Robert Ashfield were probably John Grant and Thomas Bates under incorrect names.[33] There was no mention of Keyes, Digby or Tresham in the proclamation.

After the raid on Warwick Castle Catesby led the party to John Grant's house at Norbrook, which had been used to store munitions. After collecting their prepared arms the conspirators continued to the home of Robert Wintour at Huddington Court. Bates was assigned a new mission at this stage. At some point during the course of the previous day Catesby and Digby had hastily written to Father Garnet, who was at Coughton Court, explaining the failure of the plot while attempting to rouse the Jesuit's support for rallying Catholic resistance from Wales. Bates was assigned the task of delivering the letter and thereafter separated from the conspirators. On his arrival, Bates found Garnet with Father Tesimond. On reading the letter Garnet is recorded as having said to Tesimond: 'We are all utterly undone.'[34]

Catesby and company arrived at Huddington at around two in the afternoon of the 6th where they were greeted by Gertrude Wintour. By dinner time Thomas Wintour had also joined up with the party after learning of their whereabouts from his sister at Norbrook. In the early hours of the following morning the conspirators went to confession before attending mass. Soon after, those who had remained with the conspirators following their meeting at Dunchurch – about thirty-six – departed the house on a damp, grey day in the Midlands. After travelling through the rainy countryside they reached the home of Lord Windsor, the ward of the Earl of Northampton, at Hewell Grange in Worcestershire. In the lord's absence the conspirators helped themselves to his gunpowder before continuing further north. Evidently the locals showed no sympathy towards their cause. When told that the conspirators stood for 'God and Country' some locals replied that they, in turn, stood for 'King James as well as God and Country'.[35]

By ten that evening the conspirators arrived at Holbeche House, near Kingswinford in Staffordshire, property of one Stephen Littleton, possibly a cousin of the Wintour brothers, who had turned up for the hunt at Dunchurch and stayed in their company for the subsequent attempted rising. There is some indication that Littleton was largely unaware of the plot and that Catesby had instead acquainted him with his proposed expedition to join up with the archduke in Flanders and had promised him control of a company among the three hundred troops stationed there.[36] Holbeche was an imposing mansion abundant in priest-holes constructed during the tenure of its recusant owners. It is likely that Catesby had chosen it because of its fine defensive qualities at a time when he believed the conspirators were being followed. Undoubtedly he was already aware that a posse comitatus led by the Sheriff of Worcestershire, Sir Richard Walsh, was in close pursuit.[37]

Thomas Wintour departed from the rest to seek to revive their fortunes by acquiring the aid of his brother's father-in-law, Sir John Talbot of Grafton in Shropshire. Stephen Littleton accompanied Wintour on his 10-mile (16-kilometre) journey and they found Sir John at home. Unfortunately for Wintour, Talbot was not pleased to see him, and rather than offering his backing he bitterly criticized them for their treachery and ordered them to 'get hence'.

Meanwhile, in Wintour's absence the conspirators met with misfortune. The new supplies of gunpowder acquired from the home of Lord Windsor earlier that day had been soaked by the downpour they had endured during their journey to Holbeche, rendering it completely ineffective. Attempting to recover the situation, the desperate men placed the powder in front of the fire to dry it out. Tesimond stresses that this was carried out with considerable care.[38] As one of the men was taking a hot coal from the fire to be placed on the brazier to help warm the pans containing gunpowder, which had been placed on top of the coals in the brazier, he caught his foot against one of his colleagues, causing him to drop the coal into the pans containing the powder.[39] The resulting explosion severely damaged not only the room but resulted in permanent injuries to Catesby, Rookwood, Grant and Henry Morgan. In his translation of Tesimond's work, Father Edwards questions the exact circumstances, pointing out that gunpowder spread out in a pan will flash but not explode, which might suggest that the pan was standing on another bag of powder placed in front of the fire.[40] Equally possible is that it caused the floor to catch fire, resulting in an explosion. However it occurred, those who condemned the activities of these men would undoubtedly have found some ironic satisfaction in the knowledge that those who endeavoured to rid England of its government through the use of such a 'desperate remedy' should themselves become the biggest casualties of the Gunpowder Plot.

12

GUY FAWKES, GUY FAWKES, T'WAS HIS INTENT

Unaware of the events in Staffordshire, Guy Fawkes continued to withstand unbearable pain within the walls of the White Tower. By Thursday 7 November the Privy Council had established that his real name was Guy Fawkes, not Johnson, and that he was the same Guido Fawkes who had served in the army of the archduke in the Spanish Netherlands.[1] On 8 November Guy's resolve to withstand the torture was at last starting to weaken. Under examination he confessed that he had been made aware of at least some aspects of the plot at Easter 1604 after having discussions with a 'lay-man', who was also an Englishman, in the Low Countries. This was clearly a reference to Thomas Wintour, although he did not name him at that stage. Guy then admitted that he returned to England in the company of the same man, where he met three others resolved to take drastic action to aid the Catholic cause. He also confirmed that one of the three – he did not specifically name Catesby – proposed the deed should be performed using gunpowder either 'in or near the place of the sitting of the Parliament, wherein religion had been unjustly suppressed'.

By 8 November Guy had provided some detail of the events that preceded the hiring of the house from Ferris. He also went into some detail of the mine itself, describing the wall to the

Parliament building as some 3 yards (2.75 metres) thick and being difficult to dig. As a result of their slow progress, Guy revealed that the plotters increased their number to seven, yet he still refused to mention any names. He confirmed that dirt was deposited in the garden of the house and that work continued on the mine until Candlemas. Shortly after that time the conspirators by chance found that the nearby cellar had become available and Percy subsequently leased it. After the cellar had been secured they moved into it twenty barrels of gunpowder, which were then covered with firewood. Guy told them that he then travelled to the Low Countries and stayed there between Easter and September 1605 but did not elaborate on his purpose. He also revealed that he left the key to the cellar with Percy and that another five or six barrels of gunpowder were moved in at the end of September.

Guy confirmed that after the explosion the conspirators had planned to abduct Lady Elizabeth and proclaim her as queen but that the fate of Prince Charles had not been decided. When asked why 'they did not surprise the King's person and draw him to the effecting of their purpose' – that is, threaten him – Guy replied that such a task would have required the cooperation of too many people to keep the matter secret. He also confessed that they had discussed the idea of kidnapping the Princess Mary, the youngest daughter of King James and Anne and the first of their offspring born in England, but they were unsure how they could gain access to her. Finally, he said that the gunpowder had been bought out of a common purse.[2]

The strength of Guy's resistance during the questioning under torture was remarkable. In a letter to the Ambassador to Spain, Sir Charles Cornwallis, Cecil remarked of him:

> He carrieth himself without any feare or pertur-

bation . . . in all this action he is noe more dis-
mayed, nay scarce any more troubled, than if he
were taken for a poor robbery upon the highway .
. . he is ready to die, and rather wisheth 10,000
deaths, than willingly to accuse his master or any
other.[3]

It was almost certainly because Guy was so resolute that
the decision was made to resort to more drastic measures.
Accounts of Guy's torture are limited. If the report of Sir Edward
Hoby, writing to Sir Thomas Edmondes, the Ambassador to
Brussels, is correct Fawkes was never tortured by the rack but
'only by his arms upright'.[4] An account preserved in the
Libraria Magliabechiana, a library in Florence, however, paints
a different picture, stating that 'he was first suspended in the
air by his thumbs . . . and then placed on the rack, and as he
still refused to name his accomplices, he was stretched naked
on a heated stone'.[5]

Although the authenticity of the document in Florence cannot be assumed, it is a generally accepted view that the rack was
used in Guy's interrogation. Father Gerard's account is perhaps
the most interesting:

All that day the Council could get nothing out of him
concerning his complices, refusing to answer to any
such questions which he thought might discover the
plot and laying all the blame upon himself . . . and
would acknowledge no other name to himself but John
Johnson, servant to Thomas Percy. But after he had
been three or four days in the Tower and was threatened the rack only, as the printed book saith (though
the common voice was, that he was extremely racked

the first days), then, whether to avoid torments, or for
that he might understand that the gentlemen had discovered themselves by rising up in arms in the country,
he then named some of his complices, with his own
name also, and how the matter was broken unto him.[6]

The printed book Gerard referred to was presumably the
King's Book. Taking into account the seriousness of the charges
that Guy faced and his continued resolution not to implicate his
fellow conspirators nor dishonour his oath of secrecy, it seems
likely that he was tortured to the fullest extent. Coincidentally,
the only rack in existence in England at the time was located in the
White Tower. Raised several inches from the ground and at an
angle, this device was of rectangular assembly and constructed
from oak. It had rollers at both ends with a fixed bar at the
bottom where the feet were attached and a moving bar at the top
which would be fastened to the victim's hands. A handle and
ratchet were used to tighten the ropes as the interrogation proceeded, eventually resulting in excruciating pain and the tortured
man's bones separating from one another. One of the more gruesome effects was that continued pressure on the ropes often
produced vile popping sounds caused by the snapping of a
victim's cartilage, muscle or bones. Once the body was stretched
beyond a certain point the joints would be damaged permanently.[7]

For Robert Cecil and William Waad use of the rack might
have been the only means of extracting from Guy Fawkes the
information they were seeking. It is clear that in using the words
'and so by degrees proceeding to the worst' in the letter granting
permission to torture Guy that the king had authorized the use
of the rack should all else fail. Further evidence of Guy's lack of
cooperation can be found in a letter from Waad to Cecil dated
8 November:

My Lord,

I do think it my duty to give your Lordship daily account of what temper I find this fellow, who this day is in a most stubborn and perverse humour, as dogged as if he were possessed. Yesternight I had persuaded him to set down a clear narration of all his wicked plots, from the first entering on the same to the end they pretended, with the discourses and projects that were thought upon amongst them, which he undertook to do, and craved time this night to bethink him the better. But this morning he hath changed his mind, and is so sullen and obstinate as there is no dealing with him.[8]

The date of the letter coincides with Guy's deposition on 8 November in which he finally revealed several details of the plot. While still mentioning no names, within a day of the letter being written Waad had, at least, extracted some information from him.[9] Curiously, his deposition was not signed by him at that stage; only the signatures of his examiners are present. Within a day of that deposition Waad, in better spirits than the previous day, wrote again to Cecil:

My honourable good Lord,

I have prevailed so much at the length with my prisoner, by plying him with the best persuasions I could use, as he hath faithfully promised me by narration to discover to your Lordship only all the secrets of his heart, but not to be set down in writing. Your Lordship will not mislike the exception; for when he hath confessed himself to your lordship I will undertake he shall acknowledge it before such as you shall

call, and then he will not make dainty to set his hand
to it. Therefore it may please your good lordship, if
any of the Lords do come with you, that at first your
lordship will deal with him alone. He will conceal no
name nor matter from your lordship, to whose ears he
will unfold his bosom. And I know your lordship will
think it the best journey you ever made upon so evil
occasion. Thus in haste, I thank God my poor labour
hath advanced a service of this importance. From the
Tower of London, the 9th of November, 1605

    At the commandment of your Lordship,

    W.G. Waad.[10]

The wording is intriguing. The implication is that Guy was
prepared to make a verbal deposition but not a written one. This
may also explain the absence of his signature. On the other
hand, when comparing Guy's signature before he was tortured
to one given afterwards, the latter is noticeably shaky. Gerard
states that Guy 'is supposed to have fainted before completing'
it.[11] It must be concluded that Waad used the most severe torture
available. His use of the words 'by plying him with the best persuasions I could use' almost certainly confirms use of the rack.
Cecil made his way to the Tower soon after, where it seems
probable that Guy made a revealing and long-awaited confession.[12] Evidence of this can be found in two depositions Guy
made, one on 9 November and another on the 17th, which cor-
responds to a large extent with his examination of 8 November,
only now revealing the names of several of his co-conspirators,
including Thomas Wintour, whom he identified as the 'lay-man'
who came to collect him. Jack Wright, Catesby and Percy were
also mentioned as being involved from the outset, while Keyes and
Christopher Wright were identified as co-conspirators. For

Cecil, the biggest victory was probably Guy's admission that he travelled to the Low Countries to inform Hugh Owen of the plot. However, it has also been suggested that the accusation against Owen was a later addition by Cecil.[13]

Guy's decision to reveal the names of his colleagues was of little benefit to the Privy Council by this stage, as by that time evidence against the conspirators at Holbeche was already mounting. The explosion was devastating, and John Grant was particularly badly injured, almost completely losing his sight. For those who were still part of the hunt, the first thought was that all inside the room must have been killed. In the confusion that followed, news began to spread that Catesby, Grant and Rookwood had lost their lives. Those who had remained with the hunting party had given up hope of continuing the uprising and had begun to flee on horseback. There is even some sugges- tion that they were encouraged in taking flight by the remaining conspirators who had not been hurt in the blast. With the sheriff's men approaching Holbeche, and with the leader of the conspiracy thought to be dead, any flickering embers of hope for success were well and truly extinguished.[14]

While fleeing from Holbeche some members of the party came across Thomas Wintour and Stephen Littleton returning from Shropshire. Although Wintour and Littleton had failed in their attempt to obtain help from Talbot, their journey into the country had made them aware that the Sheriff of Worcestershire was heading in their direction with a posse comitatus. Wintour had been unaware of the powder disaster until this time, and he heard some inaccurate reports that a number of conspirators, including Catesby, had been killed. For Littleton, this was the last straw. Convinced that there was no chance of overcoming the sheriff's men, he attempted to convince Wintour to flee. 'This I will not do!' Wintour replied. 'Even now! I owe my friend

Robert Catesby the last services that one man can do for another in this world. That is, I must bury him. In any case, I must first make sure that he is dead! Whatever happens, I have decided never to leave him dead or alive!'[15]

Valiant and loyal to the last, Wintour's response to the news of his friend's possible death may have been the action of a defeated man determined to go down fighting rather than face trial. Many will argue Catesby's actions conveyed a similar message, even as early as the point at which Guy was taken. Nevertheless, with firm resolve, Thomas Wintour returned to Holbeche where he witnessed for himself the extent of the damage. While news that many had departed, including his brothers Robert and John and also Sir Everard Digby, was true, Catesby was not dead, and nor were his colleagues. Still there alongside him, Rookwood was burned but reasonably able, as was Grant's friend Henry Morgan. Grant was incapable of action, but both Wright brothers and Thomas Percy remained present and uninjured. Wintour himself must have taken some consolation in the news that his master and friend Catesby was relatively unscathed, but the situation was desperate. When asked what further he proposed to do, Catesby responded with the words: 'We mean here to die.' To this, Thomas Wintour replied equally defiantly: 'I will take such part as you do.'[16]

As Waad was preparing to interrogate Guy on the morning of 8 November, the posse comitatus led by Sir Richard Walsh arrived at Holbeche. The time was around eleven in the morning. Walsh remained close to the outer wall to direct operations, while his troops, armed with swords and muskets, advanced on the house.

Inside, Catesby and his comrades prepared for the last. In the moments before the conflict, they prayed together. Once the conspirators had said their prayers they opened the front door and faced the sheriff's men full on. Thomas Wintour was the first out into the courtyard. With little support and no defence, he was shot in the shoulder by either a crossbow or a carbine musket, losing the use of his right arm. The next of the conspirators to take to battle were the Wright brothers. Within seconds of their crossing the threshold a musket bullet hit Jack Wright. Kit Wright was hit shortly after. It is generally accepted that Jack Wright was not killed immediately but lived for up to a day in excruciating pain.[17]

Rookwood was the next to emerge from the house, also wounded but not killed. With the Wrights out of the action this left only Catesby and Percy as men able to take on the sheriff's men. Grant and Morgan remained, the biggest casualties of the explosion, while the injured Thomas Wintour was also still alive. After taking shelter from musket fire, Wintour found refuge at the side of Catesby.

'Stand by me, Mr Tom, and we will die together,' Catesby is reported to have said – now famous words. To this Wintour replied: 'I have lost the use of my right arm, and I fear that will cause me to be taken.'[18] Nevertheless, both stood together side by side, and they were joined by Percy. It is said that Catesby took a golden crucifix, one that he always wore around his neck, and crossed himself. Leader till the last, Catesby maintained that all that he had undertaken had been for the 'honour of the cross' and that, while he now accepted that it was not the will of God that the Catholic faith be restored to England in the way he had anticipated, he would fight till the last, choosing to defend himself with his sword rather than on the stand.[19] Tesimond referred to this moment as the time when it was made apparent to Walsh that Catesby had been the author of the plot. Until that time the authorities still believed Percy to have been the leader. It is perhaps a testament to the characters of both of these men that eyewitness accounts of this final battle highlight that no one among the sheriff's company approached Catesby or Percy. Tesimond even stated that the man who had fired the bullets that saw off the Wright brothers was hidden behind a tree. It was that same man who also fired a legendary shot with his musket. While accounts vary, the general view is that Percy and Catesby were killed by the same shot – either two bullets from one shot or both by the same bullet. Thomas Wintour referred to one bullet, adding 'as far as I could guess'.[20]

Although fatally wounded, neither Catesby nor Thomas Percy died immediately. Percy, in fact, is recorded as having lingered for some time afterwards. Catesby's demise was not so drawn out, yet in his final moments he mustered the reserves and resolved to die in a manner befitting a leader of courage and faith. Fleeing the oncoming soldiers, he returned to the house, where he found a painting of the Madonna, which he kissed reverently and held tightly in his arms. With this, the man who had sought to reinstate his religion in England finally passed away, not in the manner of Guy Fawkes, having to endure hours of merciless torture, but without being taken, yet alone and in pain, silently in prayer.

While Thomas Wintour, Rookwood, Grant and Morgan were captured and taken away by the victorious countryside militia, Sir Everard Digby had already departed. Remaining in his company was one of his pages and a servant, who, despite offers of horses and money, refused to be parted from their master. By now escape was no easy feat. The roads were alive with crowds of expectant people, and Digby was a marked man. As a last resort he decided to make off into the woods, thinking he would stand a better chance of escape under cover of darkness. He discovered a dry ditch in the wood, in which he concealed himself, his men and their horses. For a short time they remained hidden, but their presence was given away by the hoof marks in close proximity to the ditch. Once they had been discovered his pursuers cried out: 'They are here! They are here!' To which the quick-witted Digby replied: 'It is true they are here! What are you going to do about it?'

For Digby the sheer numerical strength of his opponents left surrender as the only reasonable option. Tesimond states athat Digby's reasons for choosing surrender were his desire to have more time to prepare for death and to have the opportunity to tell the world his own version of the conspiracy. Digby's intention when being taken to London was to speak directly to the king on the formalities of the plan and to counsel him about the harshness of his regime. Despite not being fully informed of the details of the plot until such a late stage, Digby made no attempt to hide his own guilt. Throughout this time, if not throughout his entire adulthood, Digby had been firmly convinced that the good of his religion and those who adhered to it mattered above all things.[21]

Whether through his own sense of self-importance or through fear of facing a man involved in a conspiracy that should claim his life, James declined the opportunity to meet Digby face to face. Nevertheless, in the days following the discovery of the plot James remained surprisingly unaggressive towards Catholics. When appearing before Parliament on 9 November the king kept an open mind. He did use the opportunity to highlight his own importance and to take the praise for having deciphered the meaning of the Monteagle letter, but he was slow to condemn Catholics outright, stating: 'it does not follow that all those who profess the Roman religion have been knowing accomplices and abettors of the plot'. Nevertheless, James did not exonerate the Catholics completely. When referring to the motivation for the plot he castigated their views, claiming: 'it cannot be denied that the sole cause which brought them to such a desperate plan was blind superstition arising from their religious errors'.[22]

James also used the opportunity to condemn the harsh doctrines of the Puritans. One way or another, he was seeking to appear even-handed towards those he held in little regard. Nevertheless, even viewing the event from the perspective of the time, James's assessment seems naïve. Any indications that he might be prepared to show religious tolerance, for which hope and expectation had been encouraged by earlier statements or promises, were absent from his speech. This, combined with the added oppression of the newly introduced penalties on recusants would inevitably promote further resentment and opposition to his rule. James could not have failed to notice that by late 1605 there had been three attempts on his kingship, two of which were direct attempts on his life. In addition, he would also have been aware of the hatred displayed by Guy and Dutton towards the Scottish in 1603 and Guy's show of contempt towards the Scottish lords after his arrest.[23] Interestingly, James was careful to avoid any suggestion that the conspirators had had assistance from foreign powers. There was no reference to the Spanish Treason, still a relatively grey area to most people in the early years of James's reign, from either the king or members of the Privy Council. Cecil wrote on James's behalf to the various English ambassadors abroad – including Cornwallis, Edmondes and the English Ambassador to Paris, Sir Thomas Parry – explaining what had transpired in the previous week. Nevertheless, on hearing the news, the various foreign powers drew their own conclusions. Both the Duke of Lerma and the Spanish envoy to London maintained suspicions of involvement by Puritan and French influence, while the King of France believed the same of the Spanish, but individually each was quick to show his support for King James.[24]

Within a few days of James's speech, several other conspirators were brought to the tower, including Rookwood, Grant, Thomas

Wintour and Digby. By 9 November Guy had also named Tresham as a conspirator. This was hardly surprising. Even by the 8th suspicion had been growing against him. In a letter from Waad to Cecil, Waad referred to Lord Arundel, presently serving in Spain, Sir Griffin Markham and one Tresham, long a pensioner of the King of Spain, as 'suspicious persons'.[25] By the 12th Tresham had been arrested and while in the Tower wrote a five-page account of his dealings with the conspirators. Bates was also arrested that day. He was found in Staffordshire attempting to flee Holbeche after seeing Catesby had been injured. According to a contemporary account, while Bates was leaving the house, Kit Wright threw £100 from the window to him with the instruction that £80 be taken to Wright's wife and the rest he might keep. After his arrest Bates was briefly interrogated before being taken to London where, unlike his fellow conspirators, he was placed in the Gatehouse at the Tower as a mark of his yeoman status. Keyes was also taken in the Midlands. After briefly being separated from the remainder of his party, he had been stopped in Warwickshire, probably while on his way to Holbeche. After a three-day delay, Sir Fulke Greville of Warwick Castle questioned him. When asked of his activities, Keyes claimed he was on his way to visit Ambrose Rookwood, to whom he was related and whom he had heard had recently been captured. Shortly after this incident, Keyes was sent to London by the Sheriff of Warwickshire, Sir Richard Verney and held in the Tower.[26]

By mid November, only Robert Wintour, in the company of Stephen Littleton, remained at large. Meanwhile, back in London, interrogation moved on to the conspirators' known allies, including the Lords Montague, Mordaunt and Stourton, all of whom were taken to the Tower for questioning. Montague, as previously mentioned, might have had some idea of the plot following his brief conversation with Catesby; Mordaunt was related to Keyes and was also his patron; and Stourton had connections as Tresham's brother-in-law. It was probably Guy who implicated Stourton. Following several days of torture he admitted on the 16th that Stourton was to have been kept from attending the reopening by some form of accident.[27] Northumberland was also questioned on 27 November. Needless to say, none of these men of higher status was tortured, but all were severely compromised by their embarrassing connections to the conspirators.[28]

Through torture, the interrogators eventually extracted information from Guy about the part played by the priests. While admitting the role of his conspirators, at least verbally, by 8 November, Guy had yet to identify any role that priests may have played. For Cecil and company this was infuriating. Sir Edward Coke, the famous jurist and attorney-general for the prosecution, when speaking at the trial later, maintained, recalling the Bye Plot: 'I never yet knew a treason without a Romish priest.' Finally Guy revealed that a priest had been present to issue the sacrament at the house behind St Clements, but at first he refused to give the identity. By the 9th Guy's resolution gave way and Father Gerard was named. For Cecil this was the moment he had been waiting for. Although Guy refused to state that Gerard had any knowledge of their intentions, his presence at that crucial meeting was enough to bring both Gerard's integrity and that of the Jesuit Order into question. Gerard's alleged involvement remains one of the more controversial aspects of the plot. While Tesimond appears to have learned of its existence through Bates before passing on what he knew to Garnet around midsummer, there is no definitive evidence that Gerard was aware of its existence at this time. Gerard, even if he had been in the house when the meeting took place on 20 May 1604, was not necessarily aware of the conspiracy itself. Gerard himself, as mentioned earlier, denied that he had been there at all.[29] Perhaps, by this stage, continuous torture eventually led to Guy giving answers that the Privy Council wanted to hear. Gerard was a thorn in the side of the Government. It was now illegal for a priest to live in England, but Gerard had escaped prison in 1597 after having been detained as a Jesuit along with the now canonized Nicholas Owen, the builder of priest-holes. Both Gerard and Owen had escaped at the same time, and it was at Catesby's home in Uxbridge that they sought refuge following their escape.[30] Now under scrutiny again through his links with Digby and Catesby and having been denounced by both Guy and later Bates in early December, a thorough search began.

Gerard was not the only target. In the aftermath of the plot the recusant community at large was subject to ruthless investigation, the likes of which it had long feared. On 11 November Anne Vaux's property, White Webbs, was thoroughly searched and several secret passages discovered, although by this time Vaux and the Jesuits had moved on. The following day, a nine-day search began at Harrowden, but nothing of interest was found. It was perhaps with the greatest of luck that Gerard, hiding there in one of Owen's secret areas away from prying eyes, managed to survive for four days on nothing but two biscuits and a pot of quince jelly.[31] Eventually Gerard escaped, and after fleeing to London made his way to the Continent, living to tell the tale of the Gunpowder Plot. Tesimond also narrowly managed to escape, fleeing first to Saint-Omer. Father Garnet was not to be so lucky. When questioned of his own involvement in the plot on 4 December and then again on 13 January 1606, Bates denounced Garnet, in particular highlighting his own mission, on Catesby's orders, to Coughton Court to inform Garnet of the outcome of the plot. Bates also described a meeting between Tesimond, Gerard and Garnet at Harrowden less than two weeks before the delivery of the letter to Monteagle.[32] Proof of Garnet's implication in the plot came from Tresham, who referred to Garnet's minor role in the Spanish Treason providing letters of introduction on behalf of Thomas Wintour as Timothy Browne.[33]

Evidence was also presented against Hugh Owen, Sir William Stanley and Father William Baldwin. Owen was undoubtedly Cecil's principal target, and moves to extradite him were made quickly, albeit unsuccessfully. Writing to Sir Thomas Edmondes, the Ambassador to Brussels, Cecil insisted news of their involvement in the conspiracy be made known among Owen's closest friends and that proof of their complicity in 'this matter of the gunpowder' must be as 'evident as the sun in the clearest day'.[34] While Cecil undoubtedly saw the plot as an opportunity to stage a coup against the exiles and the Jesuits, based on the confessions of Guy and Wintour, Owen was at least aware of the Gunpowder Plot, even if he was not otherwise involved. Attempts to extradite Owen failed, while Cecil eventually pardoned Stanley – which was probably helped in no small way by the fact that Stanley had not been in Brussels during Guy's initial visit in 1605, a time when he was supposedly negotiating himself a pardon.

While Stanley and many of the conspirators' close colleagues, relatives and friends were tainted by alleged involvement in the conspiracy they did at least avoid torture. Sir Edward Coke described the questioning of the conspirators as taking place on twenty-three days over a ten-week period. During that time a separate commission was set up for minor members of the plot, notably those involved in the hunt at Dunchurch as well as the servants of the conspirators.[35] There is no further evidence that torture was used, with the exception of that employed on Guy, although whether or not the remaining conspirators faced some degree of torture, most likely by the use of manacles, is unknown. Thomas Wintour was questioned repeatedly and recorded a lengthy confession, dated 23 November. Wintour's declaration is the only account that goes into detail of the early meeting with Catesby and Jack Wright, before Guy was brought back from the Continent.

However, Wintour's declaration has since become the subject of some doubt and debate. Although his account goes into considerable detail about the plot, in some areas agreeing and overlapping with the later depositions of Guy, its authenticity has been questioned, not least because his account is signed Winter, while Thomas invariably signed his name Wintour. Interestingly, the records of Robert Wintour's examinations often show his name as Wynter, while Thomas's other brother, John, varied the spelling between Wintour and Winter. Equally curious was that Wintour's shoulder injury at Holbeche, which had allegedly lost him the use of his right arm, had clearly healed by the 23rd when it came to writing a lengthy confession. Other conspirators were questioned, yet without adding anything of significance. Rookwood and Digby were both interrogated on 2 December, two days before Bates and two days after Keyes.[36] John Wintour was also questioned over his alleged involvement, at least in the later hunt, on 22 November, yet his involvement was trivial at best.[37] Robert Wintour, who was not apprehended until the middle of January 1606, was eventually questioned on 17 January and signed a declaration on the 20th.[38]

While Bates's interrogation was possibly the most damaging, evidence that the betrayal of the conspirators was the work of Francis Tresham is another area of the conspiracy that remains shrouded in doubt. Most character witnesses refer to Tresham as being quite selfish in nature, casting doubt on any possible willingness to save Monteagle at the risk of his own safety. There is no evidence to suggest Tresham argued his innocence or bartered for his own release. Even more remarkable was that throughout the month of December Tresham's health deteriorated inexplicably. Officially, he had been suffering for some time from stranguary, an inflammation of the urinary tract. During his incarceration he was treated by at least three physicians, including Dr Richard Foster, former President of the College of Physicians, and he was probably also seen by Dr Matthew Gwinne, the Tower doctor.[39] Opinion on Tresham's failing health is divided among previous commentators. While many maintain his illness was a natural one, others, including Father Francis Edwards, suggest he was poisoned and the act covered up by physicians in collusion with the government. Others, however, maintain that he escaped to the Continent – or was freed – around late December. This could be borne out by something Edwards highlights in his work on the plot, that of a possible handwriting connection between Tresham and a Matthew Bruninge writing from Madrid in 1609. While difficult to confirm, the link is a piece of meticulous observation that merits further attention.

William Waad, however, stated that Tresham's condition grew 'worse and worse' as time wore on, and the official and generally accepted version of events is that on 23 December he died a painful death in his cell. Along with Catesby, Percy and both Wright brothers, Tresham would avoid death at the hands of the executioner. Nevertheless, in his last agonizing moments he did attempt to make some amends for his involvement. In his deathbed confession, which he dictated to his servant as he was now too weak to write himself, he desired his previous confession implicating Garnet in the Spanish Treason be retracted and that his new one 'stand for truth'. Rather than confirm Garnet as having provided Thomas Wintour, as Timothy Browne, with letters of introduction, he now stated that he had not seen Garnet for some sixteen years.[40] Sadly for both Tresham and Garnet, his words were not made public, and any corroboration by his wife Anne, still grieving for her late husband, was deemed unfit, while Tresham's servant was himself a prisoner for his possible involvement.

13

HIS JUST END SHOULD'ST BE GRIM

Parliament reconvened on 21 January 1606, marking the first gathering of the people whose lives had been in such peril since 9 November. By this time James's earlier good grace towards the majority of the 'good papists' had given way to bitter resentment, illustrated in no better way than by his words to the Venetian Ambassador that he 'shall, most certainly, be obliged to stain [his] hands with their blood'.[1] In the House of Commons the members showed good sense by considering how such an incident could be avoided in future, yet among the Commons there was a general sense of loathing towards Catholics with frequent references to 'the danger of Papistical practices' and similar sentiments.

On 27 January Father Garnet and Guy Fawkes's old school friend Father Oldcorne were arrested, along with Nicholas Owen, after two months at large. As fate would have it, the date coincided with the start of the trial of those involved in the plot. All eight survivors were present: Guy, Thomas Wintour, Robert Wintour (the last conspirator to be discovered), Rookwood and Grant (taken from Holbeche), Robert Keyes, Thomas Bates and Sir Everard Digby.[2] John Wintour, half-brother of Robert and Thomas, was also present, despite a comparatively minor role.

As was usual in trials for high treason under the Tudors and Stuarts, the proceedings bordered on the farcical, with the outcome a foregone conclusion from the start. Over the course of Sir Edward Coke's ten-week period of interrogation the government had already gathered the evidence they needed against the eight defendants. Guy Fawkes had never tried to conceal his part in the conspiracy even before he was tortured, and the guilt of his accomplices was well known, leaving the trial as a simple formality in which the public would learn at first hand the details behind the treason. Once this had been achieved, all that remained was for those accused officially to be found guilty and condemned to death.

On the morning of 27 January the conspirators were taken by boat along the Thames from the Tower of London to Westminster Hall. Following their arrival they were confined for thirty minutes in the Star Chamber as they awaited the arrival of various officials, after which they were ushered into the hall and placed upon the scaffold at the bar in view of all present, including many Members of Parliament and members of the public, who assailed them with ceaseless ridicule. From discreetly located rooms high above, other persons of note observed the proceedings in privacy, among them several foreign ambassadors, Queen Anne, Prince Henry and King James I, the principal target of the conspiracy.[3]

While James perhaps found some satisfaction in witnessing the humiliation of the eight conspirators, other details of the trial would have pleased him less. In particular, a contemporary account of the trial notes the conspirators 'taking tobacco, as if hanging were no trouble to them'. James was known for his loathing of tobacco, viewing it as 'hateful to the nose, harmful to the brain' and 'dangerous to the lungs' – an advanced view in the seventeenth century.[4] In addition, he could not have failed to notice that while some of the conspirators hung their heads in shame others stood with hardened expressions. Gerard, in particular, notes that while in the Star Chamber

> all men did note a great resolution in them, not seeming
> to fear or respect either judgement or death itself; nor
> showing any sign of sorrow for their attempt, in regard
> of their intention thereby to have pulled down heresy
> and set up the Catholic religion.[5]

Tesimond also commented on their hardened stances, suggesting they demonstrated 'determination and intrepidity', while another contemporary description described some of the conspirators as having possessed 'a stern look, as if they would fear death with a frown'.[6] The reaction of the conspirators certainly caught the attention of several onlookers. In the aftermath of the trial, a pamphlet was published entitled *A True Report of the Imprisonment, Arraignment, and Death of the Late Traitors*. Rather than being a true account, the pamphlet omitted many important features, in particular anything that might appear supportive of the cause espoused by the conspirators, while exaggerating the case against them. Nevertheless, it did highlight that the prisoners had carried out the plot with what they believed was the best of motives, offering no offence either to their own conscience or to God, in part stated by the words:

> that they spake little but in commendation of their
> conceited religion; also, that they asked no mercy either
> of God or the King for their offence, but seemed as
> though in their conscience they thought the work to
> be meritorious . . . also, that they did only pray by the
> dozens upon their beads [rosaries].[7]

Gerard commended their bravery, stating 'they were nothing daunted with that which they expected', yet he condemned their decision to embark on the endeavour, remarking 'seeing men of so excellent parts ran [sic] into so foul an error, and attempted so dangerous an enterprise against the whole State, by their own rash and heady courses, against the advice of their spiritual guides'. While Gerard also used the opportunity to glorify the reputation of the recently captured Father Garnet, who had been executed by the time of writing, he included a notable pearl of wisdom: 'that all men may see how needful it is even for the best minds to follow counsel'.[8]

The judges included the Earls of Suffolk, Worcester and Northampton as well as Cecil, Earl of Salisbury, while Popham was Lord Chief Justice and Sir Edward Coke acted for the prosecution as Attorney General.[9] When the proceedings got under way the indictments were read against the plotters, both collectively and individually, as based on their recent testimonies in the Tower. In addition to charges against the plotters themselves, indictments were also made against Gerard, Garnet, Tesimond and the Jesuit Order collectively, although no evidence of this had been found among the conspirators' own confessions. Once these had been read, the conspirators were asked whether or not they accepted the charges. To this, all answered not guilty: even Guy Fawkes denied the charge. This was undoubtedly met with surprise. Until this point the conspirators had made no attempt to conceal their guilt. Digby, on the other hand, was arraigned on a different indictment taken following his arrest and was tried separately.

For a time the attention fell squarely on Guy. Of all of the denials, his was met with the greatest surprise. Not only had he been discovered by Sir Thomas Knyvett equipped with matches and fuses to light the powder in the cellar where the gunpowder was kept, but when questioned he had admitted his intention to destroy Parliament and send those Scots present back to the Scottish mountains. When challenged by the commissioners with 'We are quite astonished that you of all people should want to deny the truth of the indictment', Guy responded: 'We have never dealt with the Jesuits in this business. Nor did they ever persuade or urge us to undertake it. This is as false as it is true that we alone began and ended the business. So I say that all reference in the indictment to our meetings with them, and the advice and consent they gave us in this, is something entirely new.'[10]

Following their pleading not guilty, Edward Phillips, Sergeant-at-law, took to the floor, using his time to emphasize the heinous nature of the crime. Tesimond condemns Phillips, stating that he exaggerated considerably. Once he had finished, Coke followed by highlighting in great detail the facts behind the indictment. His speech was lengthy and used in part as an excuse for a long-winded moral discourse, in particular against the Jesuits. In addition, he made reference to the delay between the arrests of the conspirators in November and the commencement of the trial in January, explaining that it had been necessary for many reasons, including allowing for the capture of Robert Wintour and in order to clarify doubts over Fawkes's identity, initially mistaken for Johnson. Tesimond scoffed at those reasons, highlighting the fact that Robert Wintour was discovered only by chance, while Guy's identity was known after only a few days. Instead he argued, probably correctly, that the gap was used to incriminate the Jesuits further, a recurring theme throughout the trial. In fact, Tesimond went as far as to suggest the trial only began after Garnet's capture to ensure it was over before the conspirators knew he had been taken, for if they already knew they would have surely made a greater attempt to plead his innocence.[11] Coke also explicitly denied the possibility that the conspirators were acting out of hatred towards James for failing to honour promises of religious tolerance. Cecil had earlier written to Coke to brief him on the subject. The possibility also cannot be ruled out that James himself had made his feelings clear on the matter at some stage over the past two months. Brief accusation was pointed at some of the conspirators, notably the late Francis Tresham and Guy for their attempt to rouse the support of the Spanish at the time of Elizabeth's death, yet care was made not to point the finger at any 'foreign princes', nor were they implicated by the conspirators themselves. Instead, Coke made the most of the opportunity to link the Gunpowder Conspiracy and the Spanish Treason with the foiled Bye and Main Plots against the king. All trace of Monteagle's involvement was removed from the account of the Spanish Treason put forward by Tresham before his death, while Monteagle himself was praised for his loyalty to the king. No accusations were put forward by the conspirators against Monteagle, and any suggestion that he had been involved in the conspiracy only to betray it to Cecil was carefully avoided by Coke. Coke went on to place particular emphasis on the chaos that would have resulted had the plot been successful. Besides highlighting the deaths of many key officials and the king – and the probable deaths of Prince Henry Frederick and Queen Anne – Coke also considered the damage to nearby buildings, 'churches and houses, and all places near adjoining'. The planned explosion in Westminster would have wreaked havoc and destruction at the heart of the government. Curiously, when Coke carried out a character analysis of the conspirators he praised them as being men of good families and connections, with excellent qualities, whose possessions were typical of their social standing and commented that they had resorted to such extreme action only after years of being corrupted by the Jesuits.[12]

Once Coke's lengthy speech had come to an end, the evidence gathered against the conspirators over the course of their imprisonment was read aloud before the jury.[13] Proceedings began by hearing the confessions of Guy Fawkes and Francis Tresham concerning the Spanish Treason, which contained specific references to Tesimond and Garnet being directly involved in Thomas Wintour's journey to Spain.[14] Needless to say, Tresham's deathbed recantation clearing Garnet was omitted, although it may be that its existence was not widely known. Following this came Guy's declaration of 17 November, followed by those made by the others, including Thomas Wintour, Keyes, Rookwood and the recently captured Robert Wintour, who admitted to hearing confession at Huddington on 7 November before the conspirators moved on to Holbeche.[15] Interestingly, the proceedings ended with evidence of a conversation between Robert Wintour and Guy while imprisoned in the Tower. Being placed in adjacent cells, they took the opportunity to talk at length, perhaps unaware that their discussion was overheard by a government official. While speaking of the recent capture of Nicholas Owen, another indirect victim of the plot despite no evidence of his actual involvement, Wintour is reported to have said to Guy: 'God will raise up seed to Abraham out of the very stones, although they were gone', taken to mean that the Catholic Church would rise again despite their individual deaths.[16] Exactly what Robert Wintour had in mind is a matter for speculation. Certainly nothing about this suggests evidence of an uprising. Instead, the pair were probably speaking of future hope for their religion, that their own failed endeavour might not mean all was lost for other Catholics forced to endure the harsh penalties of recusancy. Perhaps they found solace in such a thought at a time when the only thing that awaited them was further pain.

Once this was over the prisoners were given the opportunity to speak. Robert Wintour was brief, apparently resigned to death and perhaps at peace with himself. Thomas Wintour was uncharacteristically quiet. Ironically, when answering questions in the Tower Wintour had so impressed Cecil that, had the matter been less heinous, he would have attempted to convince the king to spare his life. Instead, all Thomas Wintour did was request he be executed in his brother's stead, for it was only through his persuasion that Robert had been party to the plot in the first place. Rookwood's speech was the longest. Although he did not deny his involvement or attempt to excuse himself, he attempted to seek mercy on the grounds that he had been raised as a God-fearing Catholic and had agreed to be involved in the belief that the Gunpowder Plot was the only way to restore the faith of his ancestors. He ended by asking for mercy for his wife and sons who would surely be penalized financially as a result of his treason. While John Wintour was destined to die another day – he was executed on 7 April in Worcestershire along with Father Oldcorne – when asked to speak, he denied any involvement in the plot until after its discovery and only then for the love of his brother, Thomas, who persuaded him to join the attempted uprising in the Midlands. John Grant spoke briefly and slowly, while Bates remained silent. Robert Keyes spoke of the great injustice endured by Catholics in England and claimed satisfaction that he should die in such a way rather than live in a land of tyranny. He defended his decision to join the plot on the grounds of his own experiences of persecution and still maintained the lingering hope that England would one day return to the Catholic faith. Guy Fawkes was the last to speak. Not for the first time, he defended the Jesuits and denied that they were involved at any stage of the conspiracy. As for the remainder of his brief speech, he admitted his guilt freely and ended his brief speech by stating that he would gladly die for his faith.[17]

On the order of Edward Coke it was decreed that each man would be dragged to the place of execution on his back by rope attached to a horse; the condemned man's head remaining close to the ground throughout as a mark of being unfit to breathe the air of innocents. On the scaffold his genitals would be cut off and burned before his eyes, thus symbolizing his unworthiness to have been born or to father a child who should follow him in his evil ways. Following this his bowels would be hacked out and his head cut off. After this had occurred, his body parts would be put on show in various places as a warning to future criminals and, finally, so that his unworthy parts might become 'prey for the fowls of the air'.[18]

With the fate of Guy Fawkes and his fellow conspirators decided it was now the turn of Sir Everard Digby. Since Digby had pleaded guilty his fate was a foregone conclusion, but at least he was awarded the privilege of delivering a speech. As usual, proceedings began with the reading of the indictment against the knight, this time concentrating on his pledge to support the cause with financial assistance and a supply of horses and arms for the Midlands Rising. Evidence of Digby's guilt, including £1,500 he had supposedly pledged from his own resources, was found primarily in his own confession. When asked if he had anything to say in his defence, he admitted the serious nature of the crime but defended his own involvement as being solely for the good of his faith rather than for personal ambition. This, at least, nobody seemed to doubt. It was even remarked by Cecil that Queen Elizabeth used to speak of Digby with 'great grace', and Cecil also remarked of his own once high opinion of him.[19]

When speaking in detail of his motives, Digby centred on his friendship with Catesby, described by Gerard as so great that he would have willingly 'adventured his estates and fortunes'. Equally vital to his decision to take part was his desire to end persecution of his fellow Catholics, 'for whom he saw no other remedy'. At this time Digby highlighted James's broken promises on tolerance, undoubtedly making up for not receiving the opportunity to speak to the king face to face, and expanded on his disappointment with claims that he expected only harsher laws to be introduced, thus worsening the Catholics' lot. Finally, Digby stated that for the good of his faith he would gladly sacrifice everything that was dear to him.[20] To this, Coke, Henry Howard, the Earl of Northampton, and Cecil all spoke at length. Unsurprisingly, each made a point of denying that any promises of tolerance had ever existed, while Coke condemned Digby's friendship with Catesby as 'mere folly and wicked conspiracy' before referring to Catholicism as 'error and heresy'. When answering Digby's plea that his crime should be his own and penalties for his wife and children be avoided, Coke showed little mercy. Instead, Coke condemned his recusant wife, claiming Digby should have kept her under control, while his request of compassion for his own children was a far cry from what he himself would have shown to those due to sit in Parliament, including the 'tender princes'.[21]

With the conspirators' guilt confirmed, all that remained was for them to be put to death. The executions took place in two stages. First were Digby, Bates, Grant and Robert Wintour, who were condemned to die on Thursday 30 January 1606. At some time before eight o'clock that morning the conspirators were roused from their confinements in the Tower of London and forced to step out into the dark and dreary London morning for the final time. As a mark of his lower status, Bates had been incarcerated in the Gatehouse, where he had remained in isolation since his capture, and travelled in a different way to the others. Because of the high-profile nature of the conspiracy and the overwhelming wish of the majority of the public to witness the event, it was decided that, instead of being dragged to the location by a horse, the condemned men would be strapped to the barrel of a wicker hurdle in an attempt to ensure they were still alive when they reached the scaffold.[22] While perhaps less painful than being dragged along the road, it was still both demoralizing and humiliating. With their hands bound, the conspirators were forced to lie on their backs, fully conscious during their journey through the city streets under the watchful eyes of the passing crowds. Among the onlookers were countless Catholics and perhaps some priests. The conspirators' wives were also present, watching either from the windows of buildings that lined the road or at the roadside. Martha Bates, the wife of Thomas Bates, managed to make her way through the halberdiers and throw herself on her husband. During the short space of time before she was apprehended, Bates managed to entrust to his wife the location of the money he had been given by Kit Wright when fleeing Holbeche.

At approximately eight o'clock the conspirators had been assembled at the site of the scaffold at the western end of the churchyard of St Paul's Cathedral, overlooking the house of the Bishop of London, the very location where, some eighteen years earlier, Queen Elizabeth I had praised God for her defeat of the Spanish Armada. Digby was the first to mount the scaffold. After spending some brief time in silent prayer he spoke out strongly to the gathering crowd. While admitting to high treason, he justified his role for the good of his religion, just as he had done at his trial, declaring that revenge on the government for previous acts of persecution against him had never been a motive for his actions. When offered the chance to pray with the Calvinist ministers, he refused, instead choosing to call upon those of the Catholic faith to offer up their most devout prayers for him. Tesimond said of Digby that he prayed with such devotion that none present could fail to be moved. Once all had been said and done, Digby bowed to all men of status present on the scaffold. It was later said that he demonstrated a warmth of feeling and even a certain light-heartedness and was without any hint of fear.[23]

Tesimond's account of Digby's execution describes it as a gruesome affair. While it was customary for victims who were hanged, drawn and quartered to hang by the neck until they began to lose consciousness, Digby was still clearly conscious at the time the rope was cut down – although some accounts claim that he banged his head as he fell and was left severely dazed – and when his stomach was cut into quarters and his genitals removed and thrown into the fire. When the executioner proceeded to remove Digby's heart, at which time he held it up accompanied by the words, 'Here is the heart of a traitor', Digby is said to have answered: 'Thou liest!' As life ebbed from his body his head was hacked off and held up before the people. It was also said that when his head was raised before the crowd the expression on his face was identical to that when he was alive.[24]

Next on the block was Robert Wintour. Like Digby, Wintour possessed the outward demeanour of tranquillity and calm and said little throughout. He prayed quietly before his death, described by most accounts as being largely identical to the horror already experienced by Digby. After him came the almost blinded John Grant. He, too, was asked whether he felt remorse for his actions, to which he replied that he was there to die not to debate matters of conscience and asked only the forgiveness of God. Grant's devotion and courage was admired. Because of the injuries he had sustained at Holbeche, Grant offered no resistance to the execution, instead accepting support as he climbed onto the scaffold before going swiftly to his death.[25]

Bates was the last of the first four to die. He did not utter prayers in Latin or cross himself but acted with great penitence.

When asked to speak he confessed that he had been driven to conspiracy through obedience and affection for his master, Robert Catesby. It is often suggested that Bates was the only conspirator motivated by reasons other than spiritual and that perhaps he was more sorry for his role. The pamphlet *A True Report of the Imprisonment, Arraignment, and Death of the Late Traitors* states that Bates admitted guilt against God, king and country, but Tesimond rejected this statement as being full of 'lies and blasphemies'.[26] Because of his yeoman status, Bates's execution has generally been viewed historically and by contemporary accounts as relatively unimportant compared with the others. Nevertheless, it should not detract from the memory of Bates that he went to his death with bravery and great humility, not as a zealot but as a good servant and friend, whose loyalty to his master meant more to him than his own life.[27]

Early the following day Thomas Wintour, Ambrose Rookwood, Robert Keyes and, finally, Guy Fawkes were awakened in the dim light of early morning and taken to their place of execution. They, too, were drawn on hurdles from the Tower of London and taken through the streets under the watchful eyes of curious onlookers. The location of the executions was different for these four. Rather than being put to death in the shadow of St Paul's, the place chosen was the Old Palace Yard at Westminster, the piazza adjoining the House of Lords. It seems the irony was not lost on any involved that it came to pass that Guy Fawkes would meet his end within sight of the building that he had attempted to destroy. The trip to Parliament involved a longer journey than that for the first four, something that was perhaps also in the mind of the government when deciding on the location. The choice of route also left a further legacy. In making their way to Westminster the conspirators were forced to pass through the Strand district. Among the buildings they passed were the lodgings of Ambrose Rookwood, from which his wife watched proceedings out of a window. The story told is that Rookwood kept his eyes closed for the duration of the journey, yet before they set off he asked to be prompted on passing his home to allow him to look once more upon his wife. On reaching the site he opened his eyes and cried out, 'Pray for me, pray for me', to which his wife responded: 'I will; and be of good courage and offer thyself wholly to God. I, for my part, do as freely restore thee to God as He gave thee unto me.'[28]

Thomas Wintour was the first to be led up on to the scaffold. Uncharacteristically for him, his appearance was described as 'a very pale and dead colour'. Most in the crowd, knowing he was a fluent speaker, wanted to hear a speech, yet Wintour instead declared that this was not the time or place to 'deliver discourses', and what little he did say was to excuse the Jesuit Order from any guilt and to confirm his adherence to the Catholic faith. He also made it his last wish that any Catholic priests present should pray for him.[29]

Once Wintour was dead it was the turn of Ambrose Rookwood. He spoke briefly, emphasizing his stance as a committed Catholic. He asked of the king mercy for his wife and children and asked that God should, through his divine influence, convert the king and queen in order to restore the old faith to England. It was commented by Tesimond that Rookwood's death was marked by tears in the crowd as a mark of his goodness throughout most of his life.[30]

Keyes was the third to ascend the scaffold that day. When asked about his guilt he replied that he saw no wrong in taking part in the conspiracy, except that it had 'unfortunate aspects'. Of his final moments, it was said in the *True Report* pamphlet that Keyes threw himself off the ladder in desperation, yet other accounts affirm his death was one to be admired.[31]

Finally the time came for Guy Fawkes, the last of the conspirators, to take to the scaffold. By now the crowd was greater than at any time over the two days. Guy's body was so battered from his time dangling from the manacles and countless hours forced to endure the force of the rack that he was barely able to stand. The account in Gerard's narrative describes his appearance as 'weak with torture and sickness', and so weak was he that he needed the assistance of the hangman to help him climb the ladder. Once on the scaffold – it is significant that he insisted on being hanged from the topmost rung – he crossed himself reverently before giving his cloak and doublet to the executioner as his comrades had previously done. Whether there is any truth that under Guy's doublet was a shirt of horsehair is one of the more unusual aspects of the reports of his execution and something that cannot be substantiated by other evidence.[32]

When offered the chance to make a speech, he spoke briefly. It was written in the official account that he expressed regret for his sins and asked the forgiveness of the king and the nation. Whether this was true or a fictional addition in the *True Report* pamphlet is now difficult to determine. It was stated by both Tesimond and Gerard that when faced with death Guy announced that he would die fearlessly, placing his soul in the hands of the Lord. Once this was done, Guy's head was placed in the noose and his broken body dropped. It is said that those as far back as the third row heard the snap when the fall broke his neck. It is yet another strange twist that the man described as the 'Devil of the Vault' should have been the only one of the conspirators not to be conscious when his entrails were removed, his stomach quartered and his heart removed from his chest. Equally unmoved he must have been when his head was hacked off and placed on a pike on London Bridge in the company of those of his associates.[33] In death he is said to have harboured an expression that would have 'feared death with a frown'.

14

THE AFTERMATH

With his neck broken, his body mutilated and his head on a pike on London Bridge, exposed to the ravages of the birds or destined gradually to decompose in the dirty air, the story of Guy Fawkes as a living man finally comes to an end. It is strangely ironic that Guy, the first of the conspirators to be discovered, was the last to die. Of all the thirteen who met their end for their part in the Gunpowder Plot, whether in that legendary final stand in Staffordshire or at the mercy of the gallows on those fateful days at the end of January 1606, the death of the man charged with the responsibility of lighting the powder to bring about the destruction of Parliament and all within it was also the quickest, and, ultimately, the least cruel.

Yet for Guy Fawkes the damage had been done long before that dreary day in January when his story finally ended. During those three months imprisoned in the Tower his body, no stranger to conflict from his years in service, was left to hang mercilessly from the cold stone walls while at other times his muscles were stretched beyond their limit under the watchful eyes of his inquisitors. During those first four days in particular, in which he withstood the inquisitors' probing questions regarding the whereabouts of his accomplices with clearness of conscience and loyalty to his cause, Guy must have faced pain the like of which most people cannot even begin to comprehend. His strength was tested to the utmost, both mentally and physically, and yet for over three days he triumphed. He accepted sacrifice above forsaking his friends and for that he paid a most severe price. Perhaps it was those unbearable hours within the confines of the famous White Tower that helped quicken his passing. Equally important, Guy was the only conspirator hanged from the uppermost rung of the scaffold, at which point the impact of the fall was at its greatest. Yet perhaps after everything he had been through it was a small mercy that the only conspirator to face the rack should have been dead before his organs were so vilely removed from him.

Although all thirteen of the main participants in the plot were dead and buried within three months of its discovery – their corpses resting in a disturbed peace in hastily assembled graves in the Midlands or else disposed of in unconsecrated pits without their heads – their legacy has long outlived them. Indeed, as time has passed, the way in which the plot is portrayed continues to change, often affected by the beliefs held by writers at the time in which each new investigation takes place. One fascinating feature of the historicity of the plot is that practically every commentator manages to find parallels between the Gunpowder Conspiracy and events in his or her own time. For commentators such as Henry Garnett and Eric N. Simons, writing shortly after the Second World War, the subject of Guy Fawkes and the Gunpowder Plot parallels events during the war, including the bombing of cities such as Coventry, Dresden and Hiroshima. Antonia Fraser highlights interesting parallels with the situation in pre-1997 Northern Ireland and the triumph of Nelson Mandela in South Africa in the 1990s. Furthermore, the subject has had a tendency to become manipulated by the commentator's bias. Fraser refers to the debate as something of a 'propaganda war' that has been 'long and vigorous and shows no sign of abating'.[1]

Not surprisingly, sympathy and condemnation of the conspirators often seems to depend on whether a commentator is coming from a Catholic perspective or a Protestant one. So wide is the gulf here that, certainly since the late nineteenth century, Catholic perception has at times been to dismiss the entire plot as a figment of government invention in a bid to discredit the Catholic community. In 1897 Father John Gerard, namesake of the famous Jesuit, took the discussion to another level with his work *What Was the Gunpowder Plot? The Traditional Story Tested by Original Evidence*, in which he argued that the plot was a work of fiction devised by Robert Cecil. Among his criticisms, Gerard wrote:

> In no single instance is Guy Fawkes represented as about to blow up the right house. Sometimes it is the House of Commons that he is going to destroy, more frequently the Painted Chamber, often a nondescript building corresponding to nothing in particular – but in no single instance is it the House of Lords. [2]

Within a short space of time Samuel Rawson Gardiner, a scholar of Puritan history, set about answering Gerard's 'somewhat vague' impressions of the plot by writing his own account, entitled *What the Gunpowder Plot Was*. Since then, differences of opinion have continued. In 1969 the Jesuit Father Francis Edwards built on Gerard's work in his book *Guy Fawkes: The Real Story of the Gunpowder Plot?* in which he promoted the view that the conspirators were *agents provocateurs*, employed by Cecil to diminish the Catholic influence. Twenty-three years later, following the publication of Mark Nicholls's *Investigating Gunpowder Plot*, a book centring on the plot as one of the greatest threats of security ever faced by the state, Edwards continued the debate countering Nicholls's arguments.

But the greatest controversy resulting from the fallout of the Gunpowder Plot was perhaps the punishment of innocents. It was largely down to Robert Cecil, assisted in part by an Appellant priest, that before the end of 1606 a new Oath of Allegiance had been enacted. This widened further the gulf between King James and the Papacy and placed new and more onerous restrictions on the lives of recusant Catholics, whose loyalty to the state had never been questioned. In addition to the witch-hunt against the Jesuits, resulting in the execution of Garnet and the narrow escape of Gerard and Tesimond, it became illegal for a Catholic to practise law or medicine or to serve as an officer in the army or navy without paying a £100 fee. In addition, no known recusant was allowed access to a royal palace, to venture within 10 miles (16 kilometres) of the City of London, be guardian to a minor, act as executor of a will or hold public office. It became forbidden for a Catholic to hold a weapon, self-defence being the only exception or to vote in either local or general elections.[3] It was not until 1797 that the ban on Catholics voting in local elections was lifted and 1829, the year of Catholic Emancipation, before Catholics could vote in national elections or receive degrees.

While financial penalties and restrictions of liberty could be argued as being a predictable development of the laws already in place – perhaps inevitable even before the plot – there was certainly a cruel element to the way Catholics were treated by the Protestant majority. In 1613 a bill was put forward making it compulsory for Catholics to wear multicoloured stockings or red hats in order to identify themselves. As fate would have it, the Commons threw out the bill, a rare show of common sense, yet the fact that it was even suggested highlights the attitudes of certain segments of Parliament towards Catholics. That any Member of Parliament could argue that this was a necessity in order to avoid further conspiracy against the state seems ludicrous. A similar theme in the aftermath of the plot was the continued insistence by the authorities of searching the homes of conspirators and their recusant allies. While this may seem to be a reasonable action in that the investigations were carried out in defence of the realm, it is a sad reflection of the times that abuses occurred. When Ashby St Ledgers was searched, for example, many possessions were 'requisitioned' by the government, despite the property being legally owned by Lady Catesby as part of her dowry from her late husband rather than the son she had recently lost. Robert Wintour's home at Huddington Court was looted; among the possessions confiscated were items associated with the mass, but nothing further of an incriminating nature was found. The searches were conducted when Robert Wintour was still at large, and while attempts to track down the fugitives undoubtedly required a thorough search of their homes, there are clearly questions as to why it was necessary to remove items of value. By 17 November 1605 it was remarked that nothing of value remained in Huddington Court.[4] A similar account involved Lady Digby. When Gayhurst was searched following Everard Digby's arrest, the Sheriff of Warwickshire writes: 'All goods are carried away, even to the very floor of the great parlour.' So bad was the situation that Mary Digby wrote to Cecil imploring him to take action, as the sheriff was dealing in their possessions 'as though they were absolutely his'. Even people who despised the conspiracy had their possessions taken away. When the house of Sir John Talbot, who refused the request of Thomas Wintour to aid the Midlands rising, was searched, interrogators found little of value but still requisitioned his weaponry and papers.[5]

That the recusant population would be forced to endure some form of retribution can probably be attributed to the significant impact of the event as much as to its being a measure of justice against those responsible. Certainly, the actions taken by the authorities after the plot were harsher and more repressive than those for the Main and Bye affairs that had occurred only two years earlier, one of which was also of Catholic origin. The religious motive of the plot, coupled with the inevitable regime change that would have occurred had it succeeded, is similar in many ways to those that took place during the reign of Elizabeth I, in particular those accredited to Ridolfi, Throckmorton, Parry and Babington, the Poisoned Pommel Affair and, to some extent, the Spanish Armada of 1588. However, the scale of the Gunpowder Plot and the logistics of the event far exceeded the usual plans for assassination by poison followed by an invasion by a foreign power. Judging by Catesby's own statement in the early stages of the plot, the choice of location was not only convenience, the meeting place of England's key policy-makers, but also symbolic, the chamber in which anti-Catholic legislation was created. As he said: 'In that place have they done us all the mischief, and perchance God hath designed that place for their punishment.'[6]

If Catesby's own perspective on the plot is examined, the attack could be argued as being one against James and Parliament personally as an act of vengeance for failing to live up to promises as much as it was a Catholic attack on Protestants. When planning, Catesby was not content solely to highlight religious oppression and the need for change but he also carefully identified the need to eliminate every key member of the royal family to ensure the conspirators' aims would be met. Many commentators have been quick to criticize Catesby as being somewhat rash in his planning and for failing to think things through. In contrast to the organizers of the Bye and Main Plots, Catesby was content to allow James the opportunity to set out his policies. The fact that the conspirators' early meetings did not start until 1604 after anti-Catholic policy had been put forward suggests that Catesby had no intention of being party to any form of treason while he believed that hope of tolerance truly existed. Even when James's true feelings towards Catholics became evident in early 1604, Catesby was prepared to allow Juan de Tassis and Velasco the opportunity to complete peace talks with James, still harbouring the hope that tolerance might be achieved through peaceful negotiation.

Considering Thomas Percy's own hatred for the king, James's failed promises were clearly an important motive. His famous words when meeting his fellow conspirators – 'Shall we always, gentlemen, talk and never do anything?' – demonstrated his frustration. While these alleged promises James is supposed to have made have never been identified, it is evident from the king's letters to Cecil that he viewed it as wrong that anyone should die for their faith. While this and religious freedom are hardly the same thing, Percy clearly took some encouragement from their meeting. While this may have been unrealistically optimistic, the evidence of the king's correspondence with Cecil and Northumberland suggests a willingness to tolerate Catholics provided they were otherwise loyal to the Crown.

It seems, however, this was something the king had no interest in honouring, and James's record, both prior and subsequent to the plot, call his integrity into question. As previously highlighted, James considered with interest the possibility of ruling Scotland alongside his mother, Mary, Queen of Scots, who had earlier been forced to abdicate in his favour, yet this was something he eventually rejected, choosing instead to abandon her to secure an alliance with England.[7] As his reign in Scotland continued, evidence of his tendency to favour political ambition over filial tendencies was demonstrated again, notably by his reluctance to show favour to his mother over Elizabeth in the aftermath of the Babington Plot. James's tendency to undermine the position of key Catholic and Puritan officials for his own benefit also seems a consistent feature of his early reign in England. Communicating with Cecil in 1602, less than a year before making his alleged promises to Thomas Percy, James displayed what may have been his true feelings towards Catholics, showing his reluctance, should he become king, to agree to an Anglo-Spanish alliance and offer religious tolerance to Catholics.[8] In 1601, in a letter to James Hamilton, the future king highlighted his attempts to create a good impression with England's Puritans, yet within two years of his accession he wrote a very different letter to Cecil, this time congratulating him on his policy towards Puritans, demanding that they conform or else be harried from the Kingdom.[9] In many ways this was perhaps the most significant action of James's kingship, as, had it not been for his intolerant nature, Puritan colonizing of North America, particularly New England, might never have occurred, thus having a tremendous effect on the early history of what is now the United States of America.

How different might England's history have been had Guy Fawkes successfully lit that fuse on that fateful night in 1605? Notwithstanding the immense financial ramifications of the destruction of so much property, the loss of thousands of invaluable historical and financial documents, not to mention the loss of one of England's most famous buildings and the mass murder of key personnel, the likely fallout of the plot in terms of future government of the realm is highly debatable. If the plot had been successful, James, his queen (Anne of Denmark), his son Prince Henry Frederick, all the key members of the Privy Council – notably the Earls of Salisbury, Northampton, Worcester, Nottingham and Suffolk – would all have been killed, leaving England with no governing body. While some key Protestant or Puritan officials would not have been present, it stands to reason that the majority of the surviving nobility would have been Catholic. Mordaunt, Stourton, Montague and Northumberland we know would have avoided the event, either through Catesby's 'hints' or their own lack of enthusiasm to attend. Over the years most historians have largely ignored the question of how England would have fared had the explosion occurred. Considering Catesby's failed attempts at leading an uprising in the Midlands, despite claiming the king and his key officials were dead, it is difficult to imagine that Catholic consolidation of the throne was ever going to be easy. It is the view of some previous commentators, including Professor Ronald Hutton, that the majority of the English Catholic community would have been appalled by the conspiracy and refused to join an uprising.[10] Even had Thomas Percy or any of the others succeeded in apprehending Prince Charles, they would have had a lot to overcome. The views of Princess Elizabeth after learning of the conspirators' intention to make her queen do little to suggest that she would have cooperated willingly. Any hope of taking her reign forward would have been highly dependent on the assistance of foreign powers, principally Philip III and Albert, Archduke of Austria. If Princess Elizabeth had ascended to the throne it is likely that the new Catholic regime would have sought to consolidate her position through marriage to a Catholic prince, so her actual marriage to the Protestant German Prince Frederick, later Frederick V of Bohemia, would never have occurred. The son of the Catholic convert Henri of Navarre – later Louis XIII of France – only four years old at the time of the plot, might have been a possibility. Elizabeth might even have married the infant Prince Philip, son of Philip III and later Philip IV of Spain.

For the conspirators, an even more serious problem had presented itself shortly before the reopening of Parliament, when it became clear that Henry Frederick, the eldest son of the king, would not be attending. On hearing the news, Catesby is reported to have said: 'Then must we have our horses beyond the water, and provision of more company to surprise the Prince and leave the Duke alone.'[10] While the duke, Prince Charles, was indeed left alone, Henry Frederick was in Wales at the time of the plot, further hindering the possibility of his being captured. Catesby's letter to Father Garnet, which had been entrusted to Bates after the raid on Warwick Castle, seeking Garnet's counsel on raising a rebellion in Wales, demonstrates that Catesby was still intent on capturing the prince despite the failure of the powder explosion, but evidence that any realistic plan to do so was ever in place is not to be found. Catesby would almost certainly have acted with greater commitment had Guy Fawkes succeeded in his mission.

Nevertheless, the problem of Prince Henry Frederick was a significant one. This promising young individual had already become popular with the English people during his brief time in the country, and following his death from typhoid in 1612 his passing was widely mourned. A contemporary account by the Earl of Dorset wrote of the prince's passing: 'Our rising sun is set.'[12] Should King James have perished, the young Henry Frederick had all the attributes to become a fine king, and in some quarters the prince was more popular than his father. He had made a good impression on the people of England from his first public appearance in the summer of 1603, but his rising popularity also resulted in conflict between the two men. One contemporary account tells that during a hunt with James and a party in Royston, Hertfordshire, they quarrelled, and the prince rode away from his father to be followed by the majority of the party.[13] His opinions on matters of state were worthy of respect and were often at odds with James. In particular, the prince disliked his father's management of the Court. Had this talented and likeable young man inherited the throne in the aftermath of the Gunpowder Plot, England would probably have been in good hands. The prince's down-to-earth, witty personality endeared him to others, while his interest in affairs of state, both foreign and domestic, showed him to have a rare sense of pragmatism perhaps absent in both his father and younger brother. His adherence to the faith of his tutors, Calvinism, would not have differed much from that of his father, yet he was altogether more open-minded. Should Henry Frederick have ascended to the throne it seems doubtful that the religion of the state would have changed, but with the young man's sense of fairness it seems unlikely that conditions for Catholics and Puritans would have worsened. Perhaps a bitter hatred for those responsible for the death of his father and mother might have consumed him, yet more likely he would have adopted a more conciliatory approach. Should the young prince have ascended to the throne then perhaps history would have been different, and he would not have contracted his fatal illness. While question marks over his advisers and regents are difficult to answer – perhaps other Protestant lords would have been absent from Parliament for one reason or another – the good potential he demonstrated in his first eleven years could have developed and prospered during a lengthy reign; perhaps even to rival the often highly esteemed reign of his nephew, Charles II.

Had Henry Frederick perished in the carnage along with his father, however, the conspirators would still have faced another problem, one generally overlooked by historians. If the plot had been successful it would not only have resulted in the death of the King of England but also the King of Scotland. In addition, five Scottish nobles appointed by James to the Privy Council following his accession would also have been due to attend the event.[14] Nowhere in the confessions of any of the conspirators is any indication given of a contingency plan should they have been met with a Calvinist-inspired rising from Scotland. Presumably Catesby was more concerned with the possibility of an English rebellion, and he probably viewed any threat from Scotland as unlikely to be imminent. It is also unclear whether it was Catesby's intention that Princess Elizabeth should have inherited the Crown of Scotland following her father's death. As the Stuart line was still heir to the Scottish throne, Elizabeth would have been the rightful successor. Nevertheless, any suggestion that James's own proclamation declaring himself King of Great Britain would have carried any weight in English and Scottish statute law is doubtful. Nor is it likely that Scotland's Calvinist majority would readily have accepted a situation in which Elizabeth would have ruled the country from England as the head of state of a Catholic government, perhaps resulting in Scotland claiming independence and the Crown being claimed by one of Elizabeth's Protestant relatives such as Lady Arbella Stuart.

Catesby's desire for military backing from Spain or the Spanish Netherlands would have been important in the case of any Scottish rebellion in addition to putting out fires closer to home, but the possibility of securing military aid from abroad in the aftermath of a successful execution of the plot was never clear cut. As mentioned earlier, Guy's attempts, along with those of Anthony Dutton, Thomas James and Thomas Wintour, to obtain assistance from Philip III had failed on more than one occasion, while evidence supporting Anthony Dutton's claim of having some 2,000 horses has yet to be found. In addition, assurances Catesby gave to recruits at Dunchurch regarding the strength of the regiment from Flanders is also subject to scrutiny. However, it is not impossible that military support from abroad might have been forthcoming. From what is known of the Spanish Treason, Philip III's reluctance to assist was largely based on the advice from Juan de Tassis that the majority of English Catholics were unwilling to take up arms, thus making assistance with an invasion highly risky for Spain.[15] Whether Philip would still have felt this way if an uprising had been guaranteed is another matter, and in such circumstances it is reasonable to conclude that once influential Catholic sympathizers in England became encouraged in the belief that a genuine opportunity existed to further their cause successfully their willingness to rise may have strengthened. Following Guy's capture, on the other hand, no Catholic was likely to incriminate himself by admitting complicity in, or favouring, a failed conspiracy.

With this in mind, the integrity of some of the confessions by those with aristocratic connections to the conspirators and who denied their support of the conspiracy should surely be called into question. If the conspirators had succeeded in placing Lady Elizabeth on the English throne, both Philip III and Albert, Archduke of Austria, and perhaps even Henri IV of France may all have been keen to cement a Catholic alliance, perhaps even resulting in the formation of a new Catholic League comprising England, Spain, the Spanish Netherlands, the Order of Jesuits, the Papal States and possibly France. This assessment is clearly speculative, but there can be no doubt that once the King of England had been assassinated, Philip III of Spain and Henri IV of France would have felt compelled to take action to put an end to any subsequent unrest.

From a domestic point of view, the destruction of Parliament, in addition to destroying the chamber in which matters of policy were debated and created, would have seen the deaths of practically every major national political figure in England, including members of the Privy Council and Protestant bishops. While Catesby's intention to proclaim Elizabeth as queen was to be put into effect immediately, perhaps eliminating some elements of disorder, England would, nevertheless, have been alarmingly susceptible to aggressive invasion from abroad as distinct from an invasion by forces sympathetic to the conspirators. While influential persons such as Mordaunt, Northumberland, Stourton and Montague, through their connections with the conspirators, would have helped steady the ship, regardless of whether or not they agreed with Catesby's motives, many key positions would need to be filled urgently. The likely death of Nottingham, the Lord High Admiral, would have been particularly significant. With Nottingham dead a quick appointment of a new Chief of Navy would have been imperative in case of an invasion – interestingly Catesby was reported to have dined with an unidentified admiral in the period shortly before the intended implementation of the plot.[16] Should the plot have succeeded, England as a political entity and major world power would have been severely weakened, and the danger would have existed of its becoming ungovernable. This could have dragged the country into civil war, possibly not dissimilar from the period following the Battle of Lewes in 1264 when Simon de Montfort successfully captured both Henry III and Prince Edward, leading to local skirmishes and outbreaks of guerrilla warfare.

When comparing the strategy of the Gunpowder Plot to those against Elizabeth I, plans for the latter were always backed by military aid from abroad. Although the conspirators came within a hair's breadth of achieving the destruction of Parliament, their strategy for the aftermath was ill conceived and poorly planned. The likely outcome is that they would have still faced execution at the hands of any new monarch or that they would have brought the country to civil war.

15

REMEMBER, REMEMBER ...

As fate would have it, the plot was destined to fail, and over four
hundred years later historians continue to study the event and
the annual celebration continues to capture people's imagina-
tion now as it did in the early days after 5 November 1605. As the
lonely figure of Guy Fawkes sat dejectedly within the great walls
of the Bloody Tower, the people of London celebrated the
safe delivery of their king with the lighting of bonfires and,
unbeknown to that 'desperate fellow' the streets of London were
bathed in a warm glow that evening, marking the first Bonfire
Night. On 23 January 1606 it was announced that Sir Edward
Montague, the Member of Parliament for Northamptonshire,
had put forward a bill that every 5 November should become a
day of public celebration in thanksgiving for the uncovering of
the plot. Once the Thanksgiving Act was passed, Bonfire Night
became a tradition.

For people of the twenty-first century Bonfire Night, or Guy
Fawkes Night, has little in common with those celebrations that
marked the streets of London on that night in 1605. Today it is
simply a festive occasion rather than an act of national thanksgiving. In the early years, however, the day served as a reminder
of Catholic treachery coupled with celebration that King James

had been spared from death. While the details varied slightly by location, traditional activities included the ringing of church bells and the lighting of bonfires – and even in the early days there was some use of fireworks. In 1647 Guy Fawkes Night became the only national feast day not to be abolished by Parliament, and over the coming years the people of England were obliged to celebrate it despite the fact that the event, which celebrates the saving of a king, was anomalous in a country under the guardianship of Lord Protector Cromwell following the execution of James's own son, Charles I, in 1649.[1]

While the passing of the Thanksgiving Act of 1606 made celebration of Guy Fawkes Night compulsory in England, over time the event also spread throughout the British Empire and survives in various guises in many of the countries of the Commonwealth of Nations. In Bermuda following the Boer Wars there was a brief tradition by British residents there of burning effigies of the Boer Relief Committee leader Anna Maria Outerbridge – famous for her attempts to rescue imprisoned Boers – as a sign of her 'treachery', in place of the usual effigies of Guy Fawkes.[2] In other parts of the Caribbean the event has also attracted attention. Before a fireworks ban in the 1990s celebrations were popular in Antigua and Barbuda, and Guy Fawkes Night continues to be of enjoyment for people in the Bahamas, St Vincent and the Grenadines as well as in St Kitts and Nevis. Up to the 1970s celebrations in Australia were common, while some still take place in New Zealand. In South Africa, 5 November continues to be marked, but the annual fireworks displays of today show little reference to its origins. In Canada the event continues to be celebrated in the provinces of British Columbia, Newfoundland and Labrador. In the city of Nanaimo, BC, the Guy Fawkes tradition began with British coalminers who had emigrated to Canada in the nineteenth century. In the early days, the people of Nanaimo built tall bonfires topped by an effigy of Guy, but since the 1960s this has been largely phased out, with the event simply incorporating the lighting of bonfires. In contrast, throughout Newfoundland and Labrador the Guy Fawkes element continues to survive.

South of Canada, Guy Fawkes Night was popular in Colonial America, especially in New England. Any suggestion that the day was used to mark the safe delivery of an English king, however, is doubtful; if it had not been for James's stance on religion the USA might have developed into a very different country. But, in keeping with British anti-Catholicism, much of the Puritan-based celebration focused on the Pope, and, typically, the celebration of Pope's Day – as it became known – was marked with the usual bonfires topped by an effigy of the Pope instead of Guy Fawkes. Pope's Day is remembered as little more than an occasion for mindless revelry, however. In Boston, Massachusetts, it was an occasion when the city was taken over by the lower classes and youths and was characterized by a tradition of collecting money from the city's wealthiest to finance the revellers' drinking. In some parts of the American Colonies the day was also used to register discontent at the British government: in 1773 an effigy of the British Prime Minister, Lord Bute, was burned alongside one of the Pope, while effigies of Bonnie Prince Charlie and the controversial American General Benedict Arnold (famed for his defection to the British) were among several figures of hate burned on Pope's Day throughout the colonies.[3]

In Britain the popularity of Guy Fawkes Night has remained high – with effigies of Guy Fawkes rather than the Pope placed on the bonfire (in Guy's home town of York the people tend not to burn his effigy, however) – although, as in other parts of the world, it seems its relevance has faded somewhat over the past century. Another long-standing custom that has diminished in recent times is 'penny for the Guy'. Traditionally, children would create their own stuffed effigies, or 'guys', which they would take out into the streets in the run-up to Guy Fawkes Night in order to raise money for fireworks. However, any relevance the 'guys' tradition had to the famous Gunpowder Conspirator has largely faded. In 1825 it was remarked by the English writer and bookseller William Hone that: 'It is not to be expected that poor boys should be well informed as to Guy's history, or be particular about his costume'.[4]

Despite the Thanksgiving Act having been repealed in 1859, many places in Britain continue to enjoy a particular relationship with 5 November. In Ottery St Mary, Devon, there is a local custom that residents carry burning barrels of tar through the streets, while Lewes, East Sussex, has become legendary for its Bonfire Night celebrations, the largest in the country, which attract crowds of up to 80,000 people. Typically, a procession made up of members of one of the local bonfire societies will march through the town carrying effigies, torches and other items. Another procession has seventeen burning crosses supposedly in honour of the memory of seventeen Protestant martyrs killed in the Marian Persecutions of 1555, 1556 and 1557. In keeping with the anti-Catholic tradition of the event, an effigy of Pope Paul V, pontiff at the time of the Gunpowder Plot, is burned alongside one of Guy Fawkes. Effigies of contemporary hate figures are also incinerated – in 1994 effigies of Margaret Thatcher, John Major and Michael Howard all made the pile, while in 2001 the event received a great deal of press attention for the burning of an effigy of Osama Bin Laden.

Although the tradition has lost much of its relevance, one element of the story that continues to thrive is the importance placed on the subject of this biography. Even in the early days after the Gunpowder Plot Guy Fawkes was identified as the villain of the piece. A sermon by Bishop Barlow on 10 November 1605 reiterated James's tone in Parliament the previous day, concentrating blame on evil Catholics rather than all Catholics, while Guy Fawkes, and to some extent his unnamed colleagues, was condemned as a Catholic fanatic.[5] A contemporary account of Guy's execution places particular attention on him rather than his accomplices, stating 'last of all came the great devil of all, Guy Fawkes, alias Johnson, who should have put fire to the powder'. While vilification of the individual responsible for lighting the match that should destroy Parliament might come as no great surprise, it is rather strange that in subsequent centuries effigies of his co-conspirators have seldom made it on to the pyre – Catesby, in particular, perhaps deserved similar attention. In popular culture, depictions of Guy Fawkes are similarly negative. Guy was allegedly the inspiration for John Milton's Devil in the sixth book of *Paradise Lost*, written within a century of the events of 1605, and his portrayal of Guy as a demonic figure is not isolated. A John Wilson, writing in 1612, depicted Guy as a demon in the following song about the Gunpowder Plot:

> O England praise the name of God
> That kept thee from this heavy rod!
> But though this demon e'er be gone,
> His evil now be ours upon!

In the aftermath of the Gunpowder Plot numerous works of this type were used to illustrate Guy Fawkes as the chief villain, often illustrated by a contemporary woodcut of his character snooping around the cellar with a lantern in hand. Among the popular rhymes is that written by John Rhodes contained in his publication: *A brief Summe of the Treason intended against King & State, when they should have been assembled in Parliament,*

November 5. 1605. Fit for to instruct the simple and ignorant heerein: that they not be seduced any longer by Papists:

> Fawkes at midnight, and by torchlight there was found
> With long matches and devices, underground.

Over the years negative depiction of Guy has been something of a recurring theme. The following popular rhyme referred to the tradition of guys being placed on the bonfire:

> Guy, Guy, Guy
> Poke him in the eye,
> Put him on the bonfire
> And there let him die.

And then there is the most famous chant about the Gunpowder Plot:

> Remember remember the fifth of November,
> Gunpowder treason and plot,
> I see no reason
> Why gunpowder treason
> Should ever be forgot.

> Guy Fawkes, Guy Fawkes, t'was his intent
> To blow up the King and Parli'ment.
> Three-score barrels of powder below
> To prove old England's overthrow.

> By God's providence he was catch'd
> With a dark lantern and a burning match.
> Holla boys, holla boys, let the bells ring.

Holla boys, holla boys, God safe the King!
And what should we do with him? Burn him!

Or an alternative verse:

A traitor to the Crown by his action,
No Parli'ment mercy from any faction.
His just end should'st be grim,
What should we do? Burn him.
Holla boys, holla boys, let the bells ring.
Holla boys, holla boys, God save the King!

In 1821 the humanist essayist and literary critic William Hazlitt wrote a piece to commemorate 5 November, portraying Guy Fawkes as a 'pale miner in the infernal regions, skulking in his retreat with his cloak and dark lantern, moving cautiously about among his barrels of gunpowder, loaded with death'.[6] In his work *Guy Fawkes, or the Gunpowder Treason*, the Victorian novelist William Harrison Ainsworth embellishes the story of Guy Fawkes in the lead-up to the Gunpowder Plot but in a somewhat humorous and sympathetic light. In addition, he adds many of his own inventions, including Guy being married to a fictional woman named Viviana Radcliffe.

Negative depictions of Guy Fawkes are not restricted to popular culture. Over the years many historians have offered their opinions, with descriptions of Guy as a shady cold-blooded murderer, a minor accomplice or a wronged *agent provocateur*. In other cases some have seen it fit to highlight the conspirators' finer qualities. In his epic investigation into the Gunpowder Plot, the nineteenth-century author and lawyer David Jardine states of Guy:

we are to look upon this man, not according to the
popular notion, as a mercenary ruffian, ready for
hire to perform the chief part in any tragedy of
blood, but as an enthusiast whose understanding had
been distorted by superstition, and in whom fanati-
cism had conquered the better feelings of nature.[7]

Samuel Rawson Gardiner is equally defensive of the conspirators' morals. Despite condemning their actions, he claims:

it is impossible not to feel some satisfaction that so
many of the original conspirators escaped the scaffold. Atrocious as the whole undertaking was, great
as must have been the moral obliquity of their
minds before they could have conceived such a project, there was at least nothing mean or selfish about
them. They had boldly risked their lives for what
they honestly believed to be the cause of God and
their country.[8]

This in turn makes nonsense of criticisms by some historians
that Guy Fawkes was a soldier of fortune, a mercenary. Although
fighting on the side of the Spanish Netherlands Guy fought con-
sistently for the same cause and principles throughout his career.
He had already converted to Catholicism before embarking on
his career in the Low Countries and was only ever going to fight
for his faith. Interestingly, the Jesuits, who despised the plot,
spoke kindly of him. Tesimond was particularly positive of his
schoolfriend, and Father Gerard equally so, stating:

those that have known him do affirm that as he did
bear office in the camp under the English coronell

on the Catholic side – Stanley – so he was a man every
way deserving it whilst he stayed there, both for
devotion more than is ordinarily found in soldiers,
and especially for his skill in martial affairs and
great valour, for which he was there much esteemed.[9]

Nowhere in any of the popular rhymes is it mentioned that
Guy Fawkes was well liked and knowledgeable, a man loyal to
his friends and one who had acquired a respected reputation as
a soldier. Not only had Guy remained loyal to Catesby throughout the plot but he refused to implicate any of his fellow
conspirators until he was eventually broken under the strain of
the rack. His willingness to investigate the cellar in the wake of
the Monteagle letter, despite the possibility that he could be
caught, also highlights this. The suggestion that his decision to
fight in the Spanish Netherlands was unpatriotic is also open
to question. For a Catholic living in England during the reign of
Elizabeth, career prospects were limited, and for a 23-year-old
looking to better himself the army was an obvious choice. By
joining the English Regiment of the Spanish Army Guy could
earn a regular income and receive accommodation and food as
well as striking a blow for his faith. In addition, he would have
avoided paying the recusancy fees that he had been forced to
endure back in England. Had he remained at home it is likely
that he would have been restricted to working on his stepfather's
estates or have sought to make his way in a house of the nobility,
as he briefly did at Cowdray.

When looking at Guy's life as a whole, little negative emerges
until his decision to join the plot at the age of thirty-four. Should
history assess him to that point, there would be little to conclude
other than that Guy Fawkes was born into a respectable household, was an excellent soldier, highly esteemed by both his

commanding officer and those who served under him, a good friend and a devout Catholic. Those who view him only as the man who attempted to destroy Parliament and all within might find it surprising to learn that this same man could also be argued to have epitomized courage, loyalty, honesty and humility. Equally surprising is that the Gunpowder Plot should be the only event associated with his life. Knowledge of his involvement in the unsuccessful Spanish Treason is somewhat limited, and had it not been for the patient study of Father Albert Loomie in the late 1960s our knowledge of the event would be still less informed. The arrests of Guy Fawkes and Thomas Wintour in the aftermath of the Gunpowder Plot threatened to call into question their activities in Spain, although less attention was given to this than might have been expected. James made brief reference to 'errors in religion', yet the subject of Spanish complicity was treated with extreme care.[10] For Cecil, the Spanish Treason was used as little more than another excuse to attempt to have Owen, Stanley and Baldwin extradited. Perhaps the most significant controversy surrounding the Spanish Treason was the willingness of Guy and Thomas Wintour to seek a Spanish invasion of their native land. In the minds of some, this could be seen as an act of betrayal of one's homeland – the Spanish invasion in 1588 seemed to unite the people of England rather than give impetus to a Catholic rebellion. By way of example, the 1st Viscount Montague is one of several Catholics who showed great loyalty to the Crown against the Armada. Perhaps the biggest difference between 1588 and 1603 in the minds of some of England's Catholics was that Philip II would have been invading England for his own purposes; Philip III, on the other hand, had he invaded, would have been assisting the Catholic exiles to help place their chosen successor on the throne. Furthermore, Guy like Dutton was anti-Scottish, probably stemming from his Yorkshire upbringing where Scots were the traditional enemy.[11] When weighing up the options of having a new monarch from Scotland or a Spaniard of English descent, for the conspirators at least the Spaniard would have been a Catholic.

For many, the Gunpowder Plot was treason of incomprehensible malice against the monarchy; for others, it was an act of desperation against a king whose failed promises nearly destroyed a kingdom. Certainly James's role in the event should not be ignored. While questions over the exact assurances he offered will likely remain unanswered, had James been prepared to allow religious tolerance the plot would never have been devised. The plot was by no means inevitable. In his speech to Parliament on 9 November 1605 James highlighted difference in religion as an insufficient reason for conspiracy. Clearly some of religious minority did not agree with this. A letter written earlier by the French Ambassador, Christophe de Harlay, the Comte de Beaumont, on 9 July 1605, stated:

> The King treats the Catholics with greater rigour than ever; and I foresee that their condition will become daily worse. All of them, as well those of the Jesuit faction as the secular priests, feel that they have been grievously deceived heretofore, and that they have been very little comforted or assisted by what the King of Spain has done.[12]

Father Gerard also provides an interesting insight into Catholic life during the latter part of Queen Elizabeth's reign and the early years of James's. Following a raid on Baddesley Clinton in Warwickshire in which Gerard and several other priests were forced to endure a period of hiding in a Nicholas Owen-devised priest-hole that involved standing knee deep in the moat, the searchers eventually left after being content with a fine of twelve gold pieces paid by Anne Vaux. 'So pitiful is the lot of the Catholics,' says Gerard,

> that those who come with a warrant to annoy them in this or in other way, have to be paid for doing so by the suffering party instead of by the authorities who send them, as though it were not enough to endure wrong, but they must also pay for their endurance of it.[13]

While most people will probably find some sympathy with the majority of the Catholic and Puritan population who were forced to suffer unjust treatment in early Stuart England, the sheer violence of the act is less easy to forgive. The immense scope of the explosion would have seen a result the likes of which had never before been experienced in England. Yet had the plot been successful the effect would have been ghastly. When viewed in the context of the twenty-first century, the destruction would surely have paralleled the terrorist attacks on New York in 2001: a key landmark reduced to rubble and the massacre of many innocents.

For the conspirators this, had they been successful, would have been their legacy. For all their good qualities, the horrendous nature of the plot is unforgivable. In terms of history, Guy Fawkes and company might have fared better had the conspiracy been against the king alone rather than the entire government. History, as a whole, has often reflected kindly on those who stood up to misery and oppression. It is a curious feature that the status of many of history's greatest heroes and villains depends on whether they won or lost. Certainly Catholic conspiracy against the monarchy was nothing new to the people of seventeenth-century England. This much, at least, has already been identified. Going back to 1569 Catholic powers had attempted to end the life of the monarch for the good of England and the 'old faith'. Conspiracy against a monarch, however, was not unique to Catholics. In 1554 Queen Mary was subject to two dethronement attempts following her desire to revert England to Rome. Similar examples are found with regard to Stephen and Matilda, Henry the Young's rebellion against Henry II, King John and Henry III who were subject to attempts by the barons to enforce acceptance of new legislation restricting the royal powers, and Wat Tyler's Peasants' Revolt of 1381, while Richard III was usurped by Henry VII at the Battle of Bosworth. All of these pre-date the controversies of differences in religion in England. Edward II, Richard II and Edward V all provide historical examples of monarchs who were murdered, either as a result of protest against the activities of their reign or else to pave the way for their replacement, while attempts to dethrone a British monarch did not end with the Gunpowder Plot. James I's grandson, James II, a Catholic, found himself facing revolution that resulted in his deposition at the hands of William of Orange and his wife Mary. Perhaps most significantly, less than fifty years after the failure of the Gunpowder Plot, Charles I, another king who claimed adherence to the doctrine of the Divine Right of Kings, met his end after failing to tolerate democratic rights.

When comparing the activities of Guy Fawkes against other individuals who attempted rebellion against a monarch there is little evidence supporting the assumption that Guy was unusually malevolent. When putting his life into perspective as a whole, there is much more to consider than his role in the plot. Based on the evidence at hand, his decision to convert to Catholicism was influenced at an early stage, and his conversion took place at a time when the new wave of Catholicism brought over by the

Seminary priests and later the Jesuits was at its height, and this almost certainly had an effect on Guy's personality. Whether the ardently Catholic and well-accomplished Montagues instilled that hardened, committed streak in him before his journey to the Low Countries, or whether his progression was gradual under the leadership of Sir William Stanley, is less easy to pinpoint. Nevertheless, when examining the influences on Guy's life it is less difficult to understand why he possessed such commitment, bravery and purpose. Certainly, commitment to the Catholic cause, or indeed the cause of the English Regiment, was no flash in the pan; it was something to which he adhered for more than half his life. Throughout his life Guy was susceptible to an overwhelming web of hatred that was later manipulated by men such as Stanley and Catesby, zealous fanatics with a desire for change. Although he was raised a Protestant, the Catholic influence of the Harringtons became deeply embedded within him. Headmaster Pulleyn perhaps nurtured it; Montague undoubtedly furthered it; Stanley provided him with an outlet for it; while Catesby proceeded to complete it. The Catholics and Puritans who lived during the reigns of Elizabeth and James were brought up in this same web of hatred – Oliver Cromwell was no exception to this. Some demanded better; the majority simply yearned for better. While no modern jury would be prepared to exonerate Guy from guilt by reason of his childhood influences, perhaps had his trial been held today the outcome might be more sympathetic. As Spink quite rightly pointed out: 'Guy Fawkes was a son of destiny, a product of his environment, a creature of circumstances – always saving his free-will and moral responsibility.'[14]

When examining Guy Fawkes's role in the Gunpowder Plot, and the plot in the context of England's history, the plot should not be viewed as an isolated event. Not only was it a direct consequence of the failure of the Spanish Treason and one of a number of attempts – motivated by differing interpretations of the Scriptures that plagued England during the sixteenth and seventeenth centuries – to dethrone a monarch, it was also a clear and powerful illustration of what good men could be driven to when forced to endure the hardships that religious minorities faced at the time. The actions of Guy Fawkes are less worthy of praise than are those who suffered quietly for their faith at a time when they were tested to the uttermost, but even his actions can be explained as a direct result of his career serving in the Low Countries. For Guy the destruction of Parliament might have been somewhat reminiscent of his work using gunpowder against fortifications such as those at Calais and Nieuwpoort. Perhaps also the plot should be viewed as an element of dissent that still lingered from the fragile Peace of Vervins in 1598 and as a continuation of the wars of religion that still engulfed the Spanish Netherlands at the time. It is, therefore, no surprise that the desire to rid the land of their birth from religious oppression continued to burn deeply in those on the losing side, even after the war had ended:

> Since God, nature, and both human and divine law, grant a defence to the innocent who are unreasonably oppressed to resist unjust violence by the lawful use of arms when no other remedy is offered ... to live and die in the defence of our honour and the liberty of our homeland against all illegitimate usurpers of an office which does not belong to them.[15]

It could easily have been a speech by George Washington or a quote from the Declaration of Independence. How different Guy Fawkes's reputation could have been. While the plot will always be viewed as a mark of religious conflict, attempted mass murder and regicide, it can also be seen to have been a predictable, albeit excessive, act of human nature. History, as we know, records numerous examples of 'wronged' individuals who were morally satisfied that their acts were justified. In the case of the Gunpowder Plot it is certainly true that there were villains on both sides of the religious divide. The reign of James I will always be criticized by some because of his failings in domestic policies, particularly his dislike of Parliament, yet he will be favourably remembered for his good foreign policies that saw so little conflict abroad. His major gifts to England ranged from the positive, such as the King James Bible, to the negative, not least his convincing his son Charles I that he was king by divine right, so inevitably paving the way for the English Civil War. For the majority of Englishmen the reign of James I was one of low taxation, little conflict, unity with Scotland, continuation of the fine literature and drama that had blessed Elizabethan England and the colonization of America. For these reasons, perhaps, it is no surprise that the majority of Englishmen mourned James as a king who died in peace after a well-spent life living in peace. Yet for those on the other side, James's reign was a time of hardships and broken promises, deprivation of rights and endless frustration.

When it comes to understanding rebellions and revolutions in the context of history, it is indeed true that many of history's desperate diseases have been solved with desperate remedies. In Russia, Vladimir Lenin is heralded in some quarters as a hero, esteemed by former Chinese Prime Minister Sun Yat-sen as a 'great man . . . [who] will live on in the memories of the oppressed people throughout the centuries', yet even he was forced to depose a royal family. In France, while the revolution of the late eighteenth century is often celebrated as the birth of the modern era and an event that permanently took away the power of the French monarchy, the Reign of Terror alone cost somewhere between 16,000 and 40,000 deaths, a far cry from the projected death toll from a successful Gunpowder Plot. Father Gerard even compared the conspirators to the Macabees, the Jewish tribe who freed their people from Syria.[16] Or perhaps Catesby took inspiration from the story of Moses, who inflicted ten plagues on Egypt before the Pharaoh's final demise in the waters of the Red Sea. But while there are many examples throughout history that the positive actions of the new regime justify the means, it is usually the case that history tends to be written by the winners. With regard to Guy Fawkes, it could be said that despite being on the losing side there is much value in understanding history from the loser's perspective, for Guy Fawkes was a man of many fine qualities. Had he seen reason at the vital time, maybe he would have been more deserving of a place among history's greatest Britons. As it is he will always be the villain of the Gunpowder Plot. Because of him effigies will continue to be burned on bonfires on 5 November. Thanks to him the vaults beneath the House of Lords continue to be searched on the eve of Parliament's reopening. It is because of him the word 'guy' is used to mean 'man'. It is because of him that a Guy Fawkes River and a Guy Fawkes National Park welcomes visitors in Australia, while an island in the Galapagos carries the name Isla Guy Fawkes. Also, writing at a time when British Members of Parliament have been subject to hideously embarrassing expenses and lobbying scandals, one can only be amused by an anarchist poster of the mid twentieth century declaring: 'Guy Fawkes – The Only Man to Enter Parliament with Honest Intentions'.

For the people of Britain, 5 November will always remain associated with Guy Fawkes. Yet while the event itself is now only tenuously linked to the activities of the historical man from York who died over four hundred years ago, perhaps he has left legacy for good. It is because of him that every year millions of people in Britain gather together in gardens and parks to watch the night sky explode with sound and colour. In this way the late-autumn night remains one of the nation's favourite annual events. Is it just possible that we are a nation of anarchists? Can it be that the British people view this man as among the most significant historical figueres that ever lived? Or is it that we simly love Bonfire Night with all its fireworks?

We will always remember 5 November for 'Gunpowder, Treason and Plot', but it is ironic that the celebration of the thwarting of the man who attempted to blow up so many of the nation's most important political and aristocratic figures of his age should have inadvertently succeeded in bringing so many people together for a celebration each year. It is perhaps for this reason that gunpowder and treason should never be forgot.

Notes and References

SP State Papers (British)
E Sección de Estado, Archivo General de Simacas
HMC Reports of the Royal Commission on Historical Manuscripts
CSP Calendar of State Papers Domestic

Preface

1 Francis Edwards (tr.), *The Gunpowder Plot: The Narrative of Oswald Tesimond Alias Greenway*, London: Folio Society, 1973, pp. 68–9.

Chapter 1: Portents of Dread

1 Michael de la Roche, *An Abridgement of Gerald Brandt's History of the Reformation in the Low Countries*, Vol. 1, London: R. Knaplock, 1725, pp. 137–8.
2 Roche, pp. 137–8; Charles Knight, *The Popular History of England*, Vol. 3, London: Bradbury and Evans, 1857, pp. 170–1.
3 Catherine Pullein, *The Pulleyns of Yorkshire*, Leeds:

Whitehead and Sons, 1915, p. 55; Henry Garnett, *Portrait of Guy Fawkes: An Experiment in Biography*, London: Robert Hale, 1962, p. 14.

4 Pullein, p. 55; Garnett, pp. 14–15.

5 ibid., p. 95; ibid., pp. 16–18; Eric Simons, *The Devil of the Vault*, London: Frederick Muller, 1963, p. 19.

6 Simons, pp. 19–20.

7 Garnett, pp. 18–19; Pullein, pp. 95–6; Robert Davies, *The Fawkes's of York in the Sixteenth Century*, London: J.B. and J.G. Nichols, 1850.

8 Will of Ellen Fawkes, 22 August 1570, from Davies; Garnett, Appendix 3, pp. 163–5.

9 Will of Thomas Fawkes, 18 February 1581, from Davies; Garnett, Appendix 4, pp. 165–6.

10 Will of Thomas Fawkes, 18 February 1581, from Davies; Garnett, Appendix 4, pp. 165–6.

11 Henry Hawkes Spink, *The Gunpowder Plot and Lord Monteagle's Letter*, London: Simpkin, Marshall, Hamilton, Kent and Co., 1902, pp. 240–1; Katharine M. Longley, 'Three Sites in the City of York', *Recusant History*, No. 12, 1973.

12 SP14/216/19, Examination of John Johnson in response to Interrogatories, 6 November 1605; SP14/216/37, Examination of Guye Fawkes, 7 November 1605.

13 Garnett, pp. 30–1; Simons, p. 23; Pullein, p. 96.

14 Dom Hugh Aveling, *The Catholic Recusants of the West Riding of Yorkshire 1558–1790*, York: Leeds Philosophical and Literary Society, 1963, p. 191.

15 William Nicholson, *The Remains of Edmund Grindal, Successively Bishop of London, and Archbishop of York and Canterbury*, Cambridge: Cambridge University Press, 1843, p. 142.

16 Pullein, p. 96.

17 Spink, pp. 248–9; Simons, pp. 22–3.

18 Spink, pp. xix–xx, 28, 40, 41, 121, 285, 377; David Jardine, *Criminal Trials, II: The Gunpowder Plot*, London: M.A. Nattali, 1846, p. 28; David Jardine, *A Narrative of the Gunpowder Plot*, London: John Murray, 1857, p. 32.

19 Pullein, p. 96.

20 Spink, pp. 32, 45; John Morris (tr.), *The Conditions of Catholics Under James I: Father Gerard's Narrative of the Gunpowder Plot*, London: Longmans, Green and Co., 1871, pp. 265–86.

21 Garnett, p. 30.

22 Spink, p. 30.

23 Simons, p. 24.

24 Garnett, p. 32.

Chapter 2: The Catholic Recusants of the West Riding of Yorkshire

1 The author would like to thank David Herber for providing this information.

2 Spink, pp. 240–2.

3 Antonia Fraser, *Mary Queen of Scots*, London: Phoenix, 2002, pp. 112–15.

4 Spink, p. 19; C. Northcote Parkinson, *Gunpowder Treason and Plot*, London: Weidenfeld and Nicolson, 1976, p. 40; Alice Hogge, *God's Secret Agents: Queen Elizabeth's Forbidden Priests and the Hatching of the Gunpowder Plot*, London: HarperCollins, 2005, p. 274; Jardine, *Criminal Trials*, p. 11; Jardine, *A Narrative of the Gunpowder Plot*, p. 9.

5 Aveling, *Catholic Recusants*, p. 192.

6   ibid., pp. 192–3.

7   ibid., pp. 203–5, 211.

8   ibid., pp. 196–201.

9   ibid., pp. 203–4.

10 ibid., pp. 212–15, 221.

11 SP14/216/17, Examination of John Johnsonne,
    6 November 1605.

12 SP14/216/19, Examination of John Johnson in Response to
    Interrogatories, 6 November 1605. When asked if he had
    been a Papist, Guy responded he 'was out amongst upper
    Catholiques by his travels'. When asked 'If otherwise,
    how was he converted, where, when and by whom?'
    Fawkes responded that he 'was raised a Catholique and
    not converted That he went out for Douex [Douai]
    amongst seminyrs, and cauled againe at Prt in Louvaine'.

13 Spink, p. 341.

14 SP14/216/19, Examination of John Johnson in Response to
    Interrogatories, 6 November 1605; Antonia Fraser,
    The Gunpowder Plot: Terror and Faith in 1605, London:
    Phoenix, 2002, pp. 84–5; Simons, p. 20; Deed Between
    Fawkes and Lumley, from Davies; Garnett, Appendix 6,
    p. 168.

15 The author would like to thank David Herber for
    providing this information.

16 Spink, pp. 248–9.

17 ibid., pp. 19, 393.

18 Madeline Hope Dodds and Ruth Dodds, *The Pilgrimage
    of Grace, 1536–37*, Vol. 1, Cambridge: Cambridge
    University Press, 1971.

19 Spink, pp. 248–9.

20 Edmund Grindal, *Memorials of Archbishop Grindal:
    Wherein the True Causes of His Suspension and Disgrace*

Are Impartially Related, London: J. How, 1710.

21 Robert Miola, *Early Modern Catholicism,* Oxford:
Oxford University Press, 2007, pp. 22, 137–8; Hogge,
pp. 210–11. The other two women to face execution were
Anne Line and Margaret Ward.

22 John Hungerford Pollen, *Unpublished Documents
Relating to the English Martyrs,* London: Catholic Record
Society, 1908, p. 384.

23 Parkinson, p. 47; Spink, p. 26.

24 Jardine, *Criminal Trials,* p. 8.

25 Pullein, p. 94.

26 ibid., pp. 94, 99; Garnett, p. 33.

27 Spink, p. 240. Alternatively, the child may have been
another son of Edward Fawkes.

28 ibid., pp. 393–5.

29 Aveling, p. 217; Simons, p. 27.

30 SP14/216/19 – Examination of John Johnson in Response
to Interrogatories, 6 November 1605.

31 *Dictionary of National Biography.*

32 Garnett, pp. 13, 40.

33 Pullein, p. 94.

34 Harry Speight, *Nidderdale and the Garden of the Nidd; a
Yorkshire Rhineland: Being a Complete Account, Historical,
Scientific, and Descriptive, of the Beautiful Valley of the Nidd,*
New York: E. Stock, 1894, p. 343; Pullein, p. 102.

35 Morris (tr.), *Gerard,* pp. 57–8.

36 Aveling, p. 212; Pullein, p. 96.

37 Deed Between Fawkes and Lumley, from Davies, *The
Fawkes's of York in the Sixteenth Century*; Garnett,
Appendix 6, p. 168.

38 Will of Thomas Fawkes, 18 February 1581, from Davies;
Garnett, Appendix 4, pp. 165–6.

39 Sale of land contract between Guy Fawkes and Anne
  Skipsey, from Davies; Garnett, Appendix 7, pp. 169–70.

40 Quit deed of Edith Fawkes, from Davies; Garnett,
  Appendix 8, pp. 170–1.

41 Davies.

Chapter 3: Cowdray, Calvinism and a Slow Boat to Flanders

1 SP14/216/19, Examination of John Johnson in Response to
  Interrogatories, 6 November 1605; Simons, p. 30.

2 Aveling, *Catholici Recusants*, p. 226.

3 Pullein, p. 55; David Herber, *The Marriage of Guy Fawkes
  and Maria Pulleyn*, Gunpowder Plot Society.

4 Pullein, pp. 78–9, 94, 99. Following Edith's second
  marriage Guy's step-grandfather was a Pulleyn of Scotton.

5 Pullein, pp. 128–9.

6 Francis Edwards (tr.), *The Gunpowder Plot: The Narrative
  of Oswald Tesimond Alias Greenway*, London: Folio
  Society, 1973, p. 69.

7 De Goffrey Goodman, *The Court of James I*, Vol. II,
  London: Samuel Bentley, 1839, pp. 118–22; Simons, p. 30;
  Fraser, *The Gunpowder Plot: Terror and Faith in 1605*,
  London: Phoenix, 2002, pp. 85–6; Parkinson, p. 47.

8 Goodman, p. 118.

9 Fraser, p. 86.

10 Sussex Archaeological Society, *Sussex Archaeological
  Collections*, Vol. 7, London: John Russell Smith, 1854;
  Recusant History, Vol. 19, Issues 1 and 2, 1988–9,
  p. 399.

11 Michael Questier, *Catholicism and Community*,
  Cambridge: Cambridge University Press, 2005, p. 109.

12 ibid., pp. 110–11.

13 ibid., p. 111.

14 ibid., pp. 114–17.

15 ibid., p. 124.

16 ibid., p. 144.

17 ibid., p. 145.

18 ibid., p. 145.

19 Roger Manning, *Anthony Browne, 1st Viscount Montague: The Influence in County Politics of an Elizabethan Catholic Nobleman*, Sussex: Sussex Archaeological Society, 1968, p. 106.

20 Questier, pp. 155–6.

21 *Acts of the Privy Council*, Vol. XXIV, pp. 328–9; Hogge, p. 203.

22 Hogge, p. 204.

23 Questier, pp. 156, 159.

24 Fraser, p. 86.

25 SP14/216/37, Examination of Guye Fawkes, 7 November 1605.

26 SP14/215/19, Examination of John Johnson in Response to Interrogatories, 6 November 1605.

27 Henry Baird, *The History of the Rise of the Huguenots of France*, New York: Charles Scribner's Sons, 1879; Natalie Davis, *Society and Culture in Early Modern France*, New York: Stanford University Press, 1975; Mack Holt, *The French Wars of Religion, 1562–1629*, Cambridge: Cambridge University Press, 2005; Edward Hulme, *The Renaissance, the Protestant Revolution, and the Catholic Reaction in Continental Europe*, New York: Century Company, 1914; Thomas Lindsey, *A History of the Reformation*, Edinburgh: T. and T. Clark, 1907; James Thompson, *The Wars of Religion in France, 1559–1576*, Chicago: University of Chicago Press, 1909; Arthur Tilley,

The French Wars of Religion, London: London Society for Promoting Christian Knowledge, 1919.

28 Aveling, *Catholic Recusants*, p. 223.

Chapter 4: A Traitor to the Crown

1 Alan Haynes, *The Gunpowder Plot*, Stroud: Sutton Publishing, 1994, p. 20.

2 Philip Sidney, *A History of the Gunpowder Plot*, London: Religious Tract Society, 1904, p. 232; Haynes, p. 20.

3 Sidney, pp. 232–3; Haynes, p. 21; Fraser, *Gunpowder Plot*, p. 87.

4 Sidney, p. 233.

5 Haynes, p. 21.

6 G. Henry, *The Irish Military Community in Flanders*, Blackrock, Co. Dublin: Irish Academic Press, 1992, p. 93.

7 Haynes, p. 21.

8 ibid., p. 22.

9 ibid., p. 21.

10 Jardine, *Criminal Trials*, p. 248; Hogge, pp. 239, 263.

11 Spink, p. 30.

12 Edwards (tr.), *Greenway*, pp. 68–9.

13 Simons, pp. 38–9.

14 Thomas Wright, *Queen Elizabeth and Her Times*, Vol. 2, London: Henry Colburn, 1838, p. 459.

15 ibid, p. 459.

16 ibid., pp. 459–60.

17 ibid., pp. 248–9; Thomas Byerley and John Timbs, *The Mirror of Literature, Amusement and Instruction*, Vol. 31, London: J. Limbird, 1838.

18 C.T. Lannuzzo (tr.), *True Discourse of the Notable and Miraculous Taking of the City and Castle of Calais by*

His Most High and Puissant Prince Albert, Archduke of Austria and Cardinal of the Holy Apostolic See, Governor and Lieutenant General of His Catholic Majesty of the Low Countries. With the Succour & Revictualment of the City of la Fère. At Bruxelles. By Rutger Velpius, Printer At the Golden Eagle, 1596; Byerley and Timbs, *The Mirror of Literature*, p. 357.

19 Lannuzzo (tr.), *True Discourse* . . .

20 Spink, p. 30; Garnett, p. 45; Simons, p. 39.

21 Adolphus William Ward, *The Cambridge Modern History Atlas*, Vol. 3, Cambridge: Cambridge University Press, p. 672.

22 Richard Bruce Wernham, *The Return of the Armadas: The Last Years of Elizabeth's War*, Oxford: Oxford University Press, 1994, p. 213.

23 Spink, pp. 393–5.

24 Jardine, *Criminal Trials*, p. 32; Garnett, pp. 45–6.

25 Francis Vere, *Commentaries of the Divers Pieces of Service*, Cambridge: W. Dillingham, 1657.

26 Garnett, pp. 51–4.

Chapter 5: A Ruthless and Unloving Land

1 Garnett, p. 47; Simons, p. 43.

2 Fraser, *Gunpowder Plot*, pp. 87–8; Sidney, p. 244.

3 Edwards (tr.), *Greenway*, p. 64; see Edwards's footnote.

4 Albert Loomie, *Toleration and Diplomacy*, Philadelphia: American Philosophical Society, 1963, pp. 22; Albert Loomie, *Spanish Elizabethans*, New York: Greenwood, 1983, pp. 178.

5 SP/14/216/116, Examination of Guido Fawkes, 25 November 1605; SP/14/216/125, Examination of Guido Fawkes, 30 November 1605; Jardine, *Criminal Trials*, pp. 139–40.

6   Fraser, *Gunpowder Plot*, pp. 5, 8–9.

7   ibid., pp. 13–15; John Bruce, *Correspondence of James with Robert Cecil and Others*, London: Camden Society, 1861, p. xvi; Wallace MacCaffrey, *Elizabeth I*, London: Edwin Arnold, 1992, p. 415.

8   Fraser, p. 15.

9   Loomie, *Guy Fawkes in Spain: The 'Spanish Treason' in Spanish Documents*, London: University of London Institute of Historical Research, 1971, pp. 4–5.

10 ibid., pp. 5–6.

11 ibid., p. 6.

12 ibid., pp. 7–9.

13 ibid., p. 9; Loomie, *Toleration and Diplomacy*, pp. 7–8.

14 ibid., pp. 9–10.

15 Morris (tr.), *Gerard*, pp. 58–9.

16 ibid., p. 58.

17 Edwards (tr.), *Greenway*, p. 62.

18 Morris (tr.), *Gerard*, pp. 58–9.

19 *HMC Salisbury*, *XVII*, p. 512.

20 ibid.; Loomie, *Guy Fawkes*, p. 11.

21 E2512/61, letter from Creswell to Philip, October 1602; Loomie, p. 12.

22 E2512/64–70, letter from Stanley to Creswell, November 1602; Loomie, pp. 12–13.

23 Loomie, pp. 12–13.

24 ibid., p. 13; R.R. Steele, *Tudor and Stuart Proclamations*, Vol. 1, Proclamation No. 930, Oxford: Oxford University Press, 1910.

25 Loomie, pp. 13–14.

26 E840/195, Letter from Creswell to Philip; *Calendar of State Papers, Spanish*, Vol. IV, London: Longman Green and Co., 1899, p. 740; Loomie, p. 15.

27 Loomie, pp. 15–16.

28 ibid., pp. 16–17.

29 Fraser, *Gunpowder Plot*, pp. xxiii–v; *Calendar of State Papers, Domestic, 1603*, Vol. VIII, London: Longman Green and Co., 1857, p. 1; Bruce, p. li.

30 Fraser, p. xxvii.

31 ibid., pp. 23–5.

32 Philip Caraman, *Henry Garnet 1555–1605 and the Gunpowder Plot*, London: Longmans, 1964, p. 306.

33 Fraser, p. xxxi.

34 Caraman, p. 305.

35 Edwards (tr.), *Greenway*, p. 58.

36 Spink, p. 22; Fraser, pp. 45–8.

37 Morris (tr.), *Gerard*, pp. 57–8.

38 Fraser, p. 50.

39 Edwards (tr.), *Greenway*, p. 58.

40 ibid., p. 58.

41 ibid., p. 59.

42 G.P.V. Akrigg, *Letters of King James VI and I*, Berkeley,: University of California Press, 1984, Letter 11, pp. 57–8.

43 ibid., Letter 47, pp. 119–21.

44 ibid., Letter 89, pp. 200–2.

45 ibid., Letter 91, pp. 204–5.

46 Edwards (tr.), *Greenway*, p. 58.

47 Fraser, p. 51; Bruce, p. 56.

48 ibid., p. 52; ibid., p. 53.

Chapter 6: A Defence to the Innocent

1 *HMC Salisbury, XIV*, pp. 245–6; Loomie, *Guy Fawkes*, p. 17.

2 SP/14/216/116, Examination of Guido Fawkes,

25 November 1605.

3 Edwards (tr.), *Greenway*, pp. 63–4, see Edwards's footnote; Morris (tr.), *Gerard*, p. 236.

4 Loomie, pp. 17–18.

5 ibid., p. 18; E840/129, Relación de Antonio Dutton, 18 May 1603.

6 ibid., p. 18.

7 ibid., p. 18.

8 E840/129, Relación de Antonio Dutton, 18 May 1603.

9 Jardine, *Criminal Trials*, pp. 136–7.

10 Loomie, p. 19.

11 Akrigg, Letter 89, pp. 200–2.

12 Loomie, *Guy Fawkes*, pp. 20–1.

13 E977, unnumbered letter from Sessa to Philip, 13 March 1603; Loomie, p. 21; Loomie, *Spanish Elizabethans*, pp. 174–5.

14 Jardine, *Criminal Trials*, p. 126.

15 Loomie, *Guy Fawkes*, p. 22.

16 ibid., pp. 17, 22.

17 ibid., p. 28.

18 ibid., p. 22.

19 Fraser, *Gunpoweder Plot*, p. xxxv; Loomie, pp. 22–3; E840/137, El Memorial que presentaron los Catholicos de Inglaterra al nuevo Rey pidiendole libertad de consciencia.

20 Loomie, pp. 23–4.

21 ibid., pp. 24–5.

22 ibid., p. 25.

23 ibid., p. 24.

24 ibid., pp. 25–6.

25 ibid., p. 27.

26 ibid., p. 28–9.

27 ibid., p. 29.

28 Akrigg, letters 5, 10, pp. 45–6, 55.

29 ibid., letter 12, pp. 58–9.

30 ibid., letter 23, pp. 77–8.

31 ibid., letters 25–7, 29, pp. 80–2, 84–7.

32 Loomie, p. 29.

33 E2512/98, Copia del Bando publicado por los titulados, caualleros y hombres buenos de Inglaterra; Loomie, p. 30.

34 Loomie, p. 30.

35 Fraser, p. 76; H.G. Stafford, *James VI of Scotland and the Throne of England*, New York: Appleton-Century, 1940, p. 284.

36 Fraser, pp. 76–7.

37 ibid., p. 77.

38 ibid., p. 77.

39 E2512/80, letter from Winter to Creswell, 30 August, 1603; Loomie, pp. 30–1.

40 E841/141, letter from Tassis to Philip, 14 Sept 1603; Loomie, p. 31.

41 E2512/154, letter from Tassis to Philip, 28 Sept 1603; Loomie, p. 32.

42 E2512/82-83, letter from Creswell to Philip, 22 and 27 November 1603; Loomie, p. 33.

43 E2512/132, 134, letter from Dutton to Creswell, 27 November 1603.

44 E2512/132, 134, letter from Dutton to Creswell, 27 November 1603.

45 ibid.

46 E2512/87, letter from Creswell to Idiáquez, 4 December 1603.

47 Loomie, pp. 34–5.

48 E2512/26, Consulta of 17 February 1604; Loomie, p. 35.

Chapter 7: A Desperate Disease

1   Edwards (tr.), *Greenway*, p. 43.
2   Fraser, *Gunpowder Plot*, p. 102; C.H. McIlwaine, *The Political Works of James I*, Cambridge, Massachusetts: Harvard University Press, 1918, pp. 269–80.
3   Morris (tr.), *Gerard*, p. 55; Edward (tr.), *Greenway*, p. 61.
4   Morris (tr.), *Gerard*, pp. 54–5.
5   Spink, p. 19.
6   British Library, Cotton Manuscript, Titus B II, fol. 294; Fraser, pp. 109–10.
7   Edward (tr.), *Greenway*, p. 61.
8   Fraser, p. 111; *Dictionary National Biography*.
9   ibid., p. 111–12.
10 Hogge, p. 329.
11 Edward (tr.), *Greenway*, p. 61.
12 ibid., p. 61.
13 Fraser, p. 112.
14 Morris (tr.), *Greenway*, p. 56.
15 SP14/216/114, Declaration of Thomas Wintour, 23 November 1605.
16 ibid.; Loomie, *Guy Fawkes*, p. 31.
17 ibid.
18 ibid.
19 Edward (tr.), *Greenway*, p. 56.
20 SP14/216/114, Declaration of Thomas Wintour, 23 November 1605
21 Edwards (tr.), *Greenway*.
22 ibid., p. 57; SP14/216/114, Declaration of Thomas Wintour, 23 November 1605.
23 Samuel Rawson Gardiner, *What the Gunpowder Plot Was*, London, New York and Bombay: Longmans, Green and

Co., 1897, Chronological Notes, pp. vii–viii.

24 Edwards (tr.), *Greenway*, pp. 65–6.

25 ibid., pp. 66–8.

26 SP14/216/114, Declaration of Thomas Wintour, 23 November 1605.

Chapter 8: To Shake the Thrones of Princes

1 SP14/216/114, Declaration of Thomas Wintour, 23 November 1605.

2 ibid.

3 Loomie, *Guy Fawkes*, p. 24.

4 Simons, p. 45.

5 SP14/216/114, Declaration of Thomas Wintour, 23 November 1605.

6 Spink, p. 31.

7 Edward (tr.), *Greenway*, pp. 68–9.

8 SP14/216/114, Declaration of Thomas Wintour, 23 November 1605.

9 ibid.

10 SP14/216/101, Deposition of Guydo Fawkes, 17 November 1605.

11 Gardiner, *Gunpowder Plot*, p. 61. Gardiner suggests the 25th as the likely time, as Easter began on 25th in 1604, and Wintour's declaration refers to the start of Easter.

12 Simons, pp. 50–1; Fraser, *Gunpowder Plot*, p. 3.

13 Edwards (tr.), *Greenway*, pp. 44–5.

14 SP14/216/114, Declaration of Thomas Wintour, 23 November 1605; SP14/216/54, Deposition of Guydo Fawkes, 9 November 1605.

15 Edwards (tr.), *Greenway*, pp. 60–1.

16 Jardine, *Criminal Trials*, p. 34.

17 Fraser, p. 120.
18 Morris (tr.), *Gerard*, pp. clxxvii–ix.
19 Garnett, pp. 83–4.
20 ibid., p. 84; Fraser, pp. 122–3.
21 Fraser, pp. 120–3.
22 Gardiner, pp. 85–6.
23 ibid., p. 29.
24 SP14/216/114, Declaration of Thomas Wintour, 23 November 1605.
25 SP77/7, Part I.
26 Gardiner, *Gunpowder Plot*, Chronological Notes, pp. vii–viii.
27 Garnett, p. 86; Fraser, pp. 123–4.
28 Garnett, pp. 86–7.
29 Fraser, pp. 123–4; Gardiner, Chronological Notes, pp. vii–viii; Jardine, *Criminal Trials*, p. 37.
30 Garnett, p. 87; Haynes, p. 44; Jardine, *Narrative*, p. 45.

Chapter 9: Three Score Barrels of Powder Below

1 John Gerard, *What Was the Gunpowder Plot? The Traditional Story Tested by Original Evidence*, London: Osgood, McIlvaine and Co., 1897, p. 251.
2 Garnett, p. 96.
3 Simons, pp. 73–4.
4 Spink, p. 313.
5 ibid., pp. 28–9; Jardine, *Criminal Trials*, pp. 35, 162–3; Jardine, *Narrative*, p. 43; Fraser, *Gunpowder Plot*, pp. 130–1; Haynes, p. 55.
6 Edwards (tr.), *Greenway*, pp. 101–2.
7 Morris (tr.), *Gerard*, p. 87.

8   SP14/216/114, Declaration of Thomas Wintour, 23 November 1605.

9   Simons, pp. 80–1.

10 ibid., p. 77.

11 ibid., pp. 73–4.

12 Edwards (tr.), *Greenway*, p. 71.

13 SP14/216/49, Examination of Guy Fawkes, 8 November 1605.

14 Edwards (tr.), *Greenway*, p. 72.

15 SP14/216/114, Declaration of Thomas Wintour, 23 November 1605.

16 ibid.; Edwards (tr.), *Greenway*, p. 73.

17 ibid.

18 ibid.

19 SP14/216/145, Examination of Thomas Bate, 4 December, 1605.

20 Fraser, *Gunpowder Plot*, pp. 131–3.

21 Edwards (tr.), *Greenway*, pp. 98–9.

22 Morris (tr.), *Gerard*, p. 84.

23 Edwards (tr.), *Greenway*, p. 83.

24 ibid., p. 83.

25 Morris (tr.), *Gerard*, p. 70.

26 SP/14/216/116, Examination of Guido Fawkes, 25 November 1605; Jardine, *Criminal Trials*, pp. 139–40.

27 Edwards (tr.), *Greenway*, pp. 63–4; see Edwards's footnote. For further reading see Albert Loomie, *Guy Fawkes in Spain*.

28 SP14/216/114, Declaration of Thomas Wintour, 23 November 1605.

29 Penne L. Restad, *Christmas in America*, Oxford: Oxford University Press, 1995, p. 6.

30 Parkinson, pp. 63–4; Simons, p. 85.

31 Simons, pp. 77–8.

32 Edwards (tr.), *Greenway*, p. 84; Sidney, p. 60.

33 Edwards (tr.), *Greenway*, p. 85.

34 ibid.; see also Edwards's footnote.

35 ibid., pp. 109–10; Jardine, *Criminal Trials*, pp. 45–6; Simons, pp. 90–1.

36 Jardine, *Criminal Trials*, pp. 45–6.

37 *King's Book: His Majesties Speech in This Last Session of Parliament . . . Together with a Discourse of the Maner of its Discouery of the Late Intended Treason, Ioyned with an Examination of Some of the Prisoners*, London, 1605, p. 293 in Sidney; Garnett, p. 102.

38 Gardiner, *Gunpowder Plot*, pp. 28–9; Fraser, pp. 145–6; Simons, p. 93.

39 SP14/216/6, Examination of John Johnson, 5 November 1605; Fraser, p. 146.

40 Gerard, *What Was the Gunpowder Plot?*, pp. 59–60; Garnett, p. 102.

41 ibid.; ibid.; Fraser, pp. 144–5; John Thomas Smith, *Antiquities of Westminster: The Old Palace, St Stephen's Chapel, Now the House of Commons*, London: John Thomas Smith, 1807, pp. 39–41.

42 SP14/216/17, Examination of John Johnsonne, 6 November 1605.

43 Gardiner, p. 104.

44 ibid.

45 SP14/216/114, Declaration of Thomas Wintour, 23 November 1605.

46 Edwards (tr.), *Greenway*, p. 84; Fraser, pp. 59–60.

47 ibid.

48 Morris (tr.), *Gerard*, p. 71.

49 Edwards (tr.), *Greenway*, pp. 100–1.

50 Morris (tr.), *Gerard*, pp. 86–7.

51 SP14/216/168, Examination of Robert Wynter, 17 January
    1605; SP14/216/169, Examination of Robert Wynter,
    17 January 1605; Jardine, *Criminal Trials*, pp. 143–4;
    Haynes, pp. 57–8; Parkinson, p. 55.

52 Morris (tr.), *Gerard*, p. 87.

Chapter 10: Spies, Soldiers, and 'Stir this Parliament'

1 Edwards (tr.), *Greenway*, p. 102.

2 SP14/216/6, Examination of John Johnson, 5 November
   1605.

3 Spink, p. 313; Simons, p. 95.

4 SP14/216/6, Examination of John Johnson, 5 November
   1605; SP14/216/17, Examination of John Johnsonne,
   6 November 1605; SP14/216/101, Deposition of Guydo
   Fawkes, 17 November 1605.

5 SP14/216/175, Declaration of Guido Faukes, 20 January
   1606; Simons, pp. 95–6; Mark Nicholls, *Investigating
   Gunpowder Plot*, Manchester: Manchester University
   Press, 1992, pp. 36–7.

6 SP14/216/163, Examination of Guido Fauke, 9 January
   1606; Simons, pp. 96–7.

7 SP14/216/6, Examination of John Johnson, 5 November
   1605; Jardine, *Narrative*, p. 316; John Lingard, *A True
   Account of the Gunpowder Plot: An Extract from Dr
   Lingard's History of England and Dodd's Church History,
   Including the Notes and Documents Appended to the
   Latter by the Rev. M.A. Tierney*, London: Cox and
   Wyman, 1851, p. 10.

8 SP14/216/6, Examination of John Johnson, 5 November
   1605.

9 ibid.

10 ibid.

11 Edwards (tr.), *Greenway*, p. 102.

12 Loomie, *Toleration and Diplomacy*, pp. 15–16; Haynes, p. 39.

13 Haynes, p. 70.

14 Fraser, *Gunpowder Plot*, pp. 148–9.

15 Haynes, pp. 71–3.

16 ibid., pp. 72–3.

17 Godfrey Anstruther, 'Powder Treason', Blackfriars, No. 33, 1952, pp. 452–6.

18 SP14/216/6, Examination of John Johnson, 5 November 1605.

19 Simons, pp. 97–8.

20 SP14/216/114, Declaration of Thomas Wintour, 23 November 1605; Edwards (tr.), *Greenway*, p. 112; Fraser, p. 159.

21 Edwards (tr.), *Greenway* p. 99; Morris (tr.), *Gerard*, pp. 85–6.

22 Fraser, p. 172.

23 Edwards (tr.), *Greenway*, pp. 99–100.

24 Morris (tr.), *Gerard*, pp. 85–6.

25 ibid., pp. 87–8.

26 Edwards (tr.), *Greenway*, pp. 104–5.

27 ibid., p. 105; Morris (tr.), *Gerard*, p. 88.

28. Morris (tr.), *Gerard*, p. 88.

29 Edwards (tr.), *Greenway*, p. 107.

30 ibid.; SP14/216/114, Declaration of Thomas Wintour, 23 November 1605.

31 Spink, p. 19; Parkinson, p. 40; Hogge, p. 274; Jardine, *Criminal Trials*, p. 11; Jardine, *Narrative*, p. 9.

32 Fraser, p. 80; David Herber, *Francis Tresham: An Incident*

in 1591, Gunpowder Plot Society.

33 Edwards (tr.), *Greenway*, p. 108.

34. Morris (tr.), *Gerard*, pp. 90–1.

35 SP14/216/114, Declaration of Thomas Wintour, 23 November 1605; Simons, p. 112.

36 Lingard, p. 17.

37 Simons, p. 101.

38 Sidney, p. 192.

39 Spink, p. 286.

40 Simons, p. 113.

41 Goodman, pp. 120–1; Fraser, p. 178; Parkinson, p. 63; Spink, p. 371; SP14/216/100, Declaration of Guydo Fawkes, 16 November 1605.

42 SP14/216/114, Declaration of Thomas Wintour, 23 November 1605; Simons, pp. 101–5.

43 Edwards (tr.), *Greenway*, p. 114.

44 ibid., p. 115, see Edwards's footnote.

45 SP14/216/2, The Monteagle Letter.

46 *King's Book*, pp. 287–9 in Sidney; Edwards (tr.), *Greenway*, pp. 116–17; Fraser, pp. 180–2.

47 Edwards (tr.), *Greenway*, p. 117.

48 Fraser, pp. 181–2.

49 Edwards (tr.), *Greenway*, pp. 117–18.

Chapter 11: With a Dark Lantern and a Burning Match

1 Edwards (tr.), *Greenway*, pp. 118–19; Spink, p. 11.

2 Edwards (tr.), *Greenway*, p. 121; Morris (tr.), *Gerard*, p. 98; *King's Book*, pp. 190–2 in Sidney.

3 Edwards (tr.), *Greenway*.

4 *King's Book*, p. 293 in Sidney; Edwards (tr.), *Greenway*, pp. 121–2; Fraser, p. 194.

5   SP14/216/11, Declaration of Thomas Wintour,
    23 November 1605.

6   Fraser, *Gunpowder Plot*, pp. 196–9.

7   ibid., pp. 199–200.

8   ibid., p. 202.

9   ibid., pp. 200–1.

10 *King's Book*, p. 296 in Sidney; Edwards (tr.), *Greenway*,
    pp. 127–8.

11 Gardiner, *Gunpowder Plot*, pp. 132–6; Spink, p. 101.

12 Gardiner , pp. 135–6.

13 Edwards (tr.), *Greenway*, pp. 127–8.

14 Jardine, *Narrative*, pp. 102–4.

15 Letter from Sir Edward Hoby to Sir Thomas Edmondes, from
    Jardine, *Criminal Trials*, p. 78; Jardine, *Narrative*, p. 104.

16 Edwards (tr.), *Greenway*, p. 128–9; Fraser, pp. 208–10.

17 James F. Larkin and Paul L. Hughes, *Stuart Royal
    Proclamations*, Oxford: Clarendon Press, 1973, p. 123.

18 SP14/216/114, Declaration of Thomas Wintour,
    23 November 1605; Fraser, p. 203.

19 Fraser, pp. 203–5.

20 SP14/216/114, Declaration of Thomas Wintour,
    23 November 1605.

21 SP14/216/22, Confession of Robert Wintour; Jardine,
    Criminal Trials, p. 145.

22 Morris (tr.), *Gerard*, p. 107.

23 Fraser, pp. 205–6.

24 Fraser, p. 207; Nicholls, p. 13; John Stow, *Annales, or,
    A Generall Chronicle of England: Begun by John Stow:
    Continued and Augmented with Matters Forraigne and
    Domestique, Ancient and Moderne, Unto the End of This
    Present Yeere, 1631*, London: Impensis Richardi Meighen,
    1631, p. 879.

25 Nicholls, p. 13.

26 Fraser, p. 211.

27 Jardine, *Narrative*, p. 130.

28 SP14/216/18, Interrogatories of James I for John Johnson, 6 November 1605.

29 Fraser, pp. 212–13.

30 SP14/216/18, Interrogatories of James I for John Johnson, 6 November 1605.

31 *HMC Salisbury, XVII*, p. 479.

32 ibid.

33 SP14/216/22, Confession of Robert Wintour; Edwards (tr.), *Greenway*, pp. 130–1; Fraser, pp. 217–18; Larkin and Hughes, pp. 124–6.

34 *CSP, Domestic, 1603–1610*, p. 288; Edwards (tr.), *Greenway*, p. 153; Morris (tr.), *Gerard*, p. 211; Fraser, p. 218; Jardine, *Criminal Trials*, p. 82; Jardine, *Narrative*, pp. 167–8.

35 SP14/216/135, Examination of Sir Everard Digby, 2 December 1605; CSP, Domestic, 1603–1610, p. 265; Fraser, pp. 220–1; SP14/216/114, Declaration of Thomas Wintour, 23 November 1605.

36 Jardine, *Narrative*, pp. 70–1.

37 Edwards (tr.), *Greenway*, pp. 131–2; Fraser, p. 221.

38 Edwards (tr.), *Greenway*, p. 133.

39 ibid.

40 ibid.; see Edwards's footnote.

Chapter 12: Guy Fawkes, Guy Fawkes, T'was His Intent

1 SP14/216/37, Examination of Guye Fawkes, 7 November 1605.

2 SP14/216/49, Examination of Guy Fawkes, 8 November

1605. Princess Mary died in 1607, aged just two years.

3   John, Nichols, *The Progresses, Processions, and Magnificent Festivities of King James the First*, London: J.B. Nichols, 1828, p. 582; Sidney, p. 191.

4   Jardine, *Criminal Trials*, p. 106; Jardine, *A Narrative of the Gunpowder Plot*, p. 132.

5   ibid.; ibid.

6   Morris (tr.), *Gerard*, p. 105.

7   Fraser, *Gunpowder Plot*, p. 215.

8   Jardine, *Criminal Trials*, p. 108; Jardine, *A Narrative of the Gunpowder Plot*, p. 134.

9   Jardine, *Criminal Trials*, p. 106.

10   ibid.; Jardine, *A Narrative of the Gunpowder Plot*, p. 135.

11   Morris (tr.), *Gerard*, p. ccxxv.

12   Jardine, *Criminal Trials*, p. 109.

13   SP14/216/54, Deposition of Guydo Fawkes, 9 November 1605; SP14/216/101, Deposition of Guydo Fawkes, 17 November 1605; Jardine, *Criminal Trials*, pp. 6, 158–9.

14   Edwards (tr.), *Greenway*, p. 133.

15   SP14/216/11, Declaration of Thomas Wintour, 23 November 1605; Edwards (tr.), *Greenway*, pp. 133–4.

16   ibid.; ibid., p. 134.

17   Edwards (tr.), *Greenway*, p. 134–5; Fraser, p. 224.

18   SP14/216/114, Declaration of Thomas Wintour, 23 November 1605.

19   Edwards (tr.), *Greenway*, pp. 134–5; Fraser, pp. 222–5; Hugh Ross Williamson, *The Gunpowder Plot*, London: Faber and Faber, 1951, p. 182.

20   SP14/216/11, Declaration of Thomas Wintour, 23 November 1605.

21   Edwards (tr.), *Greenway*, pp. 136–7.

22   9 November 1605, in *Journal of the House of Lords*, Vol. 2:

1578–1614, London: House of Lords Journal Vol. 2, 1767–1830, pp. 356–9; Edwards (tr.), *Greenway*, pp. 141–3.

23 Loomie, *Guy Fawkes*, p. 29.

24 Fraser, pp. 232–3; Francis Edwards, *Guy Fawkes: The Real Story of the Gunpowder Plot?*, London: Rupert Hart-Davis, 1969, pp. 190–1.

25 CSP, Domestic, 1603–10, p. 246.

26 Fraser, pp. 235–6; Jardine, *Criminal Trials*, p. 86, 89.

27 SP14/216/100, Declaration of Guydo Fawkes, 16 November 1605.

28 Fraser, p. 236.

29 SP14/216/54, Deposition of Guydo Fawkes, 9 November 1605; Morris (tr.), *Gerard*, pp. clxxvii–ix.

30 Hogge, p. 329.

31 Morris (tr.), *Gerard*, pp. liii–iv.

32 SP14/216/145, Examination of Thomas Bate, 4 December 1605; SP14/216/166, Examination of Thomas Bate, 13 January 1606; Fraser, p. 249.

33 CSP, Domestic, 1603–10, p. 254.

34 *HMC Salisbury*, XVII, p. 534.

35 Nicholls, p. 38; Fraser, p. 241.

36 SP14/216/126, Declaration of Robert Keyes, 30 November 1605; SP14/216/135, Examination of Everard Digby, 2 December 1605; SP14/216/136, Declaration of Ambrose Rookewoode, 2 December 1605; SP14/216/145, Examination of Thomas Bate, 4 December 1605.

37 SP14/216/109, Confession of John Wintour, 22 November 1605.

38 SP14/216/168, Examination of Robert Wynter, 17 January 1605; SP14/216/169, Examination of Robert Wynter, 17 January 1605; SP14/216/176 – Declaration of Robert Wynter, 20 January 1606.

39 Fraser, pp. 250–253.

40 SP14/216/211, Deathbed Recantation of Francis Tresame, 24 March 1605; Morris (tr.), *Gerard*, p. 259.

Chapter 13: His Just End Should'st Be Grim

1 *Calendar of State Papers, Venetian*, Vol. X, London: Longman Green and Co., 1900, pp. 308–9.

2 Fraser, *Gunpowder Plot*, pp. 262–3.

3 Nichols, p. 35; Fraser, p. 264; Morris (tr.), *Gerard*, pp. 191–3.

4 Fraser, p. 265.

5 Morris (tr.), *Gerard*, p. 192.

6 ibid.; Edwards (tr.), *Greenway*, p. 203; Fraser, p. 264.

7 Morris (tr.), *Gerard*, p. 203

8 ibid., pp. 192–3.

9 Thomas Bayley Howell, *Cobbett's Complete Collection of State Trials*, Vol. II, London: R. Bagshaw, 1809–26, pp. 159–64, 187.

10 Edwards (tr.), *Greenway*, p. 205.

11 ibid., pp. 202, 207.

12 ibid., pp. 205–13; Fraser, pp. 266–9.

13 *State Trials*, pp. 185–7.

14 SP/14/216/116, Examination of Guido Fawkes, 25 November 1605; SP/14/216/125, Examination of Guido Fawkes, 30 November 1605; Jardine, *Criminal Trials*, pp. 139–40.

15 SP14/216/168, Examination of Robert Wynter, 17 January 1605.

16 *State Trials*, pp. 186–7.

17 Edwards (tr.), *Greenway*, pp. 213–14.

18 Fraser, p. 269.

19 Morris (tr.), *Gerard*, pp. 205, 213; Edwards (tr.), *Greenway*, pp. 214–15.

20 Morris (tr.), *Gerard*, pp. 205–6.

21 *State Trials*, pp. 188–9.

22 Spink, p. 52.

23 Edwards (tr.), *Greenway*, pp. 225–7.

24 ibid., pp. 226–7; Fraser, pp. 279–80.

25 Edwards (tr.), *Greenway*, p. 227; *HMC Salisbury*, *XVIII*, p. 52; Fraser, pp. 280–1.

26 Edwards (tr.), *Greenway*, pp. 227–8.

27 Morris (tr.), *Gerard*, pp. 135–6.

28 ibid., pp. 219–20.

29 Edwards (tr.), *Greenway*, pp. 228–9.

30 ibid., p. 229.

31 ibid.

32 Morris (tr.), *Gerard*, p. 117.

33 Morris (tr.), *Gerard*, pp. 221–2; Edwards (tr.), *Greenway*, pp. 229–30; Fraser, pp. 282–3; *State Trials*, p. 218; Simons, pp. 208–9.

Chapter 14: The Aftermath

1 Fraser, *Gunpowder Plot*, pp. 339–44.

2 Gerard, *What Was the Gunpowder Plot?*, p. 228.

3 Fraser, *Gunpowder Plot*, p. 344; Hogge, p. 380.

4 *HMC Salisbury*, *XVII*, p. 534; Fraser, p. 240.

5 *HMC Salisbury*, *XVII*, p. 534; *HMC Salisbury*, *XVIII*, pp. 38–40; Fraser, pp. 240–1.

6 SP14/216/114, Declaration of Thomas Wintour, 23 November 1605.

7 Akrigg, pp. 45–6, Letter 5, p. 55, Letter 10, pp. 58–9, Letter 12.

8 ibid., pp. 200–2, Letter 89.

9 ibid., pp. 166–7, Letter 73, pp. 255–6, Letter 118.

10 Ronald Hutton, 'What If the Gunpowder Plot Had Succeeded?', BBC History website, 2005.

11 SP14/216/114, Declaration of Thomas Wintour, 23 November 1605.

12 Charles Carlton, *Charles I: The Personal Monarch*, London and New York: Routledge, 1995, p. 12.

13 ibid., p. 10.

14 Pauline Croft, *King James*, New York: Macmillan, 2003, p. 51; Parkinson, p. 32.

15 Loomie, *Guy Fawkes*, p. 32.

16 Simons, p. 103.

Chapter 15: Remember, Remember . . .

1 Ronald Hutton, *The Rise and Fall of Merrie England, The Ritual Year in Britain* 1400–1700, Oxford: Oxford University Press, 1996, p. 212; Fraser, *Gunpowder Plot*, pp. 352–3.

2 Colin H. Benbow, *Boer Prisoners of War in Bermuda*, Devonshire, Bermuda: Devonshire College, 1982, p. 28.

3 Fraser, pp. 353–4; Peter Shaw, *American Patriots and the Rituals of Revolution*, Cambridge, Massachusetts: Harvard University Press, 1981, pp. 15–18.

4 John Wardroper, *The World of William Hone*, London: Shelfmark Books, 1997, p. 157.

5 Fraser, p. 233.

6 William Hazlitt, *The Collected Works of William Hazlitt*, Vol. XI, London: J.M. Dent and Co., 1904, p. 319.

7 Jardine, *Criminal Trials*, p. 32; Jardine, *Narrative*, p. 38.

8 Samuel Rawson Gardiner, *History of England from the*

Accession of James I to the Disgrace of Chief Justice Coke, Vol. 1, London: Hurst and Blackett, 1863, p. 252.

9 Morris (tr.), *Gerard*, pp. 59–60.

10 Loomie, *Guy Fawkes*, p. 40.

11 Parkinson, p. 33.

12 Jardine, *Narrative*, p. 57.

13 Morris (tr.), *Gerard*, pp. xxxix–xl.

14 Spink, p. 30.

15 Loomie, p. 30; E2512/98, Copia del Bando publicado por los titulados, caualleros y hombres buenos de Inglaterra.

16 Morris (tr.), *Gerard*, p. 10.

BIBLIOGRAPHY

*Primary sources are acknowledged in the
Notes and References*

Akrigg, G.P.V, *Letters of King James VI and I*, Berkeley,
California: University of California Press, 1984
Anstruther, Godfrey, *The Seminary Priests: A Dictionary of
Secular Clergy of England and Wales, 1558–1850*, Vol. 1,
Durham: Ushaw, 1968
Anstruther, Godfrey, *Vaux of Harrowden*, Newport, Rhode
Island: R.H. Johns Ltd, 1953
Ashton, Robert, *James I by His Contemporaries*, London:
Hutchinson, 1968
Aveling, Hugh, *The Catholic Recusants of the West Riding
of Yorkshire 1558–1790*, York: Leeds Philosophical and
Literary Society, 1963
Aveling, Hugh, *The Handle and the Axe: The Catholic
Recusants in England from Reformation to Emancipation*,
London: Blond and Briggs, 1976
Baird, Henry M., *The History of the Rise of the Huguenots
of France*, New York: Charles Scribner's Sons, 1879
Barlow, Thomas, *The Gunpowder-Treason: With a Discourse
of the Manner of Its Discovery; and a Perfect Relation of*

the Proceedings Against those Horrid Conspirators;
Wherein Is Contained their Examinations, Trials, and
Condemnations, London: Thomas Newcomb and
H. Hills, 1679

Benbow, Colin H., *Boer Prisoners of War in Bermuda*,
Devonshire, Bermuda: Devonshire College, 1982

Bengtsen, Fiona, *Sir William Waad, Lieutenant of the Tower,*
and the Gunpowder Plot, Victoria, BC: Trafford
Publishing, 2005

Boyle, Conall, *In the Footsteps of the Gunpowder Plotters*,
Oldbury, West Midlands: Meridian Books, 1994

Bruce, John, *Correspondence of James with Robert Cecil and*
Others, London: Camden Society, 1861

Byerley, Thomas and Timbs, John, *The Mirror of Literature,*
Amusement and Instruction, Vol. 31, London: J. Limbird,
1838

Calendar of State Papers, Domestic, in the Reign of
Elizabeth I, 1601–1603, London: Longman Green and Co.,
1870

Calendar of State Papers, Domestic, 1603–10, Vol. VIII,
London: Longman Green and Co., 1857

Calendar of State Papers, Spanish, Vol. IV, London: Longman
Green and Co., 1899

Calendar of State Papers, Venetian, Vol. X, London: Longman
Green and Co., 1900

Caraman, Philip, *Henry Garnet 1555–1605 and the*
Gunpowder Plot, London: Longmans, 1964

Caraman, Philip, *The Other Face: Catholic Life Under*
Elizabeth I, New York: Sheed and Ward, 1960

Carlton, Charles, *Charles I: The Personal Monarch*, London
and New York: Routledge, 1995

Cecil, Robert, *Historical Manuscripts Commission, Calendar of the Manuscripts of the Most Honourable Marques of Salisbury,* Vols XI–XVIII, London: His Majesty's Stationery Office, 1904–40

Croft, Pauline, *King James,* New York: Macmillan, 2003

Cross, Clare, *The Puritan Earl: Henry Hastings, 3rd Earl of Huntingdon 1536–1595,* London: Macmillan, 1966

Davies, Robert, *The Fawkes's of York in the Sixteenth Century,* London: J.B. and J.G. Nichols, 1850

Davis, Natalie, *Society and Culture in Early Modern France,* New York: Stanford University Press, 1975

Dodds, Madeline Hope, and Dodds, Ruth, *The Pilgrimage of Grace, 1536–37,* Vol. I, Cambridge: Cambridge University Press, 1971

Durst, Paul, *Intended Treason: What Really Happened in the Gunpowder Plot,* London: W.H. Allen, 1970

Edwards, Francis, *Guy Fawkes: The Real Story of the Gunpowder Plot?* London: Rupert Hart-Davis, 1969

Edwards, Francis (tr.), *The Gunpowder Plot: The Narrative of Oswald Tesimond Alias Greenway,* London: Folio Society, 1973

Fraser, Antonia, *The Gunpowder Plot: Terror and Faith in 1605,* London: Phoenix, 2002

Fraser, Antonia, *Mary Queen of Scots,* London: Phoenix, 2002

Gardiner, Samuel Rawson, *History of England from the Accession of James I to the Disgrace of Chief Justice Coke,* Vol. I, London: Hurst and Blackett, 1863

Gardiner, Samuel Rawson, *What the Gunpowder Plot Was,* London, New York and Bombay: Longmans, Green and Co., 1897

Garnett, Henry, *Portrait of Guy Fawkes: An Experiment in Biography,* London: Robert Hale, 1962

Gerard, John, *The Gunpowder Plot and the Gunpowder*

Plotters, In Reply to Professor Gardiner, London: Harper
and Brothers, 1897

Gerard, John, *What Was the Gunpowder Plot? The Traditional
Story Tested by Original Evidence*, London: Osgood,
McIlvaine and Co., 1897

Goodman, De Goffrey, *The Court of James I*, Vol. II, London:
Samuel Bentley, 1839

Grindal, Edmund, *Memorials of Archbishop Grindal:
Wherein the True Causes of His Suspension and
Disgrace Are Impartially Related*, London: J. How,
1710

Haynes, Alan, *The Gunpowder Plot*, Stroud: Sutton
Publishing, 1994

Haynes, Alan, *Robert Cecil, First Earl of Salisbury: Servant of
Two Sovereigns*, London: Peter Owen, 1989

Hazlitt, William, *The Collected Works of William Hazlitt*,
Vol. XI, London: J.M. Dent, 1904

Henry, G., *The Irish Military Community in Flanders*,
Blackrock, Co. Dublin: Irish Academic Press, 1992

Hogge, Alice, *God's Secret Agents: Queen Elizabeth's
Forbidden Priests and the Hatching of the Gunpowder
Plot*, London: HarperCollins, 2005

Holt, Mack P., *The French Wars of Religion, 1562–1629*,
Cambridge: Cambridge University Press, 2005

House of Lords Journal, Vol. 2, 1578–1614, London: House of
Lords Journal, 1767–1830, pp. 356–9

Howell, Thomas Bayley, *Cobbett''s Complete Collection of State
Trials*, Vol. II, London: R. Bagshaw, 1809–26

Hulme, Edward, *The Renaissance, the Protestant Revolution,
and the Catholic Reaction in Continental Europe*, New
York: Century Company, 1914

Hutton, Ronald, *The Rise and Fall of Merrie England*,

The Ritual Year in Britain 1400–1700, Oxford: Oxford University Press, 1996

Jardine, David, *Criminal Trials, II: The Gunpowder Plot*. London: M.A. Nattali, 1846

Jardine, David, *A Narrative of the Gunpowder Plot*, London: John Murray, 1857

King's Book: His Majesties Speech in This Last Session of Parliament . . . Together with a Discourse of the Maner of Its Discouery of the Late Intended Treason, Ioyned with an Examination of Some of the Prisoners, London, 1605

Knight, Charles, *The Popular History of England*, Vol. 3, London: Bradbury and Evans, 1857

Larkin, James F., and Hughes, Paul L., *Stuart Royal Proclamations*, Oxford: Clarendon Press, 1973

Lindsay, Thomas, *A History of the Reformation*, Edinburgh: T. and T. Clark, 1907

Lingard, John, *A True Account of the Gunpowder Plot: An Extract from Dr Lingard's History of England and Dodd's Church History, Including the Notes and Documents Appended to the Latter by the Rev. M.A. Tierney*, London: Cox and Wyman, 1851

Loomie, Albert, *Guy Fawkes in Spain: The 'Spanish Treason' in Spanish Documents*, London: University of London Institute of Historical Research, 1971

Loomie, Albert, *Spanish Elizabethans*, New York: Greenwood, 1983

Loomie, Albert, *Toleration and Diplomacy*, Philadelphia: American Philosophical Society, 1963

MacCaffrey, Wallace, *Elizabeth I*, London: Edwin Arnold, 1992

McIlwaine, C.H., *The Political Works of James I*, Cambridge, Massachusetts: Harvard University Press, 1918

Manning, Roger, *Anthony Browne, 1st Viscount Montague: The Influence in County Politics of an Elizabethan Catholic Nobleman*, Sussex: Sussex Archaeological Society, 1968

Miola, Robert, *Early Modern Catholicism*, Oxford: Oxford University Press, 2007

Morey, Adrian, *The Catholic Subjects of Elizabeth I*, London: Allen and Unwin, 1978

Morris, John (tr.), *The Conditions of Catholics Under James I: Father Gerard's Narrative of the Gunpowder Plot*, London: Longmans, Green and Co., 1871

Nichols, John, *The Progresses, Processions, and Magnificent Festivities of King James the First*, London: J.B. Nichols, 1828

Nicholls, Mark, *Investigating Gunpowder Plot*, Manchester: Manchester University Press, 1992

Nicholson, William, *The Remains of Edmund Grindal, Successively Bishop of London, and Archbishop of York and Canterbury*, Cambridge: Cambridge University Press, 1843

Parkinson, C. Northcote, *Gunpowder Treason and Plot*, London: Weidenfeld and Nicolson, 1976

Pollen, John Hungerford, *Unpublished Documents Relating to the English Martyrs*, London: Catholic Record Society, 1908

Pullein, Catherine, *The Pulleyns of Yorkshire*, Leeds: Whitehead and Sons, 1915

Questier, Michael, *Catholicism and Community*, Cambridge: Cambridge University Press, 2005

Restad, Penne L., *Christmas in America*, Oxford: Oxford University Press, 1995

Roche, Michael de la, *An Abridgement of Gerald Brandt's History of the Reformation in the Low Countries*, Vol. 1,

London: R. Knaplock, 1725

Rose, Elliot, *Cases of Conscience: Alternatives Open to Recusants and Puritans Under Elizabeth I and James I*, Cambridge and New York: Cambridge University Press, 1975

Shaw, Peter, *American Patriots and the Rituals of Revolution*, Cambridge, Massachusetts: Harvard University Press, 1981

Sidney, Philip, *A History of the Gunpowder Plot*, London: Religious Tract Society, 1904

Simons, Eric N., *The Devil of the Vault*, London: Frederick Muller, 1963

Smith, John Thomas, *Antiquities of Westminster: The Old Palace, St Stephen's Chapel, Now the House of Commons*, London: John Thomas Smith, 1807

Speight, Harry, *Nidderdale and the Garden of the Nidd; a Yorkshire Rhineland: Being a Complete Account, Historical, Scientific, and Descriptive, of the Beautiful Valley of the Nidd*, New York: E. Stock, 1894

Spink, Henry Hawkes, *The Gunpowder Plot and Lord Mounteagle's Letter*, London: Simpkin, Marshall, Hamilton, Kent and Co., 1902

Stafford, H.G, *James VI of Scotland and the Throne of England*, New York: Appleton-Century, 1940

Steele, R.R., *Tudor and Stuart Proclamations*, Vol. 1, Proclamation No. 930, Oxford: Oxford University Press, 1910

Stow, John, *Annales, or, A Generall Chronicle of England: Begun by John Stow: Continued and Augmented with Matters Forraigne and Domestique, Ancient and Moderne, Unto the End of This Present Yeere, 1631*, London: Impensis Richardi Meighen, 1631

Sussex Archaeological Society, *Sussex Archaeological Collections*, Vol. 7, London: John Russell Smith, 1854

Thompson, James, *The Wars of Religion in France, 1559–1576*, Chicago: University of Chicago Press, 1909

Tilley, Arthur, *The French Wars of Religion*, London: London Society for Promoting Christian Knowledge, 1919

Vere, Francis, *Commentaries of the Divers Pieces of Service*, Cambridge: W. Dillingham, 1657

Ward, Adolphus William, *The Cambridge Modern History Atlas*, Vol. 3, Cambridge: Cambridge University Press, p. 672

Wardroper, John, *The World of William Hone*, London: Shelfmark Books, 1997

Wernham, Richard Bruce, *The Return of the Armadas: The Last Years of Elizabeth's War*, Oxford: Oxford University Press, 1994

Williamson, Hugh Ross, *The Gunpowder Plot*. London: Faber and Faber, 1951

Wills, Gary, *Witches and Jesuits*, New York and Oxford: Oxford University Press, 1995

Wright, Thomas, *Queen Elizabeth and Her Times*, Vols 1 and 2, London: Henry Colburn, 1838

Articles

Anstruther, Godfrey, 'Powder Treason', *Blackfriars*, No. 33, 1952

Edwards, Francis, 'Still Investigating Gunpowder Plot', *Recusant History*, No. 21, 1992

Herber, David, 'Francis Tresham: An Incident in 1591', Gunpowder Plot Society, www.gunpowder-plot.org

Herber, David, 'Guy Fawkes: From York to the Battlefields of Flanders', Gunpowder Plot Society, www.gunpowder-plot.org

Herber, David, 'The Marriage of Guy Fawkes', Gunpowder Plot Society, www.gunpowder-plot.org

Hutton, Ronald, 'What If the Gunpowder Plot Had Succeeded?', BBC History website, 2005

Izon, John, 'New Light on the Gunpowder Plot', *History Today*, No. 4, 1954

Lannuzzo, C.T. (tr.), Velpius, Rutger, *True Discourse of the Notable and Miraculous Taking of the City and Castle of Calais by His Most High and Puissant Prince Albert, Archduke of Austria and Cardinal of the Holy Apostolic See, Governor and Lieutenant General of his Catholic Majesty of the Low Countries. With the Succour & Revictualment of the City of la Fère. At Bruxelles. By Rutger Velpius, Printer at the Golden Eagle*, 1596

Longley, Katharine M., 'Three Sites in the City of York', *Recusant History*, No. 12, 1973

Nicholls, Mark, 'Investigating Gunpowder Plot', *Recusant History*, No. 19, 1988

Sprott, S.E., 'Sir Edmund Baynham', *Recusant History*, No. 10, 1969

Toyne S.M., 'Guy Fawkes and the Powder Plot', *History Today*, No. 1, 1951

APPENDICES

APPENDIX I: MAP OF THE LOW COUNTRIES
IN THE 17TH CENTURY

APPENDIX 2: GUY FAWKES CHRONOLOGY

1567–8 Marriage between Edward Fawkes and Edith (surname unknown) in York.

1568 Birth of a daughter, Anne, 3 October; Death of Anne, 14 November.

1570 Birth of a son, Guy Fawkes, 13 April; three days later he is baptized into the parish of St Michael-le-Belfrey in York.

1572 Birth of another daughter, also named Anne, 12 October.

1574 Fletcher, the head teacher at the free school of St Peter's in York, is dismissed after converting to Catholicism. John Pulleyn replaces him.

1575 Guy begins his education at St Peter's. Among his fellow pupils are Christopher Wright and John Wright. Another daughter, Elizabeth, is born to Edward and Edith, 27 May. Death of Guy's grandmother, Ellen Harrington.

1578 Guy's father, Edward, dies 17 January.

1581 Death of Thomas Fawkes, Guy's uncle.

1585 The War of Religion in Europe intensifies. Sir William Stanley travels to the Spanish Netherlands with Jesuits priests but delays his arrival in case of Elizabeth's death in the Babington Plot.

1587 Guy's mother marries Denis Bainbridge of Scotton; Stanley surrenders the city of Deventer in the Netherlands to the Spanish and fights on the side of the Catholics.

1587–9   Guy Fawkes moves to Scotton.

1588   Stanley travels to Spain in an attempt to advise
         Philip II on strategy for the armada. The Spanish
         Armada is defeated in this year.

1590   Guy is believed to have married Maria Pulleyn;
         Stanley returns to the court of Philip II and backs a
         further invasion of England.

1591   Guy and Maria are thought to have a son named
         Thomas. Guy inherits his late father's estates on his
         twenty-first birthday; six months later he leases
         property to Christopher Lumley.

1592   Guy sells his estates to Anne Skipsey in August.
         Guy's mother and stepfather agree to waive claim to
         Edward Fawkes's former property, and Guy finds
         employment in the household of Viscount
         Montague.

1593–4   Guy travels to Flanders with Richard Collinge
         and becomes a soldier in the service of Stanley.

1596   Guy fights in the siege of Calais on behalf of the
         Catholic Spanish. Stanley rewards him with his own
         company of soldiers.

1599   Guy is believed to have travelled to Venice to seek
         his cousin Martin Harrington. Colonel Bostock
         replaces Stanley at the head of the English
         regiment.

1600   Guy fights in the Battle of Nieuport where the
         Spanish forces, led by Albert of Austria, are defeated
         by the Calvinist Dutch, led by Prince Maurice
         of Nassau and Sir Francis Vere. Colonel Bostock
         is killed.

1601   An uprising led by the Earl of Essex is defeated.

1601–2   Thomas Wintour travels to Spain and is granted an

audience with Philip III. Wintour receives guarantees of military support from the king.

1603   Guy is dispatched to Spain in order to convince Phillip III to support an invasion of England. While in Spain Guy is considered for promotion.

1604   Robert Catesby, John Wright and Thomas Wintour meet in February and form a plot against James I. Wintour travels to Flanders in March to persuade the Constable of Castille to negotiate with James I on behalf of England's Catholics. Wintour meets Guy in Flanders, and asks him to return to England. On return to England Guy agrees to join the Gunpowder Plot. Thomas Percy also gets involved. In May Percy rents a house near Parliament to dig a mine underneath the House of Lords. Guy takes up residence in the name of John Johnson. Work on the mine starts two weeks before Christmas.

1605   In March Percy rents a cellar near the House of Lords, and work on the mine is abandoned. Guy returns to the Low Countries in May where he remains until late August/early September. Throughout October preparations are made for the plot. On 26 October an anonymous letter is sent to Lord Monteagle warning him to avoid Parliament on the night of its reopening. Monteagle shows the letter to Robert Cecil. On 5 November Guy is captured in the cellar. Three days later Catesby, Percy and the Wright brothers are killed in Staffordshire. The remaining conspirators are imprisoned in the Tower of London. Tresham dies on 23 December.

1606   The conspirators are tried on 27 January and found guilty of treason. Everard Digby, Robert Wintour, John Grant and Thomas Bates are executed on 30 January followed by Guy Fawkes, Thomas Wintour, Ambrose Rookwood and Robert Keyes on 31 January.

APPENDIX 3: HISTORICAL NOTES

1539   Dissolution of the monasteries in England and the final split with Rome.

1545   Beginning of the Catholic Counter-Reformation.

1547–53 Edward VI consolidates Protestantism as the official religion of England.

1553   Death of Edward VI; accession of Mary I.

1554   Four thousand Protestants rise against Mary in January. She imprisons Elizabeth owing to suspicions of her involvement. In March, but the plot fails.

1557   The Smithfield Fires; 277 Protestants are burned at the stake.

1558   Death of Mary I; Elizabeth I ascends to the throne.

1559   The Elizabethan Acts of Settlement are passed, confirming Protestantism as the official religion of the state. Participation in the Catholic Mass is banned.

1563   Thomas Percy is born.

1565   Robert Keyes is born. Mary Stuart marries Lord Darnley.

1566   Birth of James I.

1567   Relations between Spain and England deteriorate as a result of the repression of Protestantism in the Spanish Netherlands. In Scotland, Lord Darnley is murdered. Mary Stuart marries the 4th Earl Bothwell, leading to her capture, imprisonment and dethronement. Sir William Stanley becomes a volunteer under the Spanish General Alva. Robert Wintour and Francis Tresham are born.

1568   Mary Queen of Scots flees to England and is imprisoned in Carlisle; John Wright is born in Yorkshire.

1569 The Norfolk Conspiracy fails when the Earl of Leicester, Lord Dudley, admits the plot to Elizabeth. The Northern Rising is crushed.

1570 Guy Fawkes and Christopher Wright are born. Elizabeth is excommunicated by Rome. William Stanley leaves the Spanish service and joins Elizabeth's service in Ireland.

1571 Roberto Ridolfi encourages the Duke of Alba to send 6,000 men to England to overthrow Elizabeth and place Mary, Queen of Scots on the throne; Thomas Wintour is born.

1572 Elizabeth signs the Treaty of Blois. The St Bartholomew's Day Massacre occurs.

1573 Robert Catesby is born.

1574 Beginning of the Seminary mission.

1577 Execution of the first Seminary priest in England. Archbishop Grindal is suspended after refusing to suppress prophesying.

1578 Ambrose Rockwood and Everard Digby are born.

1579 The English College is founded in Rome.

1580 Arrival of the first Jesuit priests in England.

1581 Three Jesuit priests are captured. Among others, the Tresham, Catesby and Vaux families are found guilty of harbouring them. An act of obedience is issued by Elizabeth.

1583 The Throckmorton Plot is foiled.

1584 Sir Francis Throckmorton is executed; the Somerville Plot is uncovered.

1585 Elizabeth agrees military relief of Protestants in Spanish Netherlands. The Parry Plot against Elizabeth is foiled.

1586   Francis Ingelby is executed in York. Catholic priest
       Henry Ballard reveals details of the Babington Plot.
       William Stanley conquers Deventer in the
       Netherlands. Margaret Clitherow is executed in York
       for harbouring priests.

1587   Mary Queen of Scots is executed. The Stafford Plot
       is uncovered. Stanley surrenders Deventer to the
       Spanish.

1588   The Spanish Armada is defeated.

1594   The Lopez Plot is uncovered.

1596   A second Spanish Armada is destroyed by storms.
       Guy Fawkes is present at the siege of Calais.

1598   The Edward Squire and the Poisoned Pummel Affair.
       The peace at Vervins ends the feud between France
       and Spain

1600   Battle of Nieuport.

1601   The Essex Rebellion is put down.

1601–2 Thomas Wintour travels to obtain guarantees of
       military support from Philip III.

1603   Elizabeth I dies and is replaced by James I of England.
       In July James assures a deputation of Catholics that
       recusancy fines will be remitted. The Bye and Main
       Plots are uncovered. King James meets Thomas Percy
       and offers assurances of religious toleration.

1604   The Hampton Court conference ends with no pro-
       gress toward religious toleration for Catholics. In
       February James I issues a proclamation banning all
       Catholic priests. In July he gives his royal consent to a
       new recusancy act. In August executions occur under
       the new act. In September a commission is established
       overseeing the banishment of priests. The council
       recommends the new act is not enforced against lay

Catholics. In November fines of £20 per month are imposed against the thirteen richest Catholic families.

1605   In February King James I decrees that the recusancy act should be fully implemented. On midnight on November 5 Guy Fawkes is captured. The remaining conspirators are killed or arrested.

1606   The plotters are tried and executed in January.

1614   The 'Addled Parliament' is dissolved by James. He rules for seven years without a Parliament.

APPENDIX 3: FAMILY TREE OF GUY FAWKES

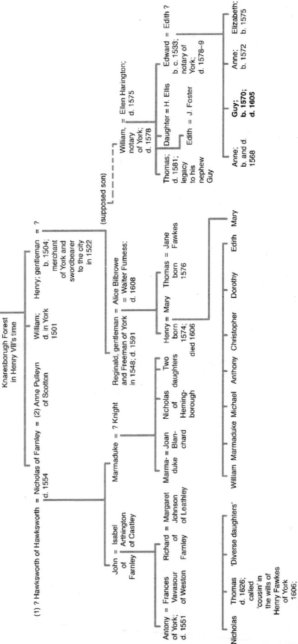

INDEX